Download the free tablet or smartphone app with your BIBLEFORCE™ purchase!

Its easy! Here's how you get your free app:

- Scan the QR code above to be taken to our registration website or go to *http://www.bibleforce.net/accesscode/* in your browser.

- Follow the prompts to receive your access code.

- Download the app from the App Store or Google Play or access links for the app at *www.bibleforce.net*

- Register, then enter the provided code into the app to unlock your free content.

With the BIBLEFORCE™ audio app you can enjoy a free read-along experience on your tablet or smartphone with the purchase of BIBLEFORCE™ *The First Heroes Bible*. Every story is included with options to read along or have the story read to you.

BIBLEFORCE™
THE FIRST HEROES BIBLE

BibleForce™ The First Heroes Bible

Copyright © 2018 North Parade Publishing Ltd., and International Publishing Services Pty Ltd.
North Parade Publishing
4 North Parade, Bath BA1 1LF, United Kingdom www.nppbooks.co.uk
International Publishing Services Pty Ltd.
Sydney, Australia www.ipsoz.com
Publisher: Wayne McKay, Peter Hicks
General editor: J. Emmerson
Editorial Team: Mark Friedman, John Perritano, Fraser Emmerson-Hicks
Design Team: QBS Learning, Delhi, India

ISBN 978-1-4003-1425-6

Printed in China

Published in Nashville, Tennessee, by Tommy Nelson. Tommy Nelson is an imprint of Thomas Nelson.
Thomas Nelson is a registered trademark of HarperCollins Christian Publishing, Inc.

Tommy Nelson titles may be purchased in bulk for educational, business, fund-raising, or sales
promotional use. For information, please e-mail SpecialMarkets@ThomasNelson.com.

Unless otherwise noted, Scripture quotations are taken from the New King James Version®.
Copyright © 1982 by Thomas Nelson, a registered trademark of HarperCollins Christian Publishing, Inc.
Used by permission. All rights reserved.
Library of Congress Control Number: 2017960986

Mfr: Dragon Sourcing (Far East) Ltd. / Chai Wan, Hong Kong / March 2018 / PO #9495111

18 19 20 21 22 23 24 25 / IPS / 10 9 8 7 6 5 4 3

BIBLEFORCE™

THE FIRST HEROES BIBLE

An Imprint of Thomas Nelson

www.bibleforce.net

Contents

AN INTRODUCTION TO THE BIBLE 1

WHAT HAPPENED WHEN? 6

THE WORLD OF THE BIBLE 8

THE OLD TESTAMENT 11

IN THE BEGINNING 13

GOD CREATES THE WORLD 14
GENESIS 1–2

THE GARDEN OF EDEN 19
GENESIS 2

BANISHED FROM EDEN 23
GENESIS 3

CAIN MURDERS ABEL 31
GENESIS 4

NOAH—THE LAST GOOD MAN 33

NOAH AND THE GREAT FLOOD 34
GENESIS 6–8

GOD'S COVENANT WITH NOAH 42
GENESIS 8–9

THE TOWER OF BABEL 45
GENESIS 11

ABRAHAM—THE CHOSEN ONE 50

THE CALL OF ABRAHAM 51
GENESIS 12

LOT LEAVES 54
GENESIS 13

GOD'S COVENANT WITH ABRAHAM 56
GENESIS 15

A SON IS BORN 59
GENESIS 16

THE DESTRUCTION OF SODOM AND
    GOMORRAH 60
GENESIS 18–19

GOD TESTS ABRAHAM 67
GENESIS 18, 21–22

ISAAC AND REBEKAH 74
GENESIS 24

JACOB—FATHER OF A NATION 78

THE BIRTH OF JACOB AND ESAU 79
GENESIS 25

ESAU SELLS HIS BIRTHRIGHT 82
GENESIS 25, 27

THE STOLEN BLESSING 87
GENESIS 27

STAIRWAY TO HEAVEN 89
GENESIS 27–32

WRESTLING WITH GOD 95
GENESIS 32–33

JOSEPH—THE DREAMER WITH A COAT 97

FAVORITE SON 98
GENESIS 37

BOUND FOR SLAVERY 102
GENESIS 37

JOSEPH IN PRISON 106
GENESIS 39

THE INTERPRETER OF DREAMS 110
GENESIS 40–41

JOSEPH FEEDS HIS FAMILY 114
GENESIS 41–45

MOSES—THE DELIVERER 123

A BABY IN A BASKET 124
EXODUS 1–2

MOSES THE PRINCE 128
EXODUS 2

THE BURNING BUSH 130
EXODUS 2–4

MOSES SPEAKS FOR GOD 136
EXODUS 4–7

THE PLAGUES 140
EXODUS 7–10

THE FINAL PLAGUE 145
EXODUS 10–12

OUT OF EGYPT 152
EXODUS 12–13

CROSSING THE RED SEA 156
EXODUS 14

MANNA FROM HEAVEN 162
EXODUS 15–17

THE TEN COMMANDMENTS 164
EXODUS 19–20

THE GOLDEN CALF 168
EXODUS 32

SIBLING JEALOUSY 174
   NUMBERS 12

MOSES AND HIS SPIES 176
   NUMBERS 13–14

WATER FROM A ROCK. 179
   NUMBERS 20

JOSHUA—ISRAELITE WARRIOR 181

A NEW LEADER EMERGES. 182
   DEUTERONOMY 31–34

JOSHUA'S SPIES 184
   JOSHUA 1–2

THE RIVER STOPS FLOWING. 186
   JOSHUA 3–4

THE CRUMBLING WALLS OF JERICHO . 188
   JOSHUA 5–6

THE DEFEAT AT AI 192
   JOSHUA 7–8

SUN STOPPER 196
   JOSHUA 9–10

CONQUEST OF CANAAN 200
   JOSHUA 11–12

GIDEON—GOD'S SOLDIER 202

GIDEON THE WARRIOR 203
   JUDGES 6–7

SAMSON—GOD'S STRONG MAN 208

SAMSON KILLS A LION 209
   JUDGES 13–15

SAMSON AND DELILAH 212
   JUDGES 16

RUTH—A FAITHFUL DAUGHTER-IN-LAW. . 215

A LOYAL WOMAN 216
   RUTH 1

RUTH AND BOAZ 218
   RUTH 2–4

SAMUEL—THE KING MAKER 222

A SON FOR HANNAH 223
   1 SAMUEL 1–3

SEIZING THE ARK. 225
   1 SAMUEL 4–6

THE MIRACLE AT MIZPAH 227
   1 SAMUEL 7

SEARCHING FOR A KING. 229
   1 SAMUEL 8–10

SAUL'S DISOBEDIENCE. 231
   1 SAMUEL 11–14

DAVID—FROM SHEPHERD TO KING 233

GOD CALLS DAVID 234
1 SAMUEL 16

DAVID AND GOLIATH 236
1 SAMUEL 16–17

SAUL'S JEALOUSY 241
1 SAMUEL 18–24

DAVID AND ABIGAIL 247
1 SAMUEL 25

THE FALL OF SAUL 249
1 SAMUEL 28–2 SAMUEL 1

KING DAVID 253
2 SAMUEL 2–6

THE WARS OF DAVID 256
2 SAMUEL 5–10; 1 CHRONICLES 14–20

DAVID AND BATHSHEBA 257
2 SAMUEL 11–12

SOLOMON—THE WISE ONE 261

SOLOMON IS CALLED 262
1 KINGS 1–2

THE WISDOM OF SOLOMON 264
1 KINGS 2–3

BUILDING THE GREAT TEMPLE 268
1 KINGS 6–8

GOD APPEARS TO SOLOMON AGAIN . . 270
1 KINGS 9

THE QUEEN OF SHEBA 272
1 KINGS 10

SOLOMON'S REIGN ENDS 274
1 KINGS 11–12

ELIJAH—SLAYER OF IDOLS 276

THE WICKED KING AND QUEEN 277
1 KINGS 12, 16–19

ELIJAH AND THE WIDOW 279
1 KINGS 17

ELIJAH AND THE PROPHETS OF BAAL . . 284
1 KINGS 18

ELIJAH GOES TO HEAVEN 288
2 KINGS 2

JERUSALEM IS DESTROYED 291
2 KINGS 24–25

ISAIAH—PROPHET OF DELIVERANCE 295

GOD CALLS ISAIAH 296
ISAIAH 6

CRISIS IN JUDAH 298
ISAIAH 7–8

THE SIEGE OF JERUSALEM 300
2 KINGS 18–20; 2 CHRONICLES 32

HEZEKIAH CRIES 303
ISAIAH 38

JEREMIAH—PROPHET OF DOOM 306

THE POTTER'S WHEEL 307
JEREMIAH 18–24

THE BASKET OF FIGS 309
JEREMIAH 24

THROWN INTO A WELL 311
JEREMIAH 37–38

EZEKIEL—PROPHET OF HOPE 313

GOD'S WARNING 314
EZEKIEL 4–5

AN ARMY OF BONES 316
EZEKIEL 37

JOB—THE SUFFERER 318

SATAN TESTS JOB 319
JOB 1–2

GOD SPEAKS TO JOB 324
JOB 38–42

GOD BLESSES JOB 326
JOB 42

DANIEL—A NOBLE PROPHET 328

DANIEL AND THE KING'S FOOD 329
DANIEL 1–2

THE KING'S FIERY FURNACE 331
DANIEL 3

WRITING ON THE WALL 332
DANIEL 5

DANIEL IN THE LIONS' DEN 334
DANIEL 6

ESTHER—A HEROIC QUEEN 338

ESTHER THE QUEEN 339
ESTHER 1–2

PLANNING THE SLAUGHTER 343
ESTHER 3–4

ESTHER SAVES HER PEOPLE 347
ESTHER 4–9

JONAH—A RELUCTANT PROPHET 351

JONAH AND THE WHALE 352
JONAH 1–4

NEHEMIAH—THE MAN BEHIND THE WALL 357

REBUILDING SOLOMON'S TEMPLE . . . 358
EZRA 1–6

WALLS IN RUIN 360
NEHEMIAH 1–7

EZRA—THE PRIEST 363

EZRA READS THE LAW 364
EZRA 9–10; MALACHI 1–4; NEHEMIAH 8

THE NEW TESTAMENT 367

JOHN THE BAPTIST 368

GABRIEL DELIVERS SOME NEWS 369
LUKE 1

GABRIEL VISITS MARY 371
LUKE 1

JOHN PREACHES 374
MATTHEW 3; LUKE 3

JESUS CHRIST—THE SON OF GOD 376

THE BIRTH OF CHRIST 378

A SPECIAL BABY 379
MATTHEW 1; LUKE 2

THE WISE MEN 385
MATTHEW 2

JESUS IN THE TEMPLE 391
LUKE 2

THE MINISTRY OF JESUS 395

THE BAPTISM OF JESUS 396
MATTHEW 3; MARK 1; LUKE 3

TEMPTATION IN THE DESERT 399
MATTHEW 4; MARK 1; LUKE 4

A PROPHET IN HIS HOMETOWN 403
LUKE 4

JESUS CALLS HIS DISCIPLES 405
MATTHEW 4, 9–10; MARK 1–3, 6; LUKE 5–6

WATER INTO WINE 415
JOHN 2

THE SAMARITAN WOMAN 419
JOHN 4

JESUS CURES THE FIRST LEPER 422
MATTHEW 8; MARK 1; LUKE 5

THE ROMAN CENTURION 425
MATTHEW 8; LUKE 7

SERMON ON THE MOUNT 428
MATTHEW 5–7; LUKE 6, 11

JESUS AND THE CHILDREN 439
MATTHEW 19; MARK 10; LUKE 18

THE PARABLE OF THE SOWER 440
MATTHEW 13; LUKE 8

THE PARABLE OF WEEDS AND WHEAT .. 443
MATTHEW 13

THE PARABLE OF THE LOST SHEEP 446
LUKE 15

THE PARABLE OF THE LOST COIN 447
LUKE 15

THE PARABLE OF THE
GOOD SAMARITAN 448
LUKE 10

THE PARABLE OF THE WISE
    AND FOOLISH GIRLS 453
    MATTHEW 25

THE PARABLE OF THE LOST SON 457
    LUKE 15

A HOLE IN THE ROOF 463
    MARK 2; LUKE 5

HEALING JAIRUS'S DAUGHTER 465
    MARK 5; LUKE 8

CALMING THE STORM 468
    MATTHEW 8; MARK 4; LUKE 8

THE HEAD OF JOHN THE BAPTIST 469
    MATTHEW 11, 14; MARK 6; LUKE 7

FEEDING THE CROWD 473
    MATTHEW 14; MARK 6; LUKE 9; JOHN 6

JESUS WALKS ON WATER 476
    MATTHEW 14

A WOMAN OF GREAT FAITH 479
    MATTHEW 15; MARK 7

THE TRANSFIGURATION OF
    JESUS CHRIST 482
    MARK 9; LUKE 9

THE DEMON-POSSESSED BOY 485
    MATTHEW 17; MARK 9; LUKE 9

HEALING TEN LEPERS 487
    LUKE 17

THE BLIND BEGGAR 489
    MARK 10; LUKE 18

ZACCHAEUS THE TAX COLLECTOR 492
    LUKE 19

MARTHA AND MARY 494
    LUKE 10

RAISING LAZARUS FROM THE DEAD . . . 495
    JOHN 11

PETER THE ROCK 499
    MATTHEW 16

THE LAST DAYS OF JESUS **500**

JESUS ARRIVES IN JERUSALEM 501
    MATTHEW 21; MARK 11; LUKE 19

THE MONEY CHANGERS 504
    MATTHEW 21; LUKE 19

BY WHAT AUTHORITY? 506
    MATTHEW 21; LUKE 20

A CONSPIRACY BREWS 508
    MATTHEW 22–23; MARK 12–15; LUKE 20–22

THE COMING PERSECUTION 512
    MATTHEW 24; MARK 13; LUKE 21

TWO GOOD WOMEN 513
    MARK 12, 14

PLANNING THE BETRAYAL 515
MATTHEW 26; MARK 14

PREPARING FOR PASSOVER 516
LUKE 22

SERVANT KING 517
JOHN 13

THE LAST SUPPER 518
MATTHEW 26; MARK 14; LUKE 22

BETRAYED WITH A KISS 522
MATTHEW 26; MARK 14; LUKE 22

PETER DENIES CHRIST 526
MATTHEW 26; LUKE 22

JESUS BEFORE THE HIGH PRIESTS 528
MARK 14–15; JOHN 18

PILATE WASHES HIS HANDS 531
MATTHEW 27; MARK 15; LUKE 23; JOHN 18–19

THE CRUCIFIXION 536
MATTHEW 27; MARK 15; LUKE 23; JOHN 18–19

THE RESURRECTION **542**

JESUS RISES 543
MATTHEW 27–28; MARK 15–16; LUKE 23–24; JOHN 19–20

THE GUARDS ARE TOLD TO LIE 549
MATTHEW 28

ON THE ROAD TO EMMAUS 550
LUKE 24

JESUS APPEARS TO THE DISCIPLES . . . 556
LUKE 24; JOHN 20

DOUBTING THOMAS 561
JOHN 20

"PETER, DO YOU LOVE ME?" 563
JOHN 21

JESUS ASCENDS TO HEAVEN 566
LUKE 24; ACTS 1

THE GOOD NEWS **568**

THE COMING OF THE HOLY SPIRIT 569
ACTS 2

PETER HEALS THE BEGGAR 575
ACTS 3–4

ARRESTED 579
ACTS 4

LYING TO GOD 580
ACTS 5

JAIL BREAK 584
ACTS 5

STEPHEN, THE MARTYR 585
ACTS 6–7

PHILIP AND THE ETHIOPIAN 586
ACTS 8

A SPECIAL WOMAN. 589
ACTS 9

A SHEET OF ANIMALS 590
ACTS 10

FREED BY AN ANGEL 593
ACTS 12

PAUL—SPREADING THE WORD **596**

SAUL SEES THE LIGHT. 597
ACTS 7–9

ESCAPE IN A BASKET. 602
ACTS 9

STRUCK BLIND. 603
ACTS 13

ON THE ROAD. 604
ACTS 13

TAKEN FOR GODS 605
ACTS 14

OFF TO MACEDONIA 607
ACTS 15–16

THE EARTHQUAKE. 610
ACTS 16–17

RIOT AT EPHESUS 612
ACTS 19

A BIG FALL. 615
ACTS 20

PLEASE DON'T GO. 618
ACTS 20

TROUBLE IN JERUSALEM. 619
ACTS 21–22

CONSPIRACY AND CONFUSION 622
ACTS 22–26

THE STORM AND THE SHIPWRECK 623
ACTS 27–28

THE EPISTLES **627**

THE GREATEST OF THESE IS LOVE. 628
ROMANS 5, 8; 1 CORINTHIANS 12–13

FAITH IN CHRIST. 629
GALATIANS 2–5; COLOSSIANS 3; EPHESIANS 6

FIGHT THE GOOD FIGHT 630
1 & 2 TIMOTHY

RUN THE RACE 631
HEBREWS; JAMES; 1 & 2 PETER; 1 JOHN

JOHN'S REVELATION **632**

AN AMAZING VISION 633
REVELATION 1–20

THE HOLY CITY 641
REVELATION 20–22

List of Maps

THE WORLD OF THE BIBLE 8

MAJOR POWERS IN OLD TESTAMENT TIMES 12

THE TWELVE TRIBES OF ISRAEL 12

THE HEBREWS' JOURNEY 154

ISRAEL DURING THE TIME OF JESUS 366

PAUL'S MISSIONARY JOURNEYS 603

THE SEVEN CHURCHES. 634

"Your word is a lamp to my feet and a light to my path."

Psalm 119:105

An Introduction to the Bible

NOT ONE BOOK, BUT A WHOLE LIBRARY!

YOU MIGHT THINK OF THE BIBLE AS ONE LARGE VOLUME, BUT IT IS ACTUALLY 66 INDIVIDUAL BOOKS, WRITTEN BY MANY DIFFERENT AUTHORS OVER MANY CENTURIES!

THERE ARE LOTS OF DIFFERENT STYLES, FROM POETRY TO LISTS AND FROM HISTORY BOOKS TO LETTERS. THERE ARE BOOKS BY KINGS, DOCTORS, PRIESTS, AND SHEPHERDS. SOME WERE WRITTEN IN THE TIME OF THE ROMAN EMPIRE. OTHERS WERE BEGUN NEARLY 3,500 YEARS AGO!

YET WHILE THESE BOOKS WERE WRITTEN BY HUMAN BEINGS, THEY WERE INSPIRED BY GOD. GOD SPOKE THROUGH ALL THESE DIFFERENT PEOPLE TO CREATE A WRITTEN VERSION OF HIS WORD. HE USED PEOPLE WHOSE WORLDS AND CULTURES WERE VASTLY DIFFERENT. BUT THROUGH IT ALL, GOD'S UNIVERSAL MESSAGE OF LOVE AND REDEMPTION IS PRESENT FROM GENESIS TO REVELATION.

SOME OF THE OLDEST SURVIVING WRITTEN PARTS OF THE BIBLE ARE FROM THE DEAD SEA SCROLLS.

IT'S LIKELY THAT MOST OF THE OLD TESTAMENT WAS PASSED DOWN BY WORD OF MOUTH THROUGH THE GENERATIONS UNTIL SCRIBES WROTE THE TEXT THAT BECAME THE BIBLE. SOME OF THE OLD TESTAMENT WAS WRITTEN IN HEBREW, WHILE A FEW PASSAGES WERE WRITTEN IN A SIMILAR LANGUAGE CALLED ARAMAIC.

THE EARLIEST TRANSLATION OF THE OLD TESTAMENT WAS FROM HEBREW MANUSCRIPTS INTO GREEK. IT WAS LATER TRANSLATED INTO LATIN AROUND THE FOURTH CENTURY AD WHILE THE FIRST ENGLISH VERSION WAS TRANSLATED AROUND 1,000 YEARS LATER, THE "KING JAMES BIBLE" (ALSO KNOWN AS THE "AUTHORIZED VERSION") WAS COMPLETED IN AD 1611.

TODAY THE FULL BIBLE HAS BEEN TRANSLATED INTO WELL OVER 600 LANGUAGES. THE NEW TESTAMENT HAS BEEN TRANSLATED INTO OVER 1,400 LANGUAGES, SPREADING THE MESSAGE OF GOD'S LOVE ALL ACROSS OUR WORLD!

THE OLD TESTAMENT

CHRISTIANS TRADITIONALLY DIVIDE THE BOOKS OF THE OLD TESTAMENT INTO FOUR GROUPINGS:

THE BOOKS OF THE OLD TESTAMENT

The Law	History	Poetry & Wisdom	The Prophets

Genesis · Exodus · Leviticus · Numbers · Deuteronomy · Joshua · Judges · Ruth · 1 Samuel · 2 Samuel · 1 Kings · 2 Kings · 1 Chronicles · 2 Chronicles · Ezra · Nehemiah · Esther · Job · Psalms · Proverbs · Ecclesiastes · Song of Solomon · Isaiah · Jeremiah · Lamentations · Ezekiel · Daniel · Hosea · Joel · Amos · Obadiah · Jonah · Micah · Nahum · Habakkuk · Zephaniah · Haggai · Zechariah · Malachi

LAW AND HISTORY

THE FIRST FIVE BOOKS OF THE BIBLE ARE KNOWN AS EITHER THE LAW, THE PENTATEUCH, OR THE TORAH. THEY COVER THE PERIOD FROM THE CREATION, THE STORY OF THE ANCESTORS OF THE ISRAELITES, AND THE EARLY HISTORY OF THE ISRAELITES. THEY OFFER MANY LAWS ABOUT HOW THEY WERE TO BUILD THEIR SOCIETY.

THE NEXT TWELVE BOOKS, OR THE HISTORICAL BOOKS, COVER ABOUT 800 YEARS OF ISRAEL'S HISTORY, FROM THE POSSESSION OF THE PROMISED LAND, THE RISE AND FALL OF THE KINGDOM, AND THE EXILE TO THE RETURN TO JERUSALEM.

TRADITIONALLY, THE FIRST FIVE BOOKS IN THE BIBLE WERE ATTRIBUTED TO MOSES.

POETRY AND WISDOM

THE FIVE POETICAL BOOKS, FROM JOB TO SONG OF SOLOMON, RELATE TO ISRAEL'S SPIRITUAL LIFE AND DEAL WITH QUESTIONS OF SUFFERING, LOVE, WISDOM, AND THE NATURE OF GOD. THEY ARE ALSO KNOWN AS THE WRITINGS OF WISDOM.

Trust in the LORD with all your heart.
Proverbs 3:5

MANY OF THE WORDS OF WISDOM IN THE BOOK OF PROVERBS ARE ATTRIBUTED TO KING SOLOMON.

The LORD is my shepherd;
I shall not want.
He makes me to lie down
  in green pastures;
He leads me beside the still waters.
He restores my soul;
He leads me in the paths of
  righteousness
For His name's sake.
Yea, though I walk through
  the valley of the shadow of death,
I will fear no evil;
For You are with me;
Your rod and Your staff,
  they comfort me.

Psalm 23:1–4

DAVID, WHO WENT FROM SHEPHERD BOY TO KING OF ISRAEL, IS BELIEVED TO HAVE WRITTEN MANY OF THE PSALMS INCLUDED IN THE OLD TESTAMENT. THE WORDS SPEAK FROM THE HEART AND OFFER COMFORT AND HOPE EVEN IN TIMES OF DESPAIR.

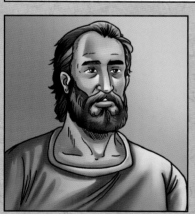

THE PROPHETS

IN THE OLD TESTAMENT, A SERIES OF BOOKS BEAR THE NAMES OF PROPHETS. THEY ARE DIVIDED INTO THE FOUR MAJOR PROPHETS (ISAIAH, JEREMIAH, EZEKIEL, AND DANIEL) AND THE TWELVE MINOR PROPHETS. THEY ARE DESIGNATED "MAJOR" AND "MINOR" MOSTLY BASED ON THE LENGTH OF THEIR WRITINGS.

PROPHETS WERE PEOPLE CHOSEN TO BE SPOKESMEN FOR GOD. THEY WERE ALSO KNOWN AS SEERS, WATCHMEN, OR SERVANTS OF THE LORD.

WHILE MANY OF THE PROPHETS' MESSAGES FOCUSED ON THE FUTURE, THEY WERE ALSO CONCERNED WITH PRESENT-DAY EVENTS, SUCH AS SOCIAL LIFE AND POLITICS.

THE NEW TESTAMENT

THE NEW TESTAMENT CAN BE DIVIDED INTO FOUR SECTIONS:

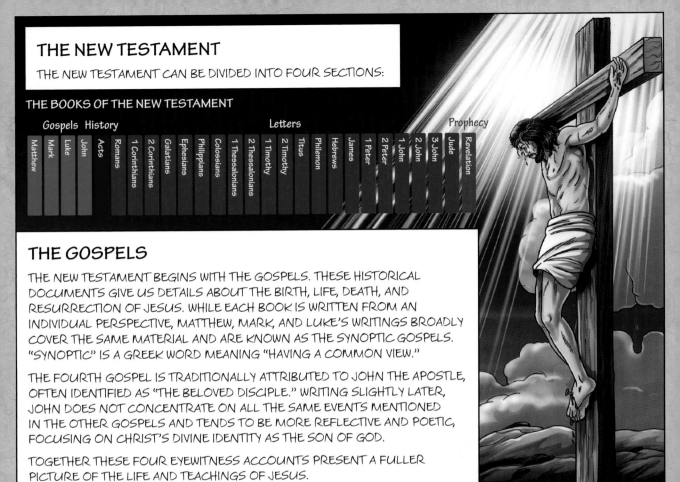

THE BOOKS OF THE NEW TESTAMENT

Gospels				History								Letters														Prophecy

Matthew · Mark · Luke · John · Acts · Romans · 1 Corinthians · 2 Corinthians · Galatians · Ephesians · Philippians · Colossians · 1 Thessalonians · 2 Thessalonians · 1 Timothy · 2 Timothy · Titus · Philemon · Hebrews · James · 1 Peter · 2 Peter · 1 John · 2 John · 3 John · Jude · Revelation

THE GOSPELS

THE NEW TESTAMENT BEGINS WITH THE GOSPELS. THESE HISTORICAL DOCUMENTS GIVE US DETAILS ABOUT THE BIRTH, LIFE, DEATH, AND RESURRECTION OF JESUS. WHILE EACH BOOK IS WRITTEN FROM AN INDIVIDUAL PERSPECTIVE, MATTHEW, MARK, AND LUKE'S WRITINGS BROADLY COVER THE SAME MATERIAL AND ARE KNOWN AS THE SYNOPTIC GOSPELS. "SYNOPTIC" IS A GREEK WORD MEANING "HAVING A COMMON VIEW."

THE FOURTH GOSPEL IS TRADITIONALLY ATTRIBUTED TO JOHN THE APOSTLE, OFTEN IDENTIFIED AS "THE BELOVED DISCIPLE." WRITING SLIGHTLY LATER, JOHN DOES NOT CONCENTRATE ON ALL THE SAME EVENTS MENTIONED IN THE OTHER GOSPELS AND TENDS TO BE MORE REFLECTIVE AND POETIC, FOCUSING ON CHRIST'S DIVINE IDENTITY AS THE SON OF GOD.

TOGETHER THESE FOUR EYEWITNESS ACCOUNTS PRESENT A FULLER PICTURE OF THE LIFE AND TEACHINGS OF JESUS.

HISTORY

THE BOOK OF ACTS IS WRITTEN BY THE SAME AUTHOR AS THE BOOK OF LUKE—THE DOCTOR AND COMPANION OF THE APOSTLE PAUL. LUKE TELLS US WHAT HAPPENED AFTER THE DEATH AND RESURRECTION OF CHRIST AND OF THE BIRTH AND GROWTH OF THE CHURCH.

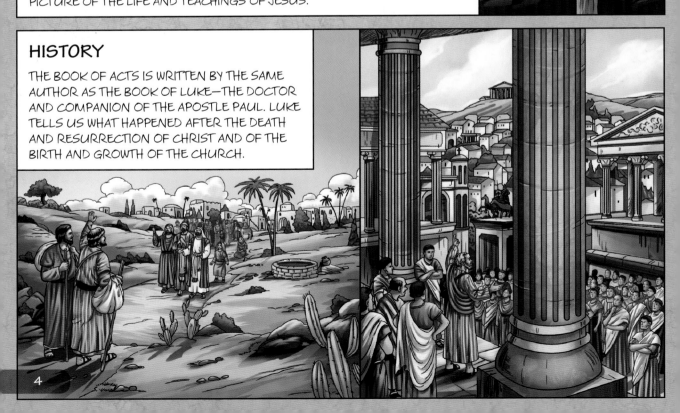

LETTERS

OF THE 27 BOOKS THAT MAKE UP THE NEW TESTAMENT, 21 ARE IN THE GROUP CALLED THE EPISTLES, OR LETTERS. MANY OF THESE WERE WRITTEN BY THE APOSTLE PAUL. SOME LETTERS WERE WRITTEN TO CHURCHES AND WERE DESIGNED TO GUIDE THE NEW BELIEVERS AND ANSWER THEIR QUESTIONS. OTHERS WERE MORE PERSONAL AND WERE DIRECTED TO INDIVIDUALS.

WHETHER PERSONAL OR GENERAL, THE LETTERS OFFERED ADVICE, GUIDANCE, COMFORT, AND HOPE TO THE NEW CHURCH. THEY CONTINUE TO BE RELEVANT AND USEFUL TO PEOPLE TODAY.

PROPHECY

JUST AS THE OLD TESTAMENT ENDS WITH PROPHECY, SO DOES THE NEW TESTAMENT. AS GENESIS IS THE BOOK OF BEGINNINGS, IN THE LAST BOOK OF THE BIBLE WE ARE SHOWN THE END OF DAYS. REVELATION IS A SERIES OF VISIONS, FILLED WITH SYMBOLISM AND PROPHECY. IT OFFERS HOPE AND CERTAINTY TO CHRISTIANS EVERYWHERE.

What Happened When?

THE STORIES IN THE BIBLE TAKE PLACE OVER MANY CENTURIES. IT IS HARD TO KNOW THE EXACT DATES OR LOCATIONS OF KEY EVENTS. HERE IS A TIMELINE OF FAMOUS BIBLE STORIES, AND ESTIMATES OF WHEN THEY HAPPENED! (ALL DATES ARE APPROXIMATE)

CREATION
DATES UNKNOWN

NOAH SURVIVES THE GREAT FLOOD
BEFORE 2500 BC

ABRAHAM IS BORN
1996 BC

SODOM IS DESTROYED
1897 BC

JACOB AND ESAU ARE BORN
1837 BC

MOSES IS BORN
1530 BC

THE ISRAELITES LEAVE EGYPT
1491 BC

GOD GIVES MOSES THE TEN COMMANDMENTS
1491 BC

DEATH OF SAUL
1010 BC

DAVID IS KING OF ISRAEL
1010 BC

SOLOMON BUILDS THE TEMPLE
960 BC

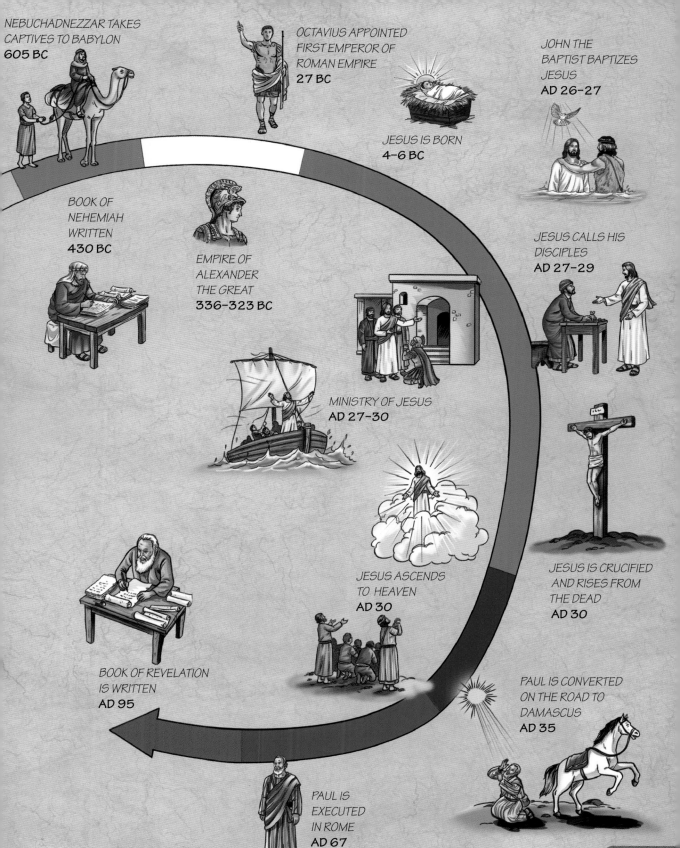

NEBUCHADNEZZAR TAKES CAPTIVES TO BABYLON
605 BC

OCTAVIUS APPOINTED FIRST EMPEROR OF ROMAN EMPIRE
27 BC

JESUS IS BORN
4–6 BC

JOHN THE BAPTIST BAPTIZES JESUS
AD 26–27

BOOK OF NEHEMIAH WRITTEN
430 BC

EMPIRE OF ALEXANDER THE GREAT
336–323 BC

JESUS CALLS HIS DISCIPLES
AD 27–29

MINISTRY OF JESUS
AD 27–30

JESUS ASCENDS TO HEAVEN
AD 30

JESUS IS CRUCIFIED AND RISES FROM THE DEAD
AD 30

BOOK OF REVELATION IS WRITTEN
AD 95

PAUL IS CONVERTED ON THE ROAD TO DAMASCUS
AD 35

PAUL IS EXECUTED IN ROME
AD 67

The World of the Bible

DACIA

ILLYRICUM

THRACE

Rome

ITALY

Adriatic Sea

MACEDONIA

Philippi

Nicopolis

Aegean Sea

AS

SICILY

Corinth

Patmos

Ephesus

LYCI

CRETE

Mediterranean Sea

AFRICA

LIBYA

Sahara Desert

CAUCASUS

Black Sea

Caspian Sea

ARMENIA

ASSYRIA

GALATIA

Anti-Taurus Mountains

PERSIA

Nineveh

Tigris

MESOPOTAMIA

Tarsus

Zagros Mountains

CILICIA

Euphrates

Antioch

CYPRUS

Paphos

SYRIA

Susah

Sidon

Damascus

Babylon

ISRAEL

Sea of Galilee

Jerusalem

Dead Sea

EGYPT

EDOM

ARABIA

Red Sea

Thebes

The Old Testament

"In the beginning God created the heavens and the earth."

Genesis 1:1

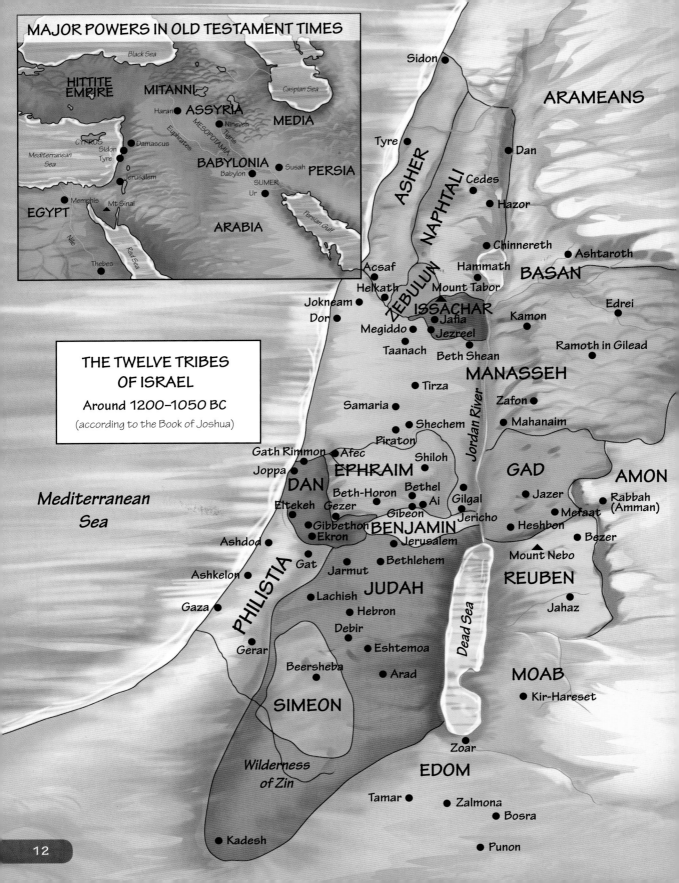

MAJOR POWERS IN OLD TESTAMENT TIMES

Black Sea

HITTITE EMPIRE

MITANNI

Caspian Sea

Haran

ASSYRIA

Nineveh

MEDIA

CYPRUS

Sidon

Damascus

Euphrates

Tigris

MESOPOTAMIA

Mediterranean Sea

Tyre

Jerusalem

BABYLONIA

Babylon

Susah

SUMER

PERSIA

Ur

EGYPT

Memphis

Mt Sinai

Nile

Red Sea

Thebes

ARABIA

Persian Gulf

THE TWELVE TRIBES OF ISRAEL

Around 1200–1050 BC

(according to the Book of Joshua)

Sidon

ARAMEANS

Tyre

Dan

ASHER

NAPHTALI

Cedes

Hazor

Chinnereth

Ashtaroth

Acsaf

Hammath

BASAN

Helkath

ZEBULUN

Mount Tabor

ISSACHAR

Edrei

Jokneam

Kamon

Dor

Megiddo

Jafia

Jezreel

Taanach

Beth Shean

Ramoth in Gilead

MANASSEH

Tirza

Zafon

Samaria

Mahanaim

Shechem

Jordan River

Piraton

Gath Rimmon

Afec

Shiloh

GAD

AMON

Joppa

EPHRAIM

Bethel

Jazer

Rabbah (Amman)

DAN

Beth-Horon

Ai

Gilgal

Mefaat

Eltekeh

Gezer

Gibeon

Jericho

Heshbon

Gibbethon

BENJAMIN

Bezer

Ekron

Jerusalem

Mediterranean Sea

Ashdod

Bethlehem

Mount Nebo

Gat

Jarmut

REUBEN

Ashkelon

Lachish

JUDAH

Jahaz

Gaza

Hebron

Debir

Eshtemoa

MOAB

Gerar

Arad

Kir-Hareset

PHILISTIA

Beersheba

SIMEON

Dead Sea

Wilderness of Zin

Zoar

EDOM

Tamar

Zalmona

Bosra

Kadesh

Punon

12

In the Beginning

EARLIEST SOURCES FOR GENESIS ARE THOUGHT TO DATE FROM 1ST MILLENNIUM BC.

THE BOOK TOOK ITS CURRENT FORM IN THE 5TH CENTURY BC.

BEHIND THE NAME

THE ORIGINAL HEBREW TITLE OF THE BOOK IS "BERESHIT," WHICH MEANS "IN BEGINNING." HOWEVER, THE NAME WE NOW KNOW IT BY, GENESIS, COMES FROM THE GREEK WORD "GENESEOS" MEANING "ORIGIN, GENERATION, OR BEGINNING," WHICH WAS USED BY GREEK SCHOLARS WHEN THEY TRANSLATED THE BOOK IN THE 3RD CENTURY BC.

BEHIND THE PEN

TRADITION ATTRIBUTES AUTHORSHIP TO MOSES FOR THE FIRST FIVE BOOKS OF THE BIBLE (ALSO KNOWN AS THE PENTATEUCH OR LAW).

God Creates the World

Genesis 1–2

IN THE BEGINNING, GOD CREATED THE HEAVENS AND THE EARTH. THE EARTH WAS WITHOUT SHAPE AND WAS COVERED IN DARKNESS.

GOD SAID, **"LET THERE BE LIGHT!"** AND THE LIGHT SHINED. GOD LIKED WHAT HE SAW. HE CALLED THE LIGHT "DAY" AND THE DARKNESS "NIGHT." EVENING CAME AND THEN MORNING. THE FIRST DAY HAD ENDED.

ON THE SECOND DAY, GOD SEPARATED THE WATER FROM THE SKY.

ON THE THIRD DAY, GOD SAID, "LET DRY LAND APPEAR." AND IT DID. HE CALLED THE DRY LAND "EARTH" AND THE WATER THE "SEAS."

GOD LIKED WHAT HE SAW.

GOD CREATED TREES, FLOWERS, AND ALL TYPES OF PLANTS.

ON THE FOURTH DAY, GOD CREATED THE SUN...

...ALONG WITH THE MOON AND STARS.

ON THE FIFTH DAY, GOD CREATED ALL THE CREATURES OF THE SEA AND THE SKY.

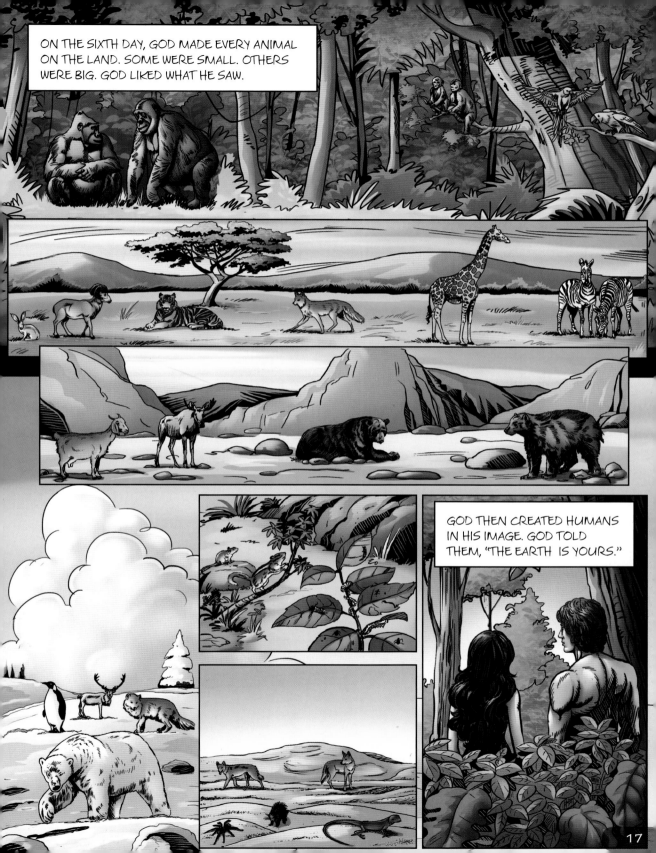

ON THE SIXTH DAY, GOD MADE EVERY ANIMAL ON THE LAND. SOME WERE SMALL. OTHERS WERE BIG. GOD LIKED WHAT HE SAW.

GOD THEN CREATED HUMANS IN HIS IMAGE. GOD TOLD THEM, "THE EARTH IS YOURS."

ON THE SEVENTH DAY, GOD SAW
WHAT HE MADE AND WAS HAPPY.
HIS WORK WAS DONE. THAT DAY
BECAME A SPECIAL DAY FOR US
TO REST AND THANK GOD.

Banished from Eden

Genesis 3

EVE AND ADAM WERE NAKED. YET THEY WERE NOT ASHAMED.

NOR WERE THEY AFRAID OF THE ANIMALS.

ONE ANIMAL, THE SNAKE, WAS THE MOST CUNNING OF ALL.

AFTER EVE ATE THE FRUIT FROM THE TREE, SHE TURNED TO ADAM...

...AND GAVE HIM THE FRUIT TO EAT. HE TOOK A BITE.

AS SOON AS ADAM BIT INTO THE FRUIT, HE AND EVE REALIZED THEY WERE NAKED. THEY WERE ASHAMED, SO THEY COVERED THEMSELVES.

GOD WAS SO ANGRY THAT HE THREW ADAM AND EVE OUT OF HIS MAGNIFICENT GARDEN.

BECAUSE ADAM AND EVE HAD SINNED, ALL HUMANS WOULD HAVE TO WORK AND SUFFER.

Hero Profile
Noah—The Last Good Man

FATHER: LAMECH, A DESCENDANT OF ADAM

SONS: SHEM, HAM, JAPHETH

LIFE SPAN: DIED AT AGE 950

GENERATION GAP

NOAH WAS THE GRANDSON OF METHUSELAH, THE OLDEST PERSON IN THE BIBLE, WHO DIED AT 969 YEARS OLD IN THE YEAR OF THE FLOOD. NOAH HIMSELF WAS ALREADY 500 YEARS OLD WHEN HE BECAME A FATHER.

WHERE IS MOUNT ARARAT?

MOUNT ARARAT, THE LANDING PLACE OF NOAH'S ARK, IS IN A MOUNTAIN RANGE IN THE EXTREME EASTERN PART OF TURKEY. ITS PEAK IS SEVERAL HUNDRED MILES NORTH OF WHERE MANY SCHOLARS BELIEVE CIVILIZATION BEGAN IN MESOPOTAMIA. FOR CENTURIES EXPLORERS HAVE SEARCHED FOR THE REMAINS OF NOAH'S GREAT BOAT ON THESE MYSTERIOUS MOUNTAIN PEAKS.

Noah and the Great Flood

Genesis 6–8

THE YEARS PASSED. PEOPLE BEGAN TO LIVE TOGETHER IN VILLAGES.

SOME WERE WICKED. THEY HURT EACH OTHER.

OTHERS TOOK WHAT THEY WANTED....

...AND DID WHATEVER PLEASED THEM.

GOD SAW THAT PEOPLE HAD BECOME EVIL. YET THERE WAS ONE GOOD MAN. HIS NAME WAS NOAH. HE HAD A WIFE AND THREE SONS—SHEM, HAM, AND JAPHETH.

NOAH

SHEM

HAM

JAPHETH

GOD SPOKE TO NOAH. HE TOLD NOAH HOW TO BUILD AN ARK—A GREAT SHIP IN WHICH NOAH AND HIS FAMILY WOULD SURVIVE THE FLOOD.

THIS IS HOW BIG THE ARK HAS TO BE.

IT CAN'T BE DONE. IT'S NOT POSSIBLE!

FATHER, IT IS TOO LARGE!

IT WILL NEVER FLOAT!

NOAH AND HIS FAMILY WORKED HARD FOR A LONG TIME BUILDING THE ARK.

NOAH DID EVERYTHING ACCORDING TO ALL THAT GOD COMMANDED HIM TO DO.

NOAH, HIS WIFE, HIS SONS, AND THEIR WIVES CARED FOR ALL THE CREATURES ON THE ARK...

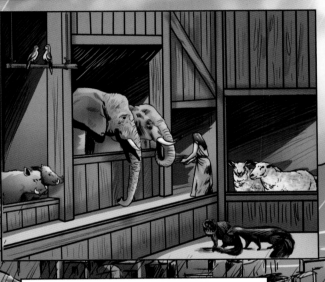

...AND THEY WAITED.

THE RAIN BEGAN TO FALL, AND THE EARTH'S SPRINGS BURST OPEN. IT RAINED FOR DAYS WITHOUT CEASING.

FLOODWATERS COVERED THE EARTH— TOWNS AND CITIES, FORESTS AND MOUNTAINS. THE FLOOD KILLED EVERY LIVING BEING ON THE PLANET.

39

THE RAIN WAS ENDLESS. GREAT WAVES SWELLED AND BATTERED THE ARK.

NOAH'S FAMILY MAY HAVE BEEN FEARFUL DURING THEIR MANY MONTHS INSIDE THE ARK. NOAH HAD A PLAN TO FIND LAND AFTER THE WATERS FINALLY STARTED TO RECEDE.

I WILL SEND OUT A BIRD TO FIND LAND.

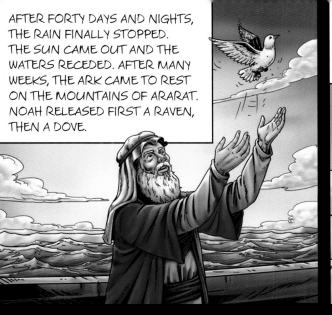

AFTER FORTY DAYS AND NIGHTS, THE RAIN FINALLY STOPPED. THE SUN CAME OUT AND THE WATERS RECEDED. AFTER MANY WEEKS, THE ARK CAME TO REST ON THE MOUNTAINS OF ARARAT. NOAH RELEASED FIRST A RAVEN, THEN A DOVE.

AT FIRST THE DOVE COULD FIND NOWHERE TO LAND, FOR THE EARTH WAS STILL COVERED IN WATER. AFTER SEVEN DAYS, NOAH TRIED AGAIN. WHEN THE BIRD RETURNED, IT CARRIED A LEAF IN ITS BEAK.

GOD TOLD NOAH TO LEAVE THE ARK WITH HIS FAMILY AND ALL THE ANIMALS. NOAH DID AS GOD ASKED.

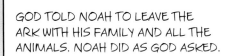

FATHER, WE HAVE BEEN DELIVERED. GOD HAS SPARED US.

WE MUST BUILD AN ALTAR AND **MAKE A SACRIFICE** TO THE LORD.

THEN GOD MADE A PROMISE—A COVENANT.

I MAKE MY COVENANT WITH YOU. NEVER AGAIN SHALL THERE BE A FLOOD TO DESTROY THE EARTH.

GOD CREATED A RAINBOW AS A SIGN OF HIS PROMISE. GOD TOLD NOAH THAT RAINBOWS WOULD APPEAR TO REASSURE HUMANS OF HIS COVENANT WITH EVERY LIVING CREATURE.

45

SO THE PEOPLE WENT TO WORK BUILDING A GREAT CITY—BABEL.

THEY LEARNED TO MAKE STRONG BRICKS. THEY USED THESE BRICKS TO BUILD TALLER BUILDINGS THAN ANYONE HAD EVER BUILT.

PUT THOSE BRICKS OVER HERE!

BUILDING A GREAT CITY IS HARD WORK!

IT IS TOUGH WORK, BUT THE CITY WILL BE BEAUTIFUL. OUR BUILDINGS WILL BE **MAGNIFICENT**!

47

Hero Profile
Abraham—The Chosen One

NAME: ABRAHAM (MEANING "FATHER OF MANY PEOPLE")

ALSO KNOWN AS: ABRAM (MEANING "GREAT FATHER") AND THE FATHER OF THE HEBREW PEOPLE, OR JEWISH NATION

AGE: LIVED TO THE AGE OF 175

FATHER: TERAH

WIFE: (SARAI) SARAH

BORN: THE CITY OF UR IN BABYLONIA

SONS: ISHMAEL AND ISAAC

NEPHEW: LOT

A FOUNDING "FATHER"

GOD USES ABRAHAM TO SHOW PEOPLE SALVATION COMES ONLY BY FAITH IN THE ONE TRUE GOD. THE NEW TESTAMENT GIVES US MORE DETAIL WHEN IT EXPLAINS THAT ABRAHAM'S TRUST IN GOD'S PROMISE WAS AN EXAMPLE OF OUR FAITH IN GOD THAT IS THROUGH HIS SON, JESUS CHRIST. (ROMANS 4)

FAMOUS ABRAHAM

MANY PEOPLE HAVE BEEN NAMED ABRAHAM IN MODERN TIMES. PERHAPS NONE HAS BEEN MORE FAMOUS THAN ABRAHAM LINCOLN, THE 16TH PRESIDENT OF THE UNITED STATES, KNOWN FOR GUIDING THE NATION THROUGH THE CIVIL WAR, FOR CHAMPIONING HUMAN RIGHTS, AND FOR BRINGING ABOUT THE EMANCIPATION OF AFRICAN AMERICANS FROM SLAVERY.

ABRAHAM HAD GREAT FAITH IN GOD. HE SET OUT FOR CANAAN WITH HIS WIFE AND HIS NEPHEW, LOT. ABRAHAM WAS 75 YEARS OLD.

ALTHOUGH ABRAHAM AND SARAH WERE OLD, GOD GUIDED THEM TO THE LAND HE PROMISED.

ABRAHAM, LOOK! I THINK WE HAVE REACHED CANAAN!

GOD IS TRULY MAGNIFICENT. WE HAVE ARRIVED! LET US THANK HIM. LET US WORSHIP HIM.

I WILL GIVE THIS LAND TO YOU AND ALL YOUR OFFSPRING.

ABRAHAM BUILT AN ALTAR AND PRAYED.

Lot Leaves

Genesis 13

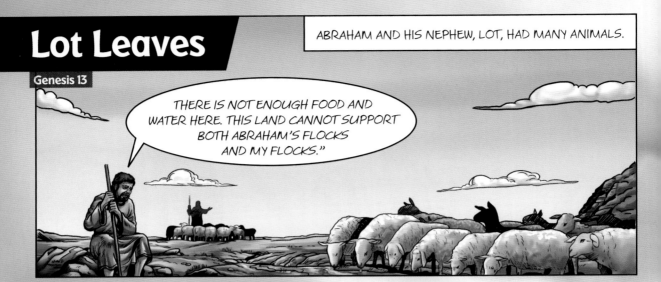

ABRAHAM AND HIS NEPHEW, LOT, HAD MANY ANIMALS.

THERE IS NOT ENOUGH FOOD AND WATER HERE. THIS LAND CANNOT SUPPORT BOTH ABRAHAM'S FLOCKS AND MY FLOCKS."

BECAUSE THEIR POSSESSIONS WERE SO GREAT, THERE WAS STRIFE BETWEEN THE HERDSMEN.

PLEASE LET THERE BE NO HARD FEELINGS BETWEEN YOU AND ME.

WE ARE **FAMILY!**

LET'S SEPARATE, AND YOU MAY CHOOSE THE LAND WHERE YOU WANT TO LIVE. I WILL DWELL ON THE OTHER SIDE.

LOT LEFT WITH HIS HERDS. HE SET OFF FOR THE FERTILE JORDAN VALLEY.

ABRAHAM STAYED IN CANAAN.

God's Covenant with Abraham

Genesis 15

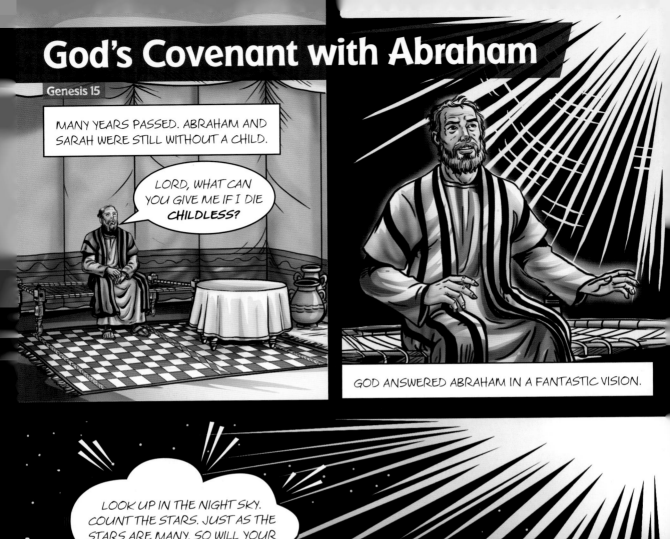

MANY YEARS PASSED. ABRAHAM AND SARAH WERE STILL WITHOUT A CHILD.

LORD, WHAT CAN YOU GIVE ME IF I DIE **CHILDLESS?**

GOD ANSWERED ABRAHAM IN A FANTASTIC VISION.

LOOK UP IN THE NIGHT SKY. COUNT THE STARS. JUST AS THE STARS ARE MANY, SO WILL YOUR DESCENDANTS BE.

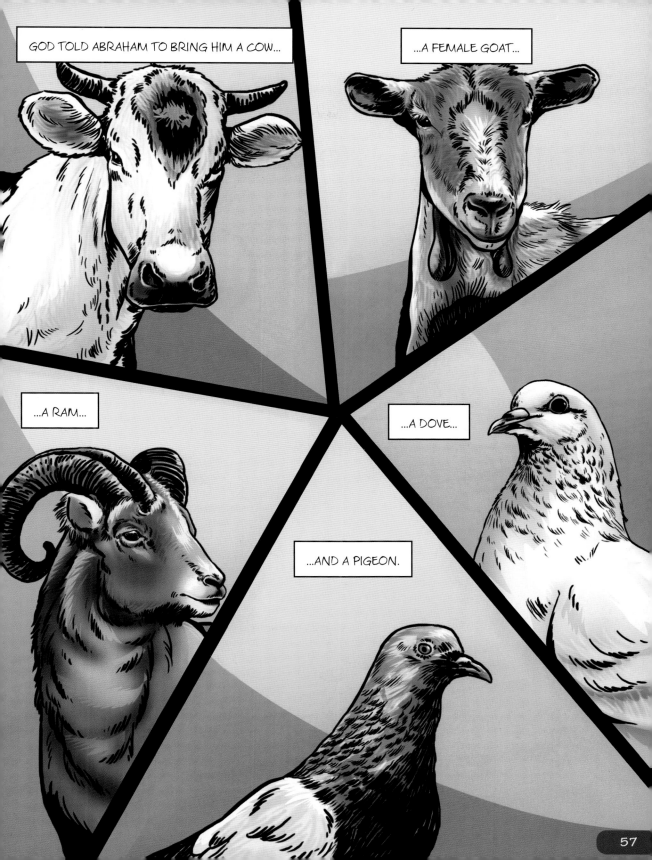

ABRAHAM DID AS GOD ASKED. HE CUT THE COW, GOAT, AND RAM IN TWO.

ABRAHAM FELL ASLEEP, AND A DARKNESS FELL OVER HIM. AS HE SLEPT, GOD TOLD HIM ABOUT THE FUTURE.

ABRAHAM, YOUR DESCENDANTS WILL BE AS STRANGERS IN A LAND THAT IS NOT THEIR OWN. THEY WILL BE SLAVES...

...BUT I WILL PUNISH THE NATION OF SLAVEHOLDERS, AND I WILL BLESS YOUR PEOPLE. I WILL LEAD THEM BACK TO CANAAN!

AS A SIGN OF HIS PROMISE, GOD PASSED A SMOKING FIREPOT WITH A BLAZING TORCH BETWEEN THE DIVIDED ANIMALS.

A Son Is Born

Genesis 16

MORE YEARS PASSED.

OH, ABRAHAM, WE WILL NEVER HAVE A BABY. I AM TOO OLD.

SARAH ASKED ABRAHAM TO FATHER A CHILD WITH THEIR SERVANT, HAGAR.

ABRAHAM AGREED, BUT SARAH TREATED HAGAR POORLY. THE YOUNG GIRL WANTED TO ESCAPE.

THE LORD'S ANGEL APPEARED.

GOD SEES HOW UNHAPPY YOU ARE.

GO BACK TO SARAH. OBEY HER. YOU WILL HAVE A SON.

HAGAR OBEYED, AND GOD KEPT HIS PROMISE. ABRAHAM HAD A SON—ISHMAEL.

59

The Destruction of Sodom and Gomorrah

Genesis 18–19

AT THAT TIME THERE WERE TWO CITIES NEAR THE DEAD SEA. THE FIRST WAS SODOM.

THE SECOND WAS GOMORRAH.

WHAT IF THERE WERE **45** RIGHTEOUS PEOPLE?

WILL YOU DESTROY THE **WHOLE** CITY?

I WILL NOT DESTROY IT IF I FIND 45 THERE.

WHAT IF **TEN** RIGHTEOUS PEOPLE WERE FOUND THERE?

GOD SAID, "FOR THE SAKE OF THE TEN, I WILL NOT DESTROY IT."

LOT, HIS WIFE, AND THEIR DAUGHTERS DID AS THE ANGELS ASKED. THEY FLED.

GOD RAINED FIRE ON SODOM AND GOMORRAH, DESTROYING BOTH CITIES AND THE PEOPLE IN THEM.

BUT LOT'S WIFE LOOKED BACK. AS SOON AS SHE LOOKED BEHIND HER, SHE WAS TURNED INTO A PILLAR OF SALT.

God Tests Abraham

Genesis 18, 21–22

THE SUMMER SUN WAS HOT AS ABRAHAM SAT AT THE ENTRANCE OF HIS TENT.

AS HE LOOKED UP, ABRAHAM SAW THREE STRANGERS.

LET ME BRING YOU SOME WATER TO WASH YOUR FEET.

LET ME BRING YOU A LITTLE FOOD TO REFRESH YOURSELVES.

...AND THE NEXT DAY, HE TOOK ISAAC TO THE MOUNTAIN CALLED MORIAH.

ABRAHAM TOLD ISAAC TO COME WITH HIM TO WORSHIP GOD.

FATHER, IF WE ARE TO MAKE A SACRIFICE TO GOD, DON'T WE NEED AN ANIMAL?

GOD WILL PROVIDE, MY SON.

THEY ARRIVED AT THE PLACE GOD HAD DESCRIBED TO ABRAHAM. THEY BUILT AN ALTAR.

ABRAHAM THEN TOOK ISAAC...

AND ABRAHAM BOUND ISAAC HIS SON AND PLACED HIM ON THE ALTAR.

Isaac and Rebekah

Genesis 24

THE YEARS PASSED. ABRAHAM DID NOT HAVE LONG TO LIVE. HIS WIFE, SARAH, HAD DIED.

ABRAHAM WAS WORRIED ABOUT ISAAC. HE DID NOT WANT HIS SON TO MARRY A CANAANITE BUT A RELATIVE FROM HIS HOMELAND.

YOU ARE MY MOST TRUSTED SERVANT. GO TO MESOPOTAMIA AND FIND MY SON A BRIDE.

MY DESCENDANTS HAVE BEEN BLESSED BY GOD. BUT ISAAC MUST MARRY IF I AM TO HAVE DESCENDANTS!

Hero Profile
Jacob—Father of a Nation

AGE: LIVED TO THE AGE OF 147

FATHER: ISAAC, SON OF ABRAHAM

MOTHER: REBEKAH

BROTHER: ESAU

WIVES: LEAH, RACHEL

CHILDREN: SONS—REUBEN, SIMEON, LEVI, JUDAH, DAN, NAPHTALI, GAD, ASHER, ISSACHAR, ZEBULUN, JOSEPH, BENJAMIN; DAUGHTER—DINAH

TWELVE TRIBES OF ISRAEL

JACOB'S TWELVE SONS WOULD BECOME THE ANCESTORS OF THE TWELVE TRIBES OF ISRAEL—CALLED "ISRAEL" BECAUSE GOD CHANGED JACOB'S NAME TO "ISRAEL."

ISRAEL

THE MODERN STATE OF ISRAEL WAS FORMED IN 1948 AS THE ONLY JEWISH COUNTRY IN THE WORLD.

The Birth of Jacob and Esau

Genesis 25

ISAAC AND REBEKAH LIVED THEIR LIVES. BUT SOMETHING WAS MISSING—A CHILD.

OH, ISAAC, HOW I LONG TO HAVE A BABY!

YES, WE MUST HAVE CHILDREN AND CONTINUE MY FATHER'S LINE.

I WILL PRAY TO GOD. HE BLESSED ME AFTER MY FATHER, ABRAHAM, DIED.

DEAR LORD, HEAR MY PRAYERS.

MY WIFE WANTS A SON TO LOVE.

GOD HEARD ISAAC'S PRAYERS, AND REBEKAH BECAME PREGNANT WITH TWINS.

THE TWINS REBEKAH CARRIED STRUGGLED TOGETHER INSIDE HER. SHE WONDERED WHY THEY WERE LIKE THIS, SO SHE SOUGHT ANSWERS FROM GOD.

LORD, WHAT IS HAPPENING WITH MY CHILDREN?

TWO NATIONS ARE IN YOUR WOMB. TWO SEPARATE PEOPLES WILL COME FROM YOU.

ONE WILL BE STRONGER THAN THE OTHER, AND THE OLDER SHALL SERVE THE YOUNGER.

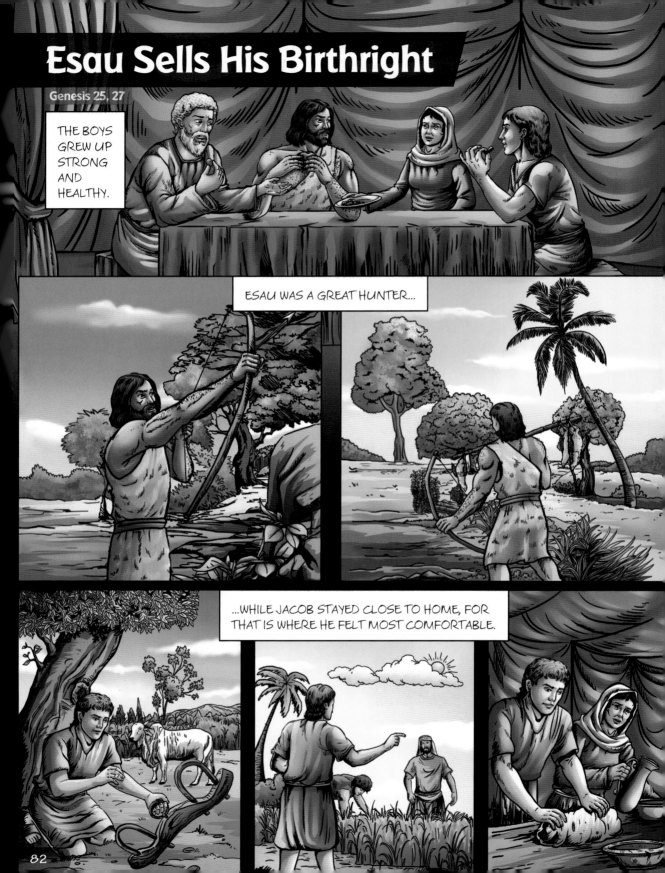

ISAAC CALLED FOR ESAU AND TOLD HIM TO GO OUT AND HUNT FOR SOME GAME.

THE YEARS PASSED, AND ISAAC GREW SICK AND BLIND.

AFTER YOU HUNT, PREPARE MY FAVORITE FOOD...

...SO THAT I MAY GIVE YOU MY BLESSING BEFORE I DIE.

SO ESAU WENT OUT TO HUNT AS HIS FATHER REQUESTED.

REBEKAH, HOWEVER, WAS MAKING OTHER PLANS.

The Stolen Blessing

Genesis 27

JACOB DID AS HIS MOTHER ASKED. HE BROUGHT HER TWO YOUNG GOATS.

REBEKAH PREPARED ISAAC'S MEAL...

...AND WRAPPED THE ANIMALS' SKINS AROUND JACOB'S ARMS AND NECK. SHE ALSO DRESSED HIM IN ESAU'S CLOTHES.

JACOB THEN BROUGHT THE FOOD TO HIS FATHER.

Stairway to Heaven

Genesis 27–32

ISAAC HAD BLESSED JACOB, AND ESAU WAS FURIOUS. HE VOWED REVENGE.

I'LL **KILL** MY BROTHER!

REBEKAH OVERHEARD ESAU AND WARNED HER BELOVED JACOB.

YOU MUST **LEAVE**. NOW!

GO VISIT YOUR UNCLE IN HARAN. I WILL SEND WORD WHEN IT IS SAFE FOR YOU TO RETURN.

JACOB LEFT, ALTHOUGH HE DID NOT WANT TO.

JACOB STOPPED IN A PLACE CALLED BETHEL AND FELL ASLEEP.

AS HE SLEPT, JACOB DREAMED OF A STAIRWAY TO HEAVEN. ANGELS WALKED UP AND DOWN THE STEPS.

THEN GOD SPOKE TO HIM.

JACOB, I AM THE GOD OF ABRAHAM AND THE GOD OF ISAAC. THIS LAND WILL BE YOURS. YOUR DESCENDANTS WILL BE AS NUMEROUS AS THE DUST OF THE EARTH.

THE NEXT MORNING JACOB WOKE UP INSPIRED BY HIS DREAM.

HE CONTINUED HIS JOURNEY. ONE DAY HE CAME UPON A GROUP OF SHEPHERDS AT A WELL.

BROTHERS, DO YOU KNOW MY UNCLE, LABAN?

YES, WE DO! AND HERE COMES HIS DAUGHTER, RACHEL.

LABAN IS MY FATHER. I WILL TAKE YOU TO MEET HIM.

RACHEL AND JACOB FELL IN LOVE.

JACOB ASKED LABAN IF HE COULD MARRY HIS DAUGHTER.

I WILL WORK FOR YOU **BECAUSE I LOVE RACHEL** WITH ALL MY HEART.

YOU CAN MARRY RACHEL, BUT ONLY IF YOU WORK FOR ME FOR **SEVEN YEARS**.

HOWEVER, LABAN TRICKED JACOB. INSTEAD OF MARRYING RACHEL, JACOB HAD TO MARRY THE ELDEST DAUGHTER, LEAH.

...BUT ONLY IF JACOB AGREED TO WORK FOR FREE FOR ANOTHER SEVEN YEARS.

LABAN SAID JACOB COULD MARRY RACHEL TOO...

JACOB NOW HAD TWO WIVES, BUT HE LOVED RACHEL MORE.

JACOB WORKED FOR LABAN ANOTHER SEVEN YEARS.

YEARS PASSED, AND JACOB HAD MANY CHILDREN WITH LEAH AND TWO SERVANT WOMEN. BUT RACHEL COULD NOT BEAR CHILDREN.

FINALLY, SHE HAD A BOY, JOSEPH.

Hero Profile
Joseph—The Dreamer with a Coat

FATHER: JACOB, SON OF ISAAC

MOTHER: RACHEL

BROTHERS: REUBEN, SIMEON, LEVI, JUDAH, DAN, NAPHTALI, GAD, ASHER, ISSACHAR, ZEBULUN, BENJAMIN

INTERPRETER OF DREAMS

JOSEPH IS ONE OF MANY OLD TESTAMENT HEROES WHO ARE GIVEN THE SKILL OF INTERPRETING THE MEANING OF DREAMS OR OTHER VISIONS. IN LATER STORIES, PROPHETS SUCH AS DANIEL, ISAIAH, AND EZEKIEL ARE SHOWN FUTURE EVENTS OR MESSAGES FROM GOD THROUGH VISIONS OR DREAMS.

MOVIE SCRIPT

THE STORY OF JOSEPH AND HIS FAMILY READS LIKE A SCRIPT OF A CLIFFHANGER MOVIE. HIS LIFE IS A SNAPSHOT OF HOW MESSY, COMPLICATED, AND PAINFUL FAMILY LIFE CAN BE. BUT GOD HAD ANOTHER PLAN. FROM HURT AND SADNESS GOD BROUGHT FORGIVENESS, BLESSING, AND HEALING TO JOSEPH AND HIS FAMILY.

Favorite Son

Genesis 37

JACOB AND RACHEL TRAVELED TO WHERE HIS FATHER HAD BEEN SO MANY YEARS BEFORE.

GOD HAD TOLD ABRAHAM, JACOB'S GRANDFATHER, THAT CANAAN WOULD ONE DAY BECOME THE PROMISED LAND WHERE GOD'S CHOSEN PEOPLE WOULD LIVE.

GOD TOLD JACOB TO TRAVEL TO BETHEL. ON THE WAY, RACHEL DIED GIVING BIRTH TO BENJAMIN.

OF ALL HIS SONS, JACOB LOVED JOSEPH THE BEST, FOR HE WAS THE FIRST BORN TO RACHEL.

JOSEPH WALKED INTO THE DESERT, NOT KNOWING HIS FATE.

MEANWHILE, HIS BROTHERS CONTEMPLATED WHAT THEY HAD DONE AND HOW THEY WOULD EXPLAIN IT TO THEIR FATHER, JACOB.

THEY TOOK JOSEPH'S COAT, DIPPED IT INTO THE BLOOD OF A SLAIN GOAT...

...AND TOOK IT TO JACOB.

FATHER, WE FOUND THIS COAT IN THE FIELD. IS IT JOSEPH'S?

IT IS! IT IS THE COAT OF MY BELOVED SON! A WILD BEAST MUST HAVE **DEVOURED** HIM!

Joseph in Prison

Genesis 39

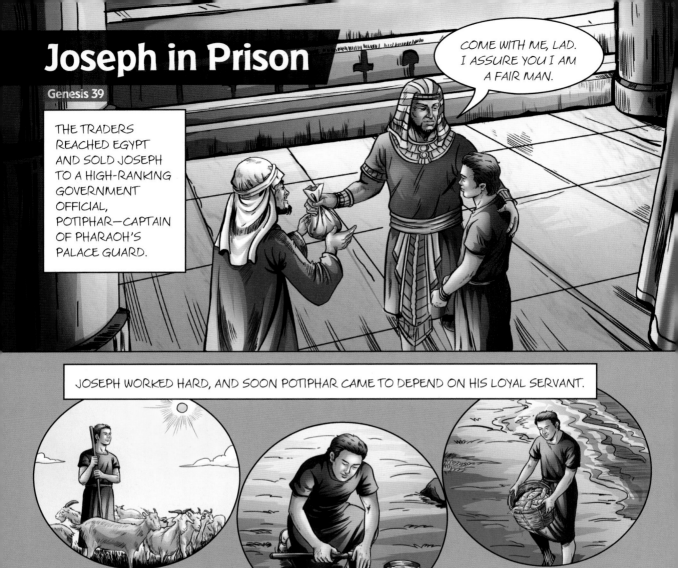

THE TRADERS REACHED EGYPT AND SOLD JOSEPH TO A HIGH-RANKING GOVERNMENT OFFICIAL, POTIPHAR—CAPTAIN OF PHARAOH'S PALACE GUARD.

COME WITH ME, LAD. I ASSURE YOU I AM A FAIR MAN.

JOSEPH WORKED HARD, AND SOON POTIPHAR CAME TO DEPEND ON HIS LOYAL SERVANT.

FROM THE MOMENT JOSEPH ARRIVED, POTIPHAR COULD FEEL THAT GOD HAD BLESSED HIS HOUSEHOLD BECAUSE OF JOSEPH'S PRESENCE. POTIPHAR DIDN'T HAVE TO WORRY ABOUT A THING.

THE HEAD JAILER LIKED JOSEPH...

...AND PUT HIM IN CHARGE OF ALL THE PRISONERS.

The Interpreter of Dreams

Genesis 40–41

TIME PASSED, AND PHARAOH'S CUPBEARER AND BAKER WERE THROWN INTO PRISON BECAUSE PHARAOH BECAME ANGRY WITH THEM.

THE HEAD JAILER ASSIGNED JOSEPH TO TAKE CARE OF THEM.

THANK YOU, JOSEPH!

ONE NIGHT THE CUPBEARER HAD A STRANGE DREAM...

...AS DID THE BAKER.

111

Joseph Feeds His Family

Genesis 41–45

PHARAOH THANKED JOSEPH.

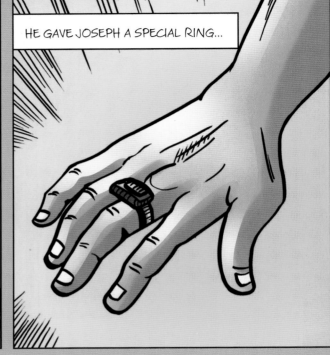

HE GAVE JOSEPH A SPECIAL RING...

...A GOLD NECKLACE, A WARDROBE OF FINE ROBES...

...AND PERMISSION TO MARRY THE DAUGHTER OF A PRIEST.

PHARAOH GAVE JOSEPH THE JOB OF PREPARING ALL OF EGYPT FOR THE FAMINE HE HAD PREDICTED. HE BECAME MORE POWERFUL THAN ANY MAN IN EGYPT OTHER THAN PHARAOH.

JOSEPH TRAVELED ACROSS EGYPT, COLLECTING FOOD FROM THE FIELDS AND STORING IT IN THE CITIES.

FOR SEVEN YEARS, JOSEPH COLLECTED THE FOOD. THERE WAS SO MUCH THAT HE HAD TO STOP MEASURING IT.

FINALLY, THE SEVEN YEARS OF ABUNDANCE CAME TO AN END.

THE YEARS OF PLENTY WERE FOLLOWED BY SEVEN YEARS OF FAMINE.

BECAUSE OF JOSEPH, HOWEVER, THE PEOPLE HAD ENOUGH TO EAT.

IN OTHER NEARBY LANDS, PEOPLE STARVED AND DIED.

THE FAMINE HIT CANAAN HARD, FORCING JACOB TO MAKE A DECISION.

SONS, GO TO EGYPT, WHERE FOOD IS PLENTIFUL. BUY SOME SO WE ALL MAY EAT AND LIVE.

YOUR BROTHER BENJAMIN WILL STAY HERE WITH ME. I FEAR FOR HIS SAFETY.

AND SO THE SONS OF ISRAEL, JOSEPH'S BROTHERS, TRAVELED TO EGYPT.

119

SO JACOB AND HIS FAMILY MOVED TO EGYPT, WHERE HE WAS REUNITED WITH HIS FAVORITE SON.

JACOB AND HIS FAMILY WERE GIVEN GOOD GRAZING LAND FOR THEIR ANIMALS AND WERE TREATED WELL. BUT JACOB'S DESCENDANTS WERE DESTINED TO SUFFER THE SAME FATE AS A YOUNGER JOSEPH. THEY WOULD EVENTUALLY BECOME SLAVES.

EVENTUALLY, THE FAMILY RAN OUT OF GRAIN AND HAD NOTHING TO EAT. IN DESPERATION, THEY RETURNED TO EGYPT, BRINGING BENJAMIN AS JOSEPH HAD DEMANDED.

JOSEPH WAS SO HAPPY THAT HE HELD A MAGNIFICENT FEAST.

JOSEPH THEN TESTED HIS BROTHERS A FINAL TIME. HE TOLD HIS SERVANTS TO FILL THEIR SACKS WITH GRAIN...

...AND JOSEPH PLACED HIS OWN SILVER CUP IN BENJAMIN'S SACK.

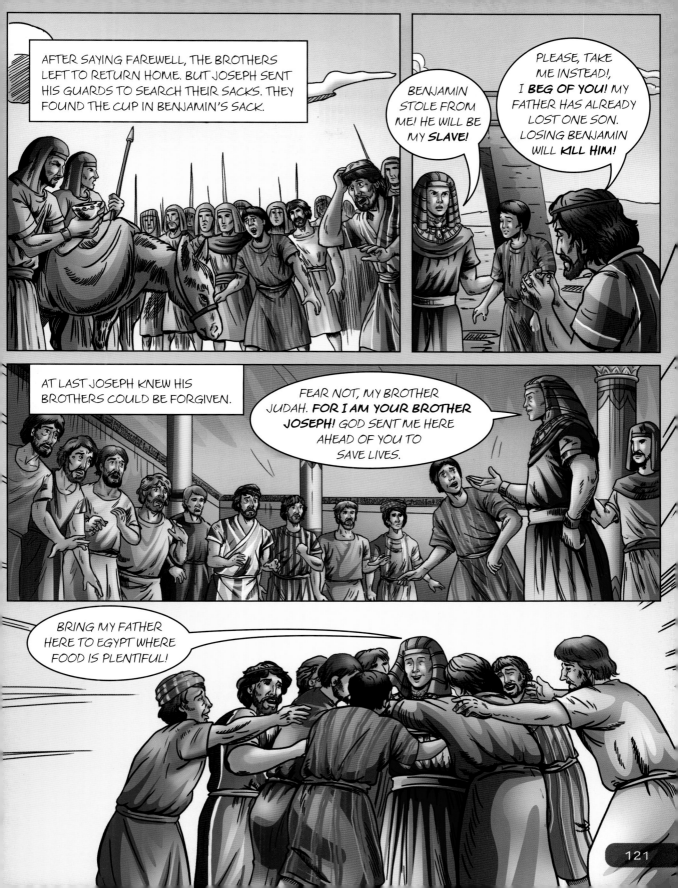

SO JACOB AND HIS FAMILY MOVED TO EGYPT, WHERE HE WAS REUNITED WITH HIS FAVORITE SON.

JACOB AND HIS FAMILY WERE GIVEN GOOD GRAZING LAND FOR THEIR ANIMALS AND WERE TREATED WELL. BUT JACOB'S DESCENDANTS WERE DESTINED TO SUFFER THE SAME FATE AS A YOUNGER JOSEPH. THEY WOULD EVENTUALLY BECOME SLAVES.

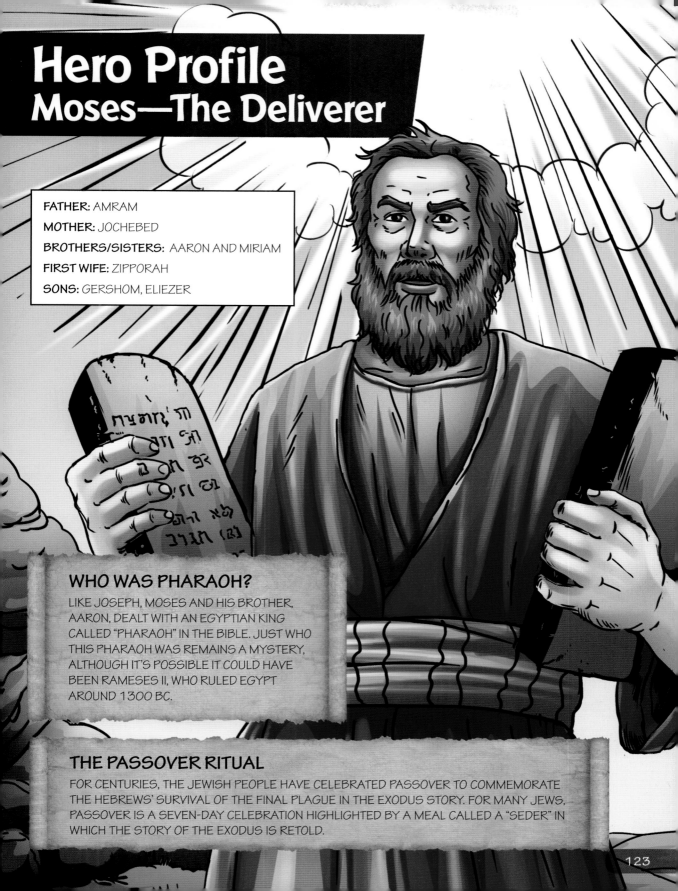

Hero Profile
Moses—The Deliverer

FATHER: AMRAM

MOTHER: JOCHEBED

BROTHERS/SISTERS: AARON AND MIRIAM

FIRST WIFE: ZIPPORAH

SONS: GERSHOM, ELIEZER

WHO WAS PHARAOH?

LIKE JOSEPH, MOSES AND HIS BROTHER, AARON, DEALT WITH AN EGYPTIAN KING CALLED "PHARAOH" IN THE BIBLE. JUST WHO THIS PHARAOH WAS REMAINS A MYSTERY, ALTHOUGH IT'S POSSIBLE IT COULD HAVE BEEN RAMESES II, WHO RULED EGYPT AROUND 1300 BC.

THE PASSOVER RITUAL

FOR CENTURIES, THE JEWISH PEOPLE HAVE CELEBRATED PASSOVER TO COMMEMORATE THE HEBREWS' SURVIVAL OF THE FINAL PLAGUE IN THE EXODUS STORY. FOR MANY JEWS, PASSOVER IS A SEVEN-DAY CELEBRATION HIGHLIGHTED BY A MEAL CALLED A "SEDER" IN WHICH THE STORY OF THE EXODUS IS RETOLD.

123

A Baby in a Basket

Exodus 1–2

A NEW PHARAOH HAD COME TO POWER IN EGYPT AND KNEW NOTHING OF WHAT JOSEPH HAD DONE TO HELP EGYPT IN THE PAST. A GROWING NUMBER OF JOSEPH'S PEOPLE, THE ISRAELITES, LIVED AND THRIVED IN THE NEARBY LAND OF GOSHEN. THEY CAUSED GREAT CONCERN FOR THE KING.

THE HEBREWS ARE MORE NUMEROUS THAN WE ARE!

THEY MIGHT JOIN OUR ENEMIES TO FIGHT AGAINST US.

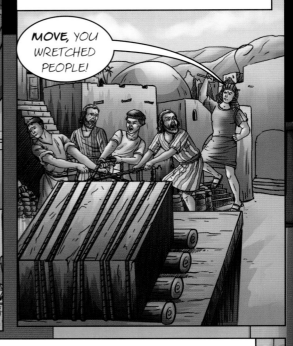

PHARAOH ENSLAVED MANY OF THE ISRAELITES AND FORCED THEM TO BUILD CITIES. IT WAS BACK-BREAKING WORK.

MOVE, YOU WRETCHED PEOPLE!

STILL, THE ISRAELITE POPULATION CONTINUED TO GROW, FORCING PHARAOH TO TAKE MORE DRASTIC ACTION.

YOU ARE MIDWIVES TO THE HEBREW WOMEN.

IF THE WOMEN GIVE BIRTH TO BOYS, **KILL THEM!**

AS YOU COMMAND.

BUT THE MIDWIVES FEARED GOD AND REFUSED TO OBEY PHARAOH'S EVIL ORDER.

PHARAOH DECREED THAT EVERY HEBREW BOY IN EGYPT BE DROWNED IN THE NILE RIVER.

NO! DO NOT KILL MY BABY! PLEASE, I'LL DO ANYTHING!

IN ONE SLAVE FAMILY'S HOME, A NEW MOTHER, JOCHEBED, HID HER CHILD FROM PHARAOH'S SOLDIERS. FOR THREE MONTHS SHE KEPT THE BABY SAFE. BUT HE GREW FAST AND SOON BECAME TOO BIG TO HIDE.

TO SAVE HER SON'S LIFE, THE MOTHER PLACED HER CHILD IN A BASKET MADE OF BULRUSHES AND PUT IT IN THE RIVER.

MAY THE LORD PROTECT YOU, MY SON.

THE BOY'S SISTER, MIRIAM, WATCHED AS THE CHILD FLOATED DOWN THE RIVER. AT THAT TIME, PHARAOH'S DAUGHTER WAS BATHING. SHE SAW THE BASKET.

IT IS ONE OF THE HEBREW BABIES!

MIRIAM APPEARED FROM THE REEDS.

SHALL I SUMMON A HEBREW WOMAN TO NURSE HIM?

YES, GO!

TAKE THIS CHILD AND NURSE HIM UNTIL HE IS OLDER, AND I WILL PAY YOUR WAGES.

AS YOU WISH!

THE BABY'S OWN MOTHER BECAME HIS NURSE IN THE COURT OF PHARAOH.

THE BOY GREW OLDER, AND PHARAOH'S DAUGHTER NAMED HIM MOSES, FOR SHE SAID, "I DREW HIM OUT OF THE WATER."

OH, MOSES, YOU WILL BE A GREAT MAN IN A GREAT LAND—A PRINCE WHO WILL LEAD HIS PEOPLE.

YEARS PASSED, AND EGYPT'S RULER EVENTUALLY DIED.

A NEW PHARAOH RULED EGYPT, BUT THE HARD TIMES OF THE ISRAELITES DID NOT CHANGE.

THEY SUFFERED GREATLY DURING THEIR SLAVERY TO PHARAOH.

THEY PRAYED FOR THEIR DELIVERANCE AND FREEDOM...

...AND GOD HEARD THEIR PRAYERS.

133

Moses Speaks for God

Exodus 4–7

MOSES DID AS THE LORD ASKED. HE PACKED HIS FAMILY'S BELONGINGS AND HEADED WEST INTO EGYPT.

GOD TOLD MOSES IT WOULD NOT BE EASY TO CONVINCE PHARAOH TO LET THE ISRAELITES GO.

I WILL HARDEN HIS HEART. SEE THAT YOU PERFORM BEFORE PHARAOH ALL THE WONDERS I HAVE PUT IN YOUR POWER.

MOSES WAS REUNITED WITH HIS BROTHER, AARON.

GOD HAS TOLD US TO DELIVER OUR PEOPLE FROM BONDAGE.

HE HAS TOLD US TO RETURN TO EGYPT, BROTHER.

MOSES AND AARON ARRIVED IN EGYPT AND MET WITH A GROUP OF HEBREW ELDERS. MOSES PERFORMED FOR THEM THE WONDERS THAT GOD HAD GIVEN HIM.

MOSES, I HAVE SEEN **THE POWER OF GOD** IN YOU!

YOU MUST **GO TO PHARAOH** AND CONVINCE HIM TO SET US FREE!

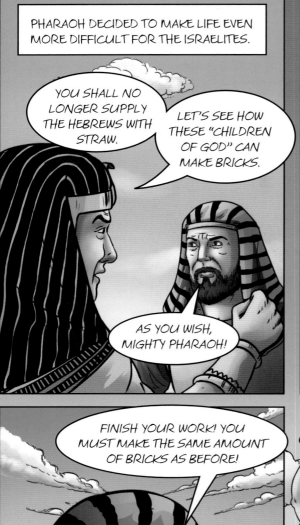

PHARAOH DECIDED TO MAKE LIFE EVEN MORE DIFFICULT FOR THE ISRAELITES.

YOU SHALL NO LONGER SUPPLY THE HEBREWS WITH STRAW.

LET'S SEE HOW THESE "CHILDREN OF GOD" CAN MAKE BRICKS.

AS YOU WISH, MIGHTY PHARAOH!

THE ISRAELITES HAD TO GATHER THEIR OWN STRAW TO MAKE PHARAOH'S BRICKS.

FINISH YOUR WORK! YOU MUST MAKE THE SAME AMOUNT OF BRICKS AS BEFORE!

WHY HAVE YOUR PEOPLE NOT MADE AS MANY BRICKS AS YESTERDAY?

IT IS IMPOSSIBLE. WE...WE...DO NOT HAVE ENOUGH STRAW!

The Plagues

141

PHARAOH'S HEART WAS STILL HARD. SO MOSES TOLD AARON TO STRETCH OUT HIS HAND WITH HIS STAFF OVER ALL OF EGYPT. SOON THE COUNTRYSIDE WAS OVERRUN WITH MILLIONS OF **FROGS**.

STILL, PHARAOH REFUSED TO LET GOD'S PEOPLE GO!

THE LORD, THROUGH MOSES, SENT DOWN PLAGUE AFTER PLAGUE ON EGYPT.

THICK SWARMS OF **FLIES** ENTERED PHARAOH'S PALACE AND THOSE OF HIS OFFICIALS AND DEVASTATED THE LAND.

MILLIONS OF **GNATS** TORMENTED BOTH HUMAN AND BEAST.

STILL, PHARAOH WOULD NOT FREE THE ISRAELITES.

A DARK **PESTILENCE** (DISEASE) THEN SWEPT OVER EGYPT, KILLING HERDS OF ANIMALS OWNED BY THE EGYPTIANS.

YET THE LIVESTOCK OF THE ISRAELITES SURVIVED.

AARON AND MOSES TOOK A HANDFUL OF SOOT FROM A KILN AND SCATTERED IT IN THE WIND...

...AND THEN FESTERING, PAINFUL **BOILS** APPEARED ON THE BODIES OF ALL EGYPTIANS.

NEXT CAME A PLAGUE OF **HAIL** THAT DESTROYED FIELDS OF CROPS...

...AND SWARMS OF **LOCUSTS** THAT ATE WHAT THE HAIL DID NOT DAMAGE.

WHEN THOSE PLAGUES FAILED TO MOVE PHARAOH, A PLAGUE OF **DARKNESS** COVERED THE LAND FOR THREE DAYS. ONLY THE ISRAELITES HAD LIGHT WHERE THEY LIVED.

The Final Plague

Exodus 10–12

MOSES CAME TO PHARAOH AGAIN, BUT PHARAOH WAS STILL NOT MOVED BY THE NINE PLAGUES. HE STILL REFUSED TO LET THE HEBREWS LEAVE.

LEAVE ME, MOSES!

MAKE SURE YOU NEVER SEE MY FACE AGAIN!

FOR THE DAY THAT YOU DO SEE IT, **YOU WILL DIE!**

BUT BEFORE HE LEFT, MOSES HAD ONE MORE THING TO TELL PHARAOH, FOR GOD HAD TOLD MOSES THAT HE WOULD SEND ONE FINAL PLAGUE.

GOD HAD INSTRUCTED MOSES TO TELL EACH HEBREW FAMILY TO FIND A ONE-YEAR-OLD MALE LAMB.

THEY WERE TO SLAUGHTER THE LAMB...

...AND PUT THE ANIMAL'S BLOOD ON THE DOORPOST OF THEIR HOUSE.

THAT NIGHT EACH FAMILY WAS TO EAT THE LAMB AND WAIT FOR DEATH TO PASS OVER.

AT MIDNIGHT, GOD'S PLAGUE SPREAD THROUGH EGYPT, STRIKING DOWN THE FIRSTBORN. AS DEATH CAME, MOTHERS AND FATHERS, SISTERS AND BROTHERS CRIED AND SCREAMED.

BUT GOD PASSED OVER THE HEBREW HOMES THAT WERE MARKED WITH LAMB'S BLOOD. THEIR LIVES WERE SPARED.

149

PHARAOH WAS AWAKENED BY THE CRIES OF HIS PEOPLE.

HE RUSHED TO HIS SON'S BEDCHAMBER...

...ONLY TO FIND THE BOY'S LIFELESS BODY.

PHARAOH KNEW HE HAD BEEN BEATEN. HIS POWER WAS NOT GREATER THAN THE GOD OF MOSES.

Out of Egypt

Exodus 12–13

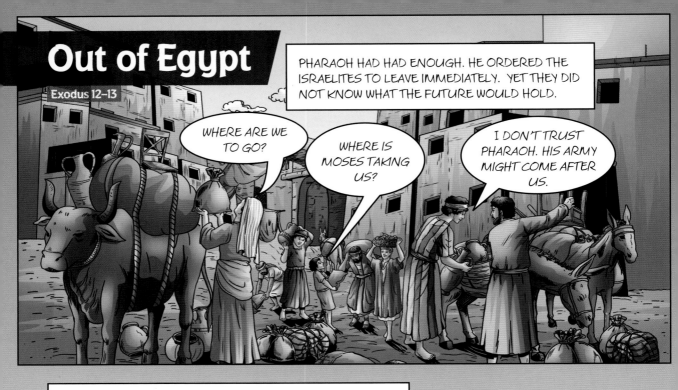

PHARAOH HAD HAD ENOUGH. HE ORDERED THE ISRAELITES TO LEAVE IMMEDIATELY. YET THEY DID NOT KNOW WHAT THE FUTURE WOULD HOLD.

WHERE ARE WE TO GO?

WHERE IS MOSES TAKING US?

I DON'T TRUST PHARAOH. HIS ARMY MIGHT COME AFTER US.

THE HEBREWS TOOK EVERYTHING THEY COULD CARRY AND QUICKLY GATHERED THEIR SHEEP, GOATS, CHICKENS, AND OTHER LIVESTOCK FOR THE JOURNEY AHEAD.

MOSES LED HIS PEOPLE OUT OF EGYPT.

GOD TOLD MOSES HE WOULD GUIDE THEM.

DURING THE DAY, A COLUMN OF WHIRLING DUST MOVED IN FRONT OF THEM, POINTING THE WAY.

AT NIGHT, A PILLAR OF FIRE GUIDED THEM.

THE HEBREWS' JOURNEY

Plague
of Frogs

EGYPT

GOSHEN

Rameses (Tanis)

Succoth
Pithom

Etham

Wilderness
of Etham

Paharaoh pursues
the exiles

Crossing of the
Red Sea

Migdol

Pi-hahiroth

Baal-Zephon

Bitter
waters
at Marah

Marah

Springs
at
Elim

Eli

Nile River

THE ISRAELITES DID NOT
TRAVEL THROUGH THE
WILDERNESS BY THE MOST
DIRECT WAY—THROUGH
THE LAND OF THE
PHILISTINES ALONG THE
COAST OF THE GREAT SEA.
INSTEAD, GOD TOLD MOSES
TO LEAD HIS PEOPLE
SOUTHEAST TOWARD THE
RED SEA BY THE WAY OF
THE WILDERNESS ROAD.
THEY WOULD THEN TRAVEL
NORTHEAST TO THE
PROMISED LAND.

Red
Sea

Water from the rock at
Horeb/Mt. Sinai

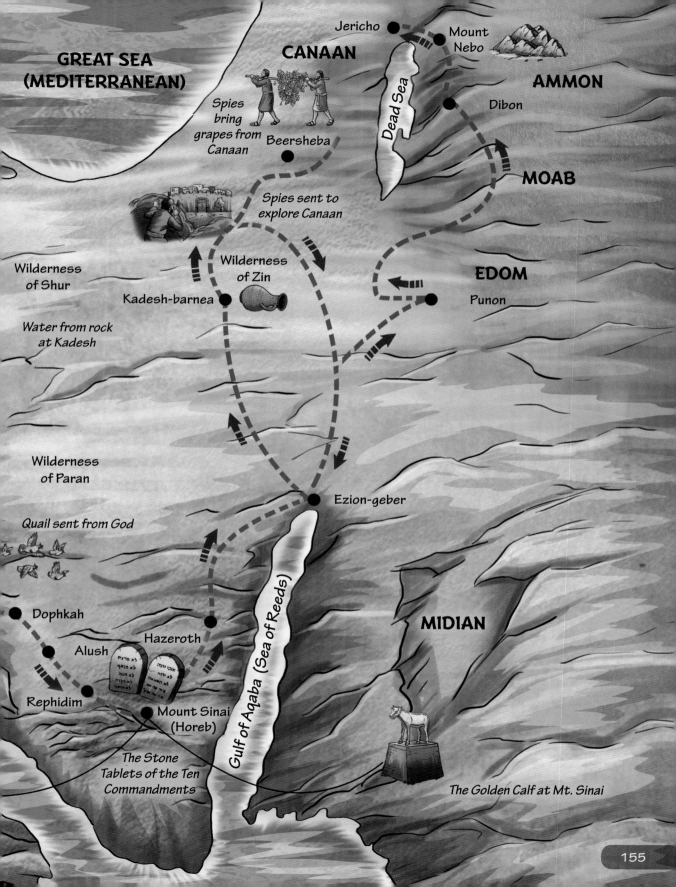

GREAT SEA
(MEDITERRANEAN)

CANAAN

Jericho

Mount
Nebo

AMMON

Spies
bring
grapes from
Canaan

Beersheba

Dibon

Dead Sea

Spies sent to
explore Canaan

MOAB

Wilderness
of Shur

Wilderness
of Zin

EDOM

Kadesh-barnea

Punon

Water from rock
at Kadesh

Wilderness
of Paran

Ezion-geber

Quail sent from God

Dophkah

MIDIAN

Hazeroth

Alush

Gulf of Aqaba (Sea of Reeds)

Rephidim

Mount Sinai
(Horeb)

The Stone
Tablets of the Ten
Commandments

The Golden Calf at Mt. Sinai

THE ISRAELITES FOLLOWED MOSES' INSTRUCTIONS AND CONTINUED MOVING TOWARD THE RED SEA...

...AS THE EGYPTIANS READIED FOR THE ATTACK.

GOD THEN MADE A PILLAR OF CLOUD APPEAR BEFORE THE EGYPTIANS, HALTING THEIR ADVANCE.

159

THE ISRAELITES WERE ASTONISHED BY GOD'S MIRACLE.

THE ISRAELITES THEN WALKED THROUGH THE PATH IN THE SEA CREATED BY GOD.

GOD RELEASED THE CLOUD, AND THE EGYPTIANS PURSUED THE HEBREWS INTO THE SEA. ALL OF PHARAOH'S HORSES, CHARIOTS, AND HORSEMEN RACED INTO THE PATH GOD HAD MADE FOR HIS PEOPLE.

WHEN ALL OF THE ISRAELITES WERE SAFELY ON THE FAR SHORE, GOD TOLD MOSES TO RAISE HIS STAFF OVER THE SEA ONCE AGAIN. GOD HAD SAVED HIS PEOPLE FROM CERTAIN DEATH...

...AS THE WATERS SWALLOWED UP THE EGYPTIAN ARMY, DROWNING EACH AND EVERY SOLDIER.

THE GRATEFUL ISRAELITES GAVE THANKS TO GOD FOR THEIR SALVATION.

Manna from Heaven

Exodus 15–17

MOSES TOOK HIS PEOPLE INTO THE WILDERNESS, BUT AFTER THREE DAYS, THEY RAN OUT OF WATER.

FATHER, I'M SO THIRSTY!

DRINK THIS LAST DROP. THERE IS NO MORE.

AT LAST THEY ARRIVED AT THE SPRING IN MARAH, BUT THE WATER WAS TOO BITTER TO DRINK.

FATHER, I CANNOT DRINK THIS WATER!

GOD SHOWED MOSES A PIECE OF WOOD, AND MOSES THREW IT INTO THE WATER. THE WATER BECAME DRINKABLE, AND IN GREAT RELIEF THE PEOPLE DRANK THEIR FILL.

GOD TOLD MOSES TO LEAD THE PEOPLE INTO THE DESERT. FINALLY, THEY CAME TO A PLACE CALLED ELIM, WHERE THEY FOUND 12 SPRINGS OF WATER AND 70 PALM TREES.

THE PEOPLE RUSHED TO QUENCH THEIR THIRST, BUT THEY WERE SOON ON THE MARCH AGAIN. THEIR HUNGER AND THIRST QUICKLY RETURNED.

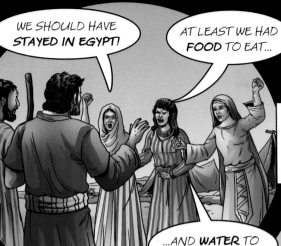

WE SHOULD HAVE **STAYED IN EGYPT!**

AT LEAST WE HAD **FOOD** TO EAT...

...AND **WATER** TO DRINK!

MOSES PROMISED THE ISRAELITES THEY WOULD HAVE MEAT AND FRESH BREAD IN THE MORNING. BEFORE THE SUN SET, QUAIL APPEARED IN THE SKY ABOVE THEIR CAMP.

IN THE MORNING, THE PEOPLE FOUND A GIFT FROM THE LORD—THE GROUND WAS COVERED WITH MANNA, A SPECIAL BREAD THEY COULD EAT.

EVERY MORNING WHILE THE ISRAELITES WERE IN THE WILDERNESS, GOD PROVIDED ENOUGH MANNA FOR THEM FOR THAT DAY, EXCEPT ON THE DAY BEFORE THE SABBATH WHEN HE PROVIDED EXTRA MANNA SO THAT THEY COULD REST AND GIVE THANKS ON THE SABBATH.

GOD TOLD MOSES TO STRIKE A ROCK AT HOREB (SINAI) WITH HIS STAFF, AND WATER FLOWED FROM IT.

MOSES DID AS GOD COMMANDED, AND WHEN THE REST OF THE HEBREWS ARRIVED, THEY HAD PLENTY OF WATER TO DRINK.

163

The Ten Commandments

Exodus 19–20

THREE MONTHS AFTER LEAVING EGYPT, THE ISRAELITES ARRIVED AT MOUNT SINAI—THE SAME PLACE WHERE MOSES HAD FIRST ENCOUNTERED GOD.

MOSES LEFT THE PEOPLE AT A SAFE DISTANCE...

...AND VENTURED ALONE UP THE MOUNTAIN TO TALK TO GOD.

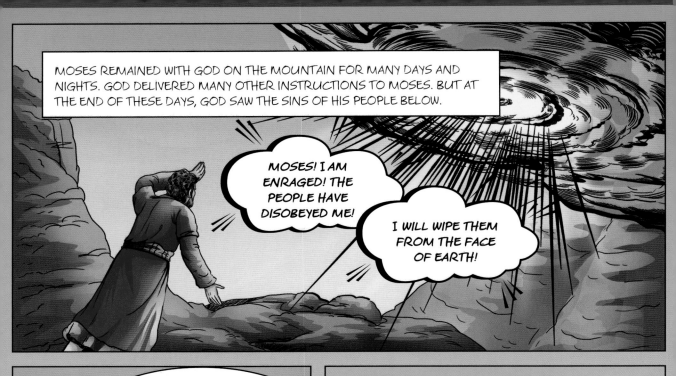

MOSES REMAINED WITH GOD ON THE MOUNTAIN FOR MANY DAYS AND NIGHTS. GOD DELIVERED MANY OTHER INSTRUCTIONS TO MOSES. BUT AT THE END OF THESE DAYS, GOD SAW THE SINS OF HIS PEOPLE BELOW.

MOSES! I AM ENRAGED! THE PEOPLE HAVE DISOBEYED ME!

I WILL WIPE THEM FROM THE FACE OF EARTH!

LORD! DO NOT LET YOUR ANGER GROW HOT AGAINST THE PEOPLE YOU HAVE DELIVERED FROM SLAVERY!

IF YOU KILL THEM NOW, THE EGYPTIANS WILL SAY YOU FREED THEM WITH EVIL INTENT— TO DESTROY THEM IN THE WILDNERNESS!

LORD, DON'T BE ANGRY, **I BEG YOU!**

REMEMBER YOUR SERVANTS: ABRAHAM, ISAAC, AND ISRAEL!

YOU TOLD THEM YOU WOULD MAKE THEIR DESCENDANTS AS NUMEROUS AS STARS. LORD, **SPARE** THESE PEOPLE!

GOD LISTENED TO MOSES AND SHOWED MERCY TO THE ISRAELITES.

FINALLY, MOSES DESCENDED THE MOUNTAIN CARRYING GOD'S COMMANDMENTS ETCHED IN TWO STONE TABLETS.

AS HE CAME DOWN THE MOUNTAIN, MOSES COULD HEAR THE SOUND OF CELEBRATION. WHEN HE SAW WHAT HIS FELLOW ISRAELITES HAD BEEN UP TO IN HIS ABSENCE, HE WAS FURIOUS AND HURLED THE TABLETS TO THE GROUND.

WHO IS RESPONSIBLE FOR THIS???

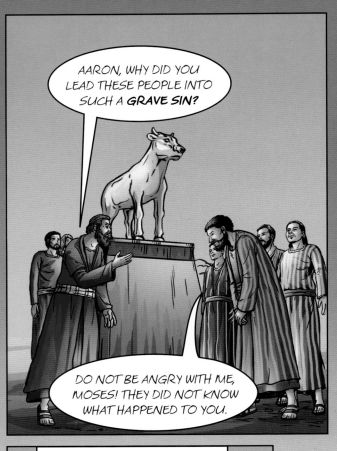

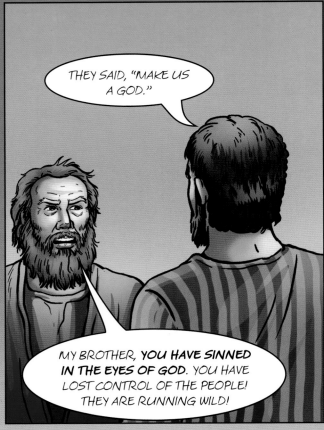

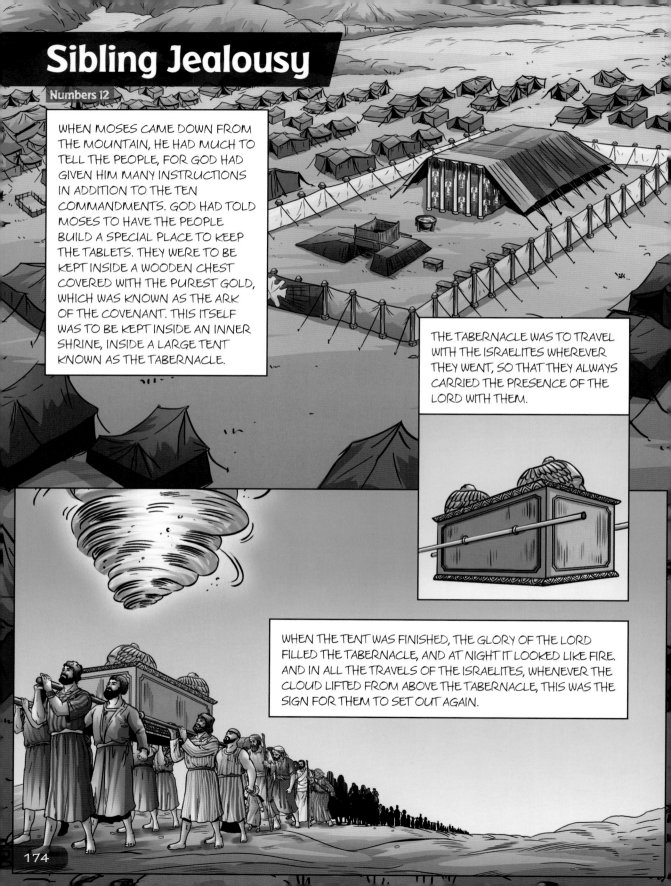

Sibling Jealousy

WHEN MOSES CAME DOWN FROM THE MOUNTAIN, HE HAD MUCH TO TELL THE PEOPLE, FOR GOD HAD GIVEN HIM MANY INSTRUCTIONS IN ADDITION TO THE TEN COMMANDMENTS. GOD HAD TOLD MOSES TO HAVE THE PEOPLE BUILD A SPECIAL PLACE TO KEEP THE TABLETS. THEY WERE TO BE KEPT INSIDE A WOODEN CHEST COVERED WITH THE PUREST GOLD, WHICH WAS KNOWN AS THE ARK OF THE COVENANT. THIS ITSELF WAS TO BE KEPT INSIDE AN INNER SHRINE, INSIDE A LARGE TENT KNOWN AS THE TABERNACLE.

THE TABERNACLE WAS TO TRAVEL WITH THE ISRAELITES WHEREVER THEY WENT, SO THAT THEY ALWAYS CARRIED THE PRESENCE OF THE LORD WITH THEM.

WHEN THE TENT WAS FINISHED, THE GLORY OF THE LORD FILLED THE TABERNACLE, AND AT NIGHT IT LOOKED LIKE FIRE. AND IN ALL THE TRAVELS OF THE ISRAELITES, WHENEVER THE CLOUD LIFTED FROM ABOVE THE TABERNACLE, THIS WAS THE SIGN FOR THEM TO SET OUT AGAIN.

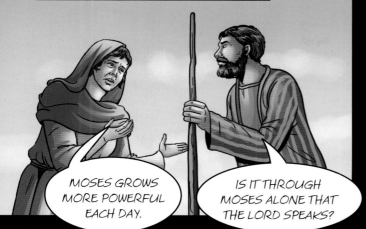

AARON AND MIRIAM GREW JEALOUS OF THEIR BROTHER, MOSES.

MOSES GROWS MORE POWERFUL EACH DAY.

IS IT THROUGH MOSES ALONE THAT THE LORD SPEAKS?

HAS GOD NOT SPOKEN TO US TOO?

GOD HEARD AARON AND MIRIAM'S COMPLAINT AND CAME TO SPEAK TO THEM IN A SWIRLING CLOUD.

THERE ARE PROPHETS AMONG YOU. I SPEAK TO THEM IN VISIONS.

I SPEAK TO THEM IN DREAMS. NOT SO WITH MOSES!

I SPEAK TO MOSES PLAINLY. WHY DO YOU SPEAK AGAINST HIM?

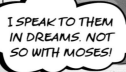

THE LORD INFLICTED MIRIAM WITH LEPROSY THAT RAVAGED HER BODY.

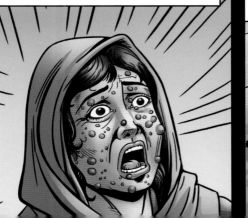

MOSES STILL LOVED HIS SISTER. HE PLEADED WITH GOD TO HEAL HER. SEVEN DAYS LATER, MIRIAM WAS HEALED, AND THE ISRAELITES CONTINUED ON THEIR JOURNEY.

Moses and His Spies

Numbers 13–14

THE ISRAELITES CONTINUED UNTIL THEY REACHED THE WILDERNESS OF PARAN. THEN GOD TOLD MOSES TO SEND OUT SOME MEN TO EXPLORE THE LAND OF CANAAN, WHICH HE HAD PROMISED TO THEM. MOSES WAS TO SEND ONE MAN FROM EACH OF THE TWELVE TRIBES TO SCOUT OUT THE LAND.

MOSES TOLD THE MEN TO SPY ON THE CANAANITES TO DISCOVER AS MUCH INFORMATION AS THEY COULD.

THE SPIES DID THEIR WORK FOR FORTY DAYS. THEY THEN RETURNED AND REPORTED TO MOSES.

GOD HAD PROMISED THIS LAND TO HIS PEOPLE, BUT THEY WERE SCARED. THEY DIDN'T PUT THEIR FAITH IN GOD EVEN THOUGH HE HAD BROUGHT THEM OUT OF EGYPT, ACROSS THE RED SEA, AND THROUGH THE WILDERNESS. GOD THREATENED TO KILL THEM ALL, BUT MOSES AGAIN PERSUADED THE LORD TO SPARE THEM.

INSTEAD, GOD CONDEMNED THE HEBREWS TO WANDER IN THE DESERT FOR 40 YEARS—ONE YEAR FOR EACH OF THE DAYS THAT THEY HAD EXPLORED THE PROMISED LAND.

WITH THE EXCEPTION OF JOSHUA AND CALEB, WHO HAD FAITH, NONE OF YOU WILL EVER SEE THE PROMISED LAND! YOU WILL ROAM AIMLESSLY UNTIL THE LAST ONE OF YOU IS BURIED!

Water from a Rock

Numbers 20

THE ISRAELITES RETREATED SOUTH FROM CANAAN TO KADESH, WHERE MIRIAM DIED AND WAS BURIED. THERE WAS NO WATER FOR THE HEBREWS TO DRINK.

MOSES, WHY DID YOU BRING US TO THIS PLACE? THERE IS NO **WATER!**

WE WILL DIE HERE! OUR LIVESTOCK WILL DIE HERE.

GOD TOLD MOSES AND AARON TO GATHER THE PEOPLE NEAR A ROCK IN THE MIDDLE OF THE DESERT.

MOSES AND AARON WERE TO SPEAK TO THE ROCK BEFORE MOSES STRUCK IT WITH HIS STAFF. GOD PROMISED THAT WATER WOULD SPEW FROM THE ROCK.

LOOK, YOU REBELLIOUS PEOPLE! MUST WE BRING YOU WATER OUT OF THIS ROCK?

BUT MOSES AND AARON DID NOT SPEAK TO THE ROCK AS GOD HAD COMMANDED. NOR DID THEY GIVE THE CREDIT TO GOD. BECAUSE THEY DISOBEYED, GOD TOLD THEM THAT THEY WOULD NOT LEAD THE ISRAELITES INTO THE PROMISED LAND.

Hero Profile
Joshua—Israelite Warrior

BORN: EGYPT

FATHER: NUN, OF THE TRIBE OF EPHRAIM

DIED: CANAAN, THE PROMISED LAND

AGE AT TIME OF DEATH: 110

BEST KNOWN FOR: BEING A LEADER AND MIGHTY WARRIOR FOR GOD

WHAT'S IN A NAME?
JOSHUA AND JESUS SHARE THE SAME NAME. "JESUS" IS A GREEK FORM OF THE HEBREW NAME. BOTH MEAN "GOD SAVES."

RUINED WALLS
JOSHUA'S GREATEST VICTORY CAME DURING THE SIEGE OF JERICHO. ARCHAEOLOGISTS HAVE UNCOVERED MUD-BRICK WALLS THAT WERE VIOLENTLY DESTROYED.

MOSES SUMMONED JOSHUA TO HIM AND TOLD HIM THAT GOD HAD CHOSEN HIM AS THE THE LEADER OF THE ISRAELITES.

BE STRONG, JOSHUA. BE BRAVE. THE ROAD IS LONG.

YOU WILL LEAD THE PEOPLE TO THE PROMISED LAND.

MOSES THEN WALKED UP MOUNT NEBO, WHERE GOD SHOWED HIM THE PROMISED LAND.

MOSES DIED ON THE MOUNTAIN. HE WAS 120 YEARS OLD. THE HEBREWS MOURNED FOR A MONTH. THERE WOULD NEVER BE ANOTHER PROPHET LIKE MOSES—A MAN WHO HAD SPOKEN FACE-TO-FACE WITH GOD.

The River Stops Flowing

JOSHUA MARCHED TO THE BANK OF THE JORDAN RIVER JUST OUTSIDE JERICHO.

PREPARE YOUR SOLDIERS AND THE PEOPLE. TOMORROW THE LORD WILL PERFORM A GREAT MIRACLE! WE **WILL** CROSS THE RIVER!

JOSHUA, THE RIVER IS MOVING TOO FAST FOR US TO CROSS!

JOSHUA TOLD THE PRIESTS TO TAKE THE ARK OF THE COVENANT TO THE WATER'S EDGE. HE THEN SPOKE TO THE ISRAELITES.

LISTEN TO WHAT GOD HAS TOLD ME.

THE ARK IS GOING AHEAD OF YOU.

AS THE PRIESTS STEP INTO THE WATER, THE RIVER WILL STOP FLOWING.

GOD STILLED THE WATER, AND DRY LAND APPEARED. JOSHUA THEN TOLD HIS PEOPLE...

FOLLOW THE ARK INTO THE WATER AND CROSS TO THE OTHER SIDE!

WHILE THE PRIESTS STOOD WITH THE ARK OF THE COVENANT IN THE MIDDLE OF THE RIVER, THE PEOPLE OF ISRAEL CROSSED THE RIVER IN SAFETY. WHEN EVERYONE HAD CROSSED, JOSHUA TOLD ONE MAN FROM EACH OF THE TWELVE TRIBES TO COLLECT A STONE FROM THE CENTER OF THE RIVERBED, WHERE THE PRIESTS WERE STANDING. HE SET THESE STONES IN THEIR CAMP AND TOLD THE PEOPLE THAT THEY WOULD BE FOREVER IMPORTANT TO ISRAEL.

FROM THAT DAY ON, THE ISRAELITES ACCEPTED JOSHUA AS THEIR LEADER.

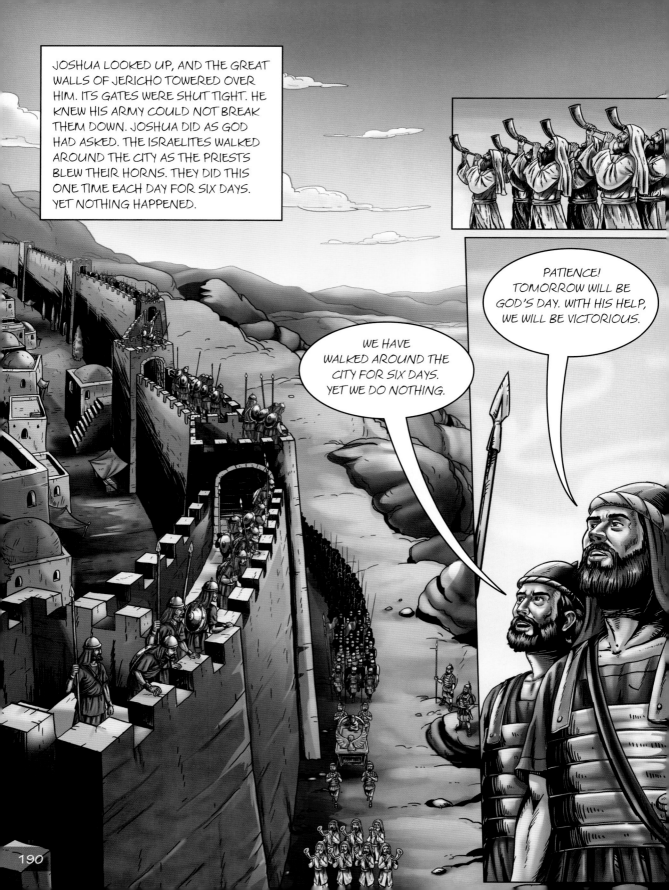

JOSHUA LOOKED UP, AND THE GREAT WALLS OF JERICHO TOWERED OVER HIM. ITS GATES WERE SHUT TIGHT. HE KNEW HIS ARMY COULD NOT BREAK THEM DOWN. JOSHUA DID AS GOD HAD ASKED. THE ISRAELITES WALKED AROUND THE CITY AS THE PRIESTS BLEW THEIR HORNS. THEY DID THIS ONE TIME EACH DAY FOR SIX DAYS. YET NOTHING HAPPENED.

WE HAVE WALKED AROUND THE CITY FOR SIX DAYS. YET WE DO NOTHING.

PATIENCE! TOMORROW WILL BE GOD'S DAY. WITH HIS HELP, WE WILL BE VICTORIOUS.

AS DAWN BROKE ON THE SEVENTH DAY, JOSHUA'S ARMY WALKED YET AGAIN AROUND THE MASSIVE CITY. THEY MARCHED SEVEN TIMES, JERICHO'S WALLS TAUNTING THEM AT EVERY STEP.

I'M TIRED OF WALKING. IT'S TIME TO ATTACK!

I HOPE JOSHUA KNOWS WHAT HE IS DOING.

THEN THE PRIESTS BLEW THEIR TRUMPETS LOUDLY, AND ON JOSHUA'S COMMAND, ALL THE ISRAELITES SHOUTED AT THE TOP OF THEIR VOICES. SUDDENLY, THE WALLS OF THE GREAT CITY TUMBLED TO THE GROUND IN A CLOUD OF DUST AND ROCK.

SHOUT! FOR THE LORD HAS GIVEN YOU THE CITY.

THE ISRAELITES DREW THEIR SWORDS AND GRABBED THEIR SPEARS. THE CITY WAS NOW OPEN.

THE ISRAELITES DID AS GOD HAD COMMANDED. THEY CHARGED INTO THE CITY AND DESTROYED EVERYTHING AND EVERYONE IN IT EXCEPT RAHAB AND HER FAMILY, ACCORDING TO GOD'S INSTRUCTIONS. NEWS OF THE VICTORY SPREAD QUICKLY. JOSHUA WAS FAMOUS, AND EVERYONE KNEW THE LORD WAS WITH HIM.

JOSHUA MOVED HIS ARMY TO THE OUTSKIRTS OF GIBEON. AS HE CAREFULLY PLANNED AN ATTACK, THE CITY'S ELDERS SENT A GROUP OF MEN DISGUISED IN TATTERED CLOTHES TO MAKE PEACE WITH JOSHUA. THE MEN POSED AS TRAVELERS WHO DID NOT LIVE IN GIBEON. THEY BROUGHT WITH THEM STALE BREAD AND BROKEN, CRACKED WINESKINS.

WE COME FROM A FAR-OFF LAND.

WE ARE YOUR SERVANTS.

LOOK AT OUR GARMENTS. THEY ARE WORN OUT FROM THE LONG JOURNEY.

PLEASE MAKE A PEACE TREATY WITH US.

JOSHUA DID NOT ASK GOD WHAT TO DO. HE LATER FOUND THE TRAVELERS WERE NATIVES OF THE LAND TO BE CONQUERED. BY THE TIME THE TRUTH CAME OUT, IT WAS TOO LATE—JOSHUA HAD MADE HIS PLEDGE. GOD WASN'T HAPPY WITH JOSHUA, BUT HE WAS PLEASED THAT JOSHUA HONORED HIS PLEDGE AND SPARED THEIR LIVES..

JOSHUA AND HIS SOLDIERS MARCHED ALL NIGHT AND CAUGHT THE ENEMY BY SURPRISE. THE ISRAELITES FOUGHT FURIOUSLY, AND WHEN THE ENEMY SOLDIERS TRIED TO FLEE, THEY WERE STRUCK DOWN BY HUGE HAILSTONES SENT BY GOD. THE HAILSTONES KILLED MORE MEN THAN THE SWORDS OF JOSHUA'S ARMY.

BUT JOSHUA KNEW THAT NIGHT WAS COMING AND THAT MANY OF HIS ENEMIES WOULD BE ABLE TO ESCAPE UNDER COVER OF DARKNESS. HE PRAYED TO GOD AND SAID...

SUN, STAND STILL OVER GIBEON, AND MOON, STAND STILL OVER THE VALLEY OF AIJALON!

AND ON THAT DAY, THE LORD LISTENED TO JOSHUA, AND THE SUN STOPPED IN THE MIDDLE OF THE SKY UNTIL ALL THE FIGHTING WAS OVER. AND EVERYONE SAW THAT THE LORD WAS FIGHTING FOR ISRAEL.

Conquest of Canaan

Joshua 11–12

THE KING OF HAZOR MOBILIZED THE ARMIES OF SEVERAL KINGDOMS IN THE MOUNTAINS TO ATTACK THE ISRAELITES, INCLUDING...

...THE AMORITES, HITTITES, AND THE PERIZZITES.

THEY MARCHED TO THE WATERS OF MEROM, WHERE THEY CAMPED. THERE THEY WAITED TO FIGHT AGAINST ISRAEL.

THE COMBINED ARMIES WERE AS NUMEROUS AS GRAINS OF SANDS ON A SEASHORE.

BUT IN SPITE OF THEIR ENEMY'S NUMBERS, THE ISRAELITES DEFEATED ALL THEIR FOES, AS JOSHUA, HIMSELF, CAPTURED THE CITY OF HAZOR AND STRUCK DOWN ITS KING...

...AND ORDERED THE CITY BURNED.

IN ALL THE CAPTURED LANDS, THE ISRAELITES TOOK TREASURES AND LIVESTOCK. JOSHUA WAS PLEASED WITH HIS VICTORY.

Hero Profile
Gideon—God's Soldier

FATHER: JOASH

SONS: GIDEON HAD 70 SONS. ONE, ABIMELECH, KILLED ALL THE OTHERS EXCEPT THE YOUNGEST, JOTHAM.

ORIGINAL OCCUPATION: FARMER

AGAINST ALL ODDS

GIDEON ASSEMBLED A MILITARY FORCE OF 32,000 MEN TO DEFEAT THE MIDIANITES. THE ARMY WAS THEN PARED DOWN TO 10,000, AND THEN TO 300. GIDEON WAS OFFERED A CHANCE TO BE KING AFTER HIS VICTORY, BUT HE REFUSED.

TRUMPET CALL

GIDEON'S MEN BLEW TRUMPETS IN THEIR FIGHT AGAINST THE MIDIANITES. SCHOLARS BELIEVE THEY PROBABLY USED HOLLOWED-OUT RAM'S HORNS SIMILAR TO THE SHOFAR THAT IS BLOWN IN TODAY'S JEWISH SYNAGOGUES TO SIGNAL THE START OF THE JEWISH NEW YEAR, ROSH HASHANAH.

Gideon the Warrior

Judges 6–7

THE ISRAELITES SETTLED IN THE PROMISED LAND BUT SOON FORGOT ABOUT GOD. THEY DISOBEYED HIS COMMANDMENTS AND FELL INTO EVIL WAYS.

GOD DELIVERED THE ISRAELITES INTO THE HANDS OF MIDIANITES TO TEACH THEM A LESSON. THE MIDIANITES RULED OVER THE ISRAELITES FOR SEVEN YEARS.

DEAR LORD, DELIVER US FROM THE MIDIANITES.

WE HAVE LOST OUR WAY. **SAVE US!**

THE BATTLE BETWEEN ISRAEL AND ITS ENEMIES GREW CLOSER. THE MIDIANITES AND THEIR ALLIES CAMPED IN THE VALLEY OF JEZREEL ON THE BANKS OF THE RIVER. THERE THEY PREPARED TO ATTACK.

GIDEON BLEW A HORN TO SUMMON HIS SOLDIERS TO BATTLE. HE ALSO SENT OUT MESSENGERS TO DISTANT LANDS TO RALLY MORE TROOPS.

BUT DESPITE THIS, GIDEON STRUGGLED TO BELIEVE HE WAS THE RIGHT MAN FOR THE JOB. HE ASKED GOD FOR A SIGN.

IF TOMORROW THIS FLEECE IS WET WITH DEW, THEN I KNOW GOD WILL SAVE ISRAEL.

THE NEXT MORNING, THE FLEECE WAS WET BUT THE GROUND WAS DRY.

STILL, GIDEON ASKED FOR ONE MORE SIGN.

GIDEON AGAIN PUT THE FLEECE ON THE GROUND. IF ISRAEL WERE TO TRIUMPH IN BATTLE THE NEXT DAY, THE GROUND WOULD BE WET AND THE WOOL DRY.

THIS IS EXACTLY WHAT HAPPENED. NOW GIDEON WAS CONVINCED!

TENS OF THOUSANDS OF SOLDIERS ANSWERED GIDEON'S CALL. BUT GOD WARNED GIDEON THAT THERE WERE TOO MANY. GOD WANTED THE WORLD TO KNOW THAT IT WAS NOT BY THE MIGHT OF MEN BUT BY THE MIGHT OF GOD THAT VICTORY WOULD BE ACHIEVED.

ANYONE WHO IS FRIGHTENED MUST LEAVE NOW.

THOUSANDS LEFT. GOD THEN TOLD GIDEON TO TAKE THOSE WHO REMAINED DOWN TO THE RIVER BANK.

GOD SAID THOSE WHO DRANK THE RIVER WATER WITH CUPPED HANDS COULD REMAIN AND FIGHT. THOSE WHO KNELT DOWN TO DRINK HAD TO LEAVE. IN THE END, GIDEON WENT TO WAR WITH 300 SOLDIERS.

THAT NIGHT GIDEON FELT SCARED. GOD TOLD HIM TO GO DOWN TO THE MIDIANITES' CAMP. THERE HE OVERHEARD SOME SOLDIERS TALKING ABOUT ONE OF THEIR DREAMS THAT FORETOLD A VICTORY FOR GIDEON. THEY WERE EVEN MORE SCARED THAN HE WAS!

GIDEON'S CONFIDENCE GREW AS HE RETURNED TO HIS CAMP. HE GAVE EACH OF HIS MEN A TRUMPET AND A TORCH INSIDE A JAR. THE 300 ENCIRCLED THE CAMP.

THEY LIT THEIR TORCHES...

...AND THEY BLEW THEIR TRUMPETS AND BROKE THEIR JARS. THE MIDIANITES THOUGHT THEY WERE SURROUNDED. THEY WERE TERRIFIED AND FLED IN CONFUSION. GIDEON HAD RESTORED ISRAEL.

Hero Profile
Samson—God's Strong Man

FATHER: MANOAH

NOTABLE WOMEN IN SAMSON'S LIFE:
HIS WIFE, A PHILISTINE WOMAN FROM TIMNAH (A CITY IN CANAAN) AND DELILAH, A BEAUTIFUL WOMAN FROM THE VALLEY OF SOREK

NAZIRITE STRENGTH

SAMSON WAS A NAZIRITE. A NAZIRITE WAS AN ANCIENT HEBREW HOLY MAN WHO HAD MADE A SPECIAL PROMISE TO GOD. HE WAS TO SERVE GOD BY FOLLOWING SPECIAL RULES. SAMSON HAD A TREMENDOUS STRENGTH, WHICH WAS IN HIS UNCUT HAIR.

SAMSON AND DELILAH

SAMSON AND DELILAH HAVE LONG BEEN THE SUBJECT OF MANY POPULAR POEMS, BOOKS, AND MOVIES. PERHAPS THE RELATIONSHIP HAS BEEN SO FASCINATING BECAUSE OF THE MYSTERIOUS STRENGTH OF SAMSON AND DELILAH'S DECEIT TO FIND OUT WHY HE WAS SO STRONG. IN THE END SHE BETRAYS HIM, BUT GOD STILL PROVES HIS POWER AT THE END OF THE STORY!

Samson Kills a Lion

Judges 13-15

THE ISRAELITES ONCE AGAIN FELL OUT OF GOD'S FAVOR, AND FOR 40 YEARS THEY WERE DOMINATED BY THE PHILISTINES. ONE DAY AN ANGEL APPEARED TO A MAN NAMED MANOAH AND HIS WIFE. THEY HAD BEEN TRYING FOR YEARS TO HAVE A CHILD.

YOU WILL SOON HAVE A SON.

HE MUST NEVER CUT HIS HAIR. HE WILL BE A CHAMPION OF GOD.

THEY SOON HAD A SON, WHOM THEY NAMED SAMSON. HE NEVER CUT HIS HAIR AND GREW UP TO BE VERY STRONG.

OUR FRIEND IS UNBELIEVABLY STRONG!

YES, HE IS. HE HAS THE STRENGTH OF TEN MEN! MAYBE TWENTY!

SAMSON MET A BEAUTIFUL PHILISTINE WOMAN, AND THE TWO FELL IN LOVE. SAMSON HURRIED HOME TO TELL HIS PARENTS.

YOU WILL NOT MARRY A PHILISTINE WOMAN!

SURELY THERE IS A HEBREW WOMAN FOR YOU?

NO, FATHER! SHE IS THE ONE FOR ME. I LOVE HER!

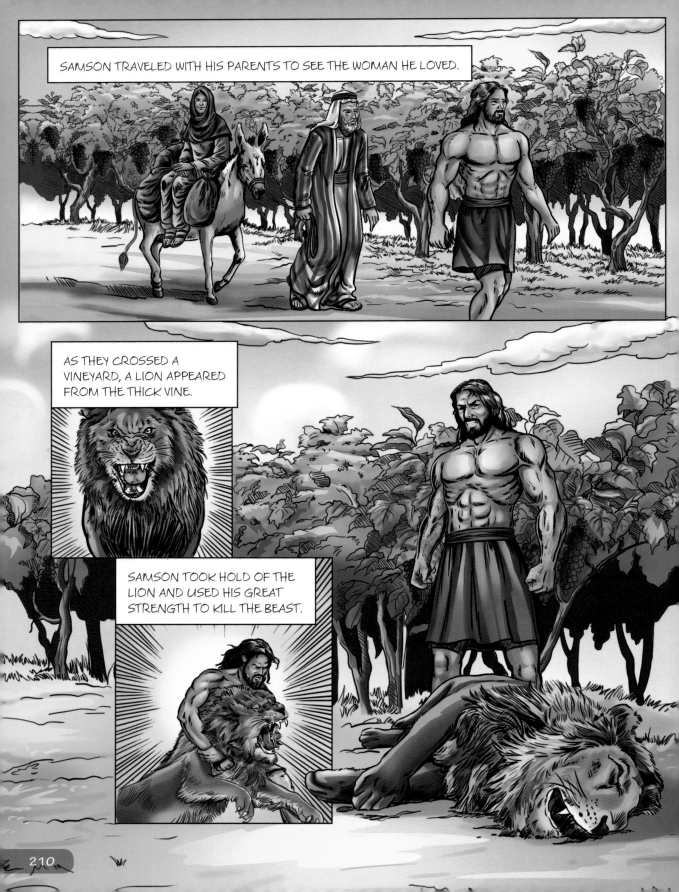

SAMSON TRAVELED WITH HIS PARENTS TO SEE THE WOMAN HE LOVED.

AS THEY CROSSED A VINEYARD, A LION APPEARED FROM THE THICK VINE.

SAMSON TOOK HOLD OF THE LION AND USED HIS GREAT STRENGTH TO KILL THE BEAST.

SOMETIME LATER, WHEN SAMSON WAS TRAVELING TO MARRY THE WOMAN, HE PASSED BY THE LION HE HAD KILLED. BEES HAD NESTED INSIDE AND MADE DELICIOUS HONEY, WHICH SAMSON SCOOPED OUT AND ATE.

ON HIS WEDDING DAY, SAMSON TOLD HIS GUESTS A RIDDLE BASED ON THE HONEY HE HAD EATEN.

I WILL GIVE YOU SEVEN DAYS TO GUESS THE ANSWER TO THIS RIDDLE.

OUT OF THE EATER CAME FOOD; OUT OF THE STRONG CAME SWEETNESS.

ON THE SEVENTH DAY, THE MEN CONFRONTED SAMSON'S WIFE.

SAMSON THEN LEFT HIS WIFE AND KILLED THIRTY OF THEIR MEN IN ASHKELON.

TELL US THE ANSWER TO THE RIDDLE OR WE WILL KILL YOU!

SAMSON'S WIFE WEPT AND CONVINCED HIM TO GIVE THE ANSWER, WHICH SHE THEN PASSED ON. LATER, WHEN THE MEN ANSWERED HIS RIDDLE, SAMSON WAS ANGRY.

LATER, THE PHILISTINES STRUCK BACK BY MURDERING SAMSON'S WIFE. SAMSON THEN VOWED TO KILL EVERY PHILISTINE IN HIS SIGHT. HIS WEAPON WAS THE JAWBONE OF A DEAD DONKEY.

I WILL NOT STOP UNTIL I **HAVE MY REVENGE!**

SAMSON RETURNED TO THE ISRAELITES AND BECAME THEIR LEADER. MEANWHILE, THE PHILISTINES HUNTED THE LEGENDARY STRONG MAN FOR YEARS.

DELILAH PLEADED, WEPT, AND PESTERED SAMSON TO REVEAL HIS SECRET. AT LAST, TO STOP HER FROM ANNOYING HIM, HE MADE UP A STORY.

TELL ME MY LOVE, WHY ARE YOU SO STRONG?

IF YOU WERE TO TIE ME UP WITH SEVEN ROPES, I WOULD BE JUST LIKE EVERYONE ELSE.

DELILAH TIED SAMSON UP AND TOLD HIM THE PHILISTINES WERE ABOUT TO ATTACK. HE QUICKLY BROKE FREE OF THE ROPES!

YOU LIED TO ME! YOUR STRENGTH IS JUST AS GREAT AS EVER!

DELILAH CONTINUED TO BEG SAMSON TO TELL THE TRUTH. OUT OF HIS LOVE FOR HER, HE FINALLY REVEALED HIS SECRET.

AS SAMSON SLEPT, THE PHILISTINES CAME AND CUT HIS HAIR.

WITH HIS STRENGTH GONE, THEY PUT OUT HIS EYES AND BLINDED HIM. SAMSON WAS BOUND AND THROWN INTO PRISON.

Hero Profile
Ruth—A Faithful Daughter-in-Law

HUSBANDS: MAHLON, BOAZ

SON: OBED (GRANDFATHER OF DAVID)

MEANING OF NAME: HEBREW NAME MEANING COMPANION, FRIEND

TOO FORWARD?

WHEN RUTH PUT ON HER FINEST CLOTHES AND WENT TO SEE BOAZ, HER FUTURE HUSBAND, SHE WAS NOT BEING TOO FORWARD. AT THAT TIME, A CHILDLESS WIDOW COULD ASK A RELATIVE TO MARRY HER.

A FOREIGNER

WHILE BOAZ MARRYING RUTH, THE MOABITE, MIGHT SEEM AT ODDS WITH THE TEACHINGS OF EZRA AND NEHEMIAH THAT FORBID JEWISH MEN FROM MARRYING NON-JEWISH WOMEN, IT IS IMPORTANT TO REMEMBER THAT WHEN RUTH VOLUNTEERED TO STAY WITH NAOMI, SHE ALSO SAID, "YOUR PEOPLE WILL BE MY PEOPLE AND YOUR GOD WILL BE MY GOD." SHE REJECTED HER PAGAN HERITAGE AND EMBRACED HER MOTHER-IN-LAW'S RELIGION AND NATIONALITY.

BOAZ RECOGNIZED THE WORTH OF HER ACTIONS. HE SAW THAT SHE WAS A GOOD WOMAN AND CHOSE TO MARRY HER.

GOD REWARDED RUTH'S LOVE AND LOYALTY TO NAOMI BY MAKING IT POSSIBLE FOR HER TO BE A GREAT-GRANDMOTHER OF DAVID, AND AN ANCESTOR OF JESUS!

A Loyal Woman

Ruth 1

THREE GENERATIONS BEFORE KING DAVID WAS BORN, A FAMINE SPREAD ACROSS JUDAH, INCLUDING THE TOWN OF BETHLEHEM. PEOPLE HAD LITTLE TO EAT. SOME BECAME SICK AND DIED. OTHERS, LIKE ELIMELECH AND HIS FAMILY, DECIDED TO LEAVE.

THIS IS THE LAST OF OUR FOOD, HUSBAND. THERE IS NO MORE.

YOU ARE A GOOD WIFE, NAOMI. YOU'VE DONE A LOT WITH SO LITTLE. IT'S TIME WE LEFT THIS PLACE FOR THE LAND OF MOAB.

AFTER ARRIVING IN MOAB, ELIMELECH DIED, LEAVING NAOMI AND HER TWO SONS TO FEND FOR THEMSELVES.

NAOMI'S SONS GREW AND PROSPERED. EACH TOOK A MOABITE WOMAN AS THEIR BRIDE.

BUT WITHIN TEN YEARS, TRAGEDY HAD STRUCK THE FAMILY AGAIN. BOTH MAHLON AND CHILION DIED, LEAVING THEIR MOTHER AND THEIR WIVES ALONE.

MY SONS ARE GONE. RUTH, WHAT AM I TO DO?

ORPAH AND I HAVE DECIDED TO RETURN TO BETHLEHEM WITH YOU.

ON THE ROAD TO JUDAH, NAOMI TOLD HER DAUGHTERS-IN-LAW TO GO BACK TO THEIR MOTHERS BECAUSE LIFE IN BETHLEHEM WOULD BE TOO HARD. ORPAH LEFT IN TEARS, BUT RUTH REMAINED.

RUTH, MY LIFE IS TOO BITTER. YOU MUST NOT STAY WITH ME!

DON'T ASK ME TO LEAVE. **I WON'T ABANDON YOU!** WHERE YOU GO, I WILL GO. YOUR PEOPLE WILL BE MY PEOPLE. YOUR GOD WILL BE MY GOD.

NAOMI AND RUTH ARRIVED IN BETHLEHEM, WHERE THEY WOULD START A NEW LIFE TOGETHER.

217

BOAZ TOOK RUTH AS HIS WIFE, AND THEY PROCLAIMED THEIR HAPPINESS IN FRONT OF NAOMI AND THE TOWN'S ELDERS.

THE COUPLE SOON HAD A CHILD, A SON NAMED OBED, WHO WOULD BECOME THE GRANDFATHER OF ISRAEL'S GREAT KING—DAVID.

Hero Profile
Samuel—The King Maker

MOTHER: HANNAH

FATHER: ELKANAH

LITERAL MEANING OF "SAMUEL"
IN HEBREW: NAME OF GOD

A MOTHER'S ANSWERED PRAYER
IN BIBLE TIMES GREAT VALUE WAS PLACED ON HAVING CHILDREN. HANNAH LONGED FOR A BABY. SHE PRAYED TO GOD AND PROMISED HER CHILD WOULD LEAD A LIFE OF SERVICE TO GOD.

THE BUILDING OF A NATION
ALTHOUGH SAMUEL WASN'T A KING, HIS EARLY LIFE IS WELL CHRONICLED IN THE BIBLE, WHILE THE LIFE OF ISRAEL'S FIRST KING, SAUL, IS NOT. THIS PROVIDES A NOTION OF HOW IMPORTANT SAMUEL IS TO THE FOUNDING OF ISRAEL AS A NATION. BEFORE SAMUEL, ISRAEL WAS A COLLECTION OF TRIBES, BUT SAMUEL PLAYS AN IMPORTANT ROLE IN ITS CHANGEOVER TO A NATION.

A Son for Hannah

1 Samuel 1–3

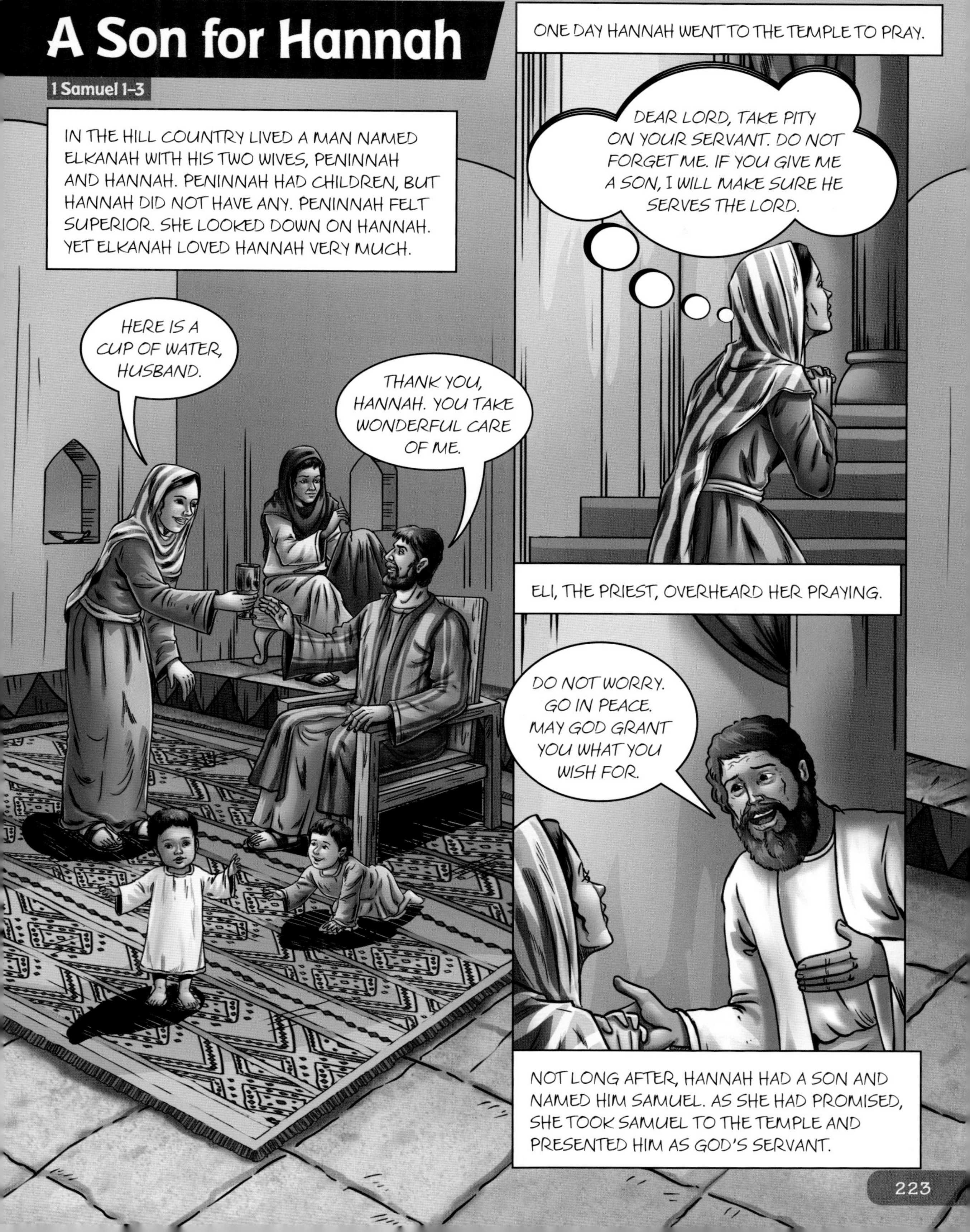

SAMUEL GREW UP IN THE TEMPLE UNDER ELI'S CARE. ONE NIGHT, SAMUEL WAS AWAKENED WHEN HE HEARD HIS NAME CALLED.

SAMUEL!

HERE I AM.

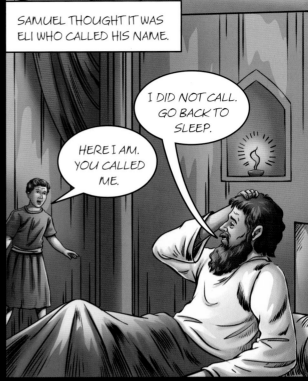

SAMUEL THOUGHT IT WAS ELI WHO CALLED HIS NAME.

I DID NOT CALL. GO BACK TO SLEEP.

HERE I AM. YOU CALLED ME.

THE LORD CALLED SAMUEL TWO MORE TIMES, AND AGAIN SAMUEL THOUGHT IT WAS ELI WHO WAS CALLING.

MY BOY, IT MUST BE THE LORD CALLING YOU! IF HE CALLS AGAIN, ANSWER AND SAY YOU ARE HIS SERVANT.

THE LORD CAME AND CALLED THE BOY AGAIN.

SAMUEL! SAMUEL!

YOUR SERVANT IS LISTENING, LORD!

GOD TOLD SAMUEL THAT HE WOULD SOON PUNISH ELI'S TWO SONS, FOR UNLIKE THEIR FATHER, THEY WERE WICKED. AND GOD WAS WITH SAMUEL AS HE GREW UP. EVENTUALLY, ALL OF ISRAEL RECOGNIZED SAMUEL AS A PROPHET OF THE LORD.

Seizing the Ark

1 Samuel 4–6

THE PHILISTINES AND THE HEBREWS WERE ONCE AGAIN AT WAR. THE PHILISTINES SLAUGHTERED THE ISRAELITES IN BATTLE.

AT THE TIME OF THE WAR, THE LORD APPEARED TO SAMUEL. SOON WORD SPREAD THAT THE SON OF HANNAH WAS A PROPHET WHO COMMUNICATED WITH GOD.

AFTER THE DEFEAT, THE HEBREWS RETREATED. IN DESPERATION, THEY BROUGHT THE ARK OF THE COVENANT TO THEIR CAMP. THEY HOPED IT WOULD BRING THEM VICTORY IN THE BATTLE.

A WILD CHEER AROSE FROM THE ISRAELITE CAMP WHEN THE ARK APPEARED.

NO ONE WILL DEFEAT US NOW!

THE ARK IS TOO POWERFUL. GOD IS TOO POWERFUL!

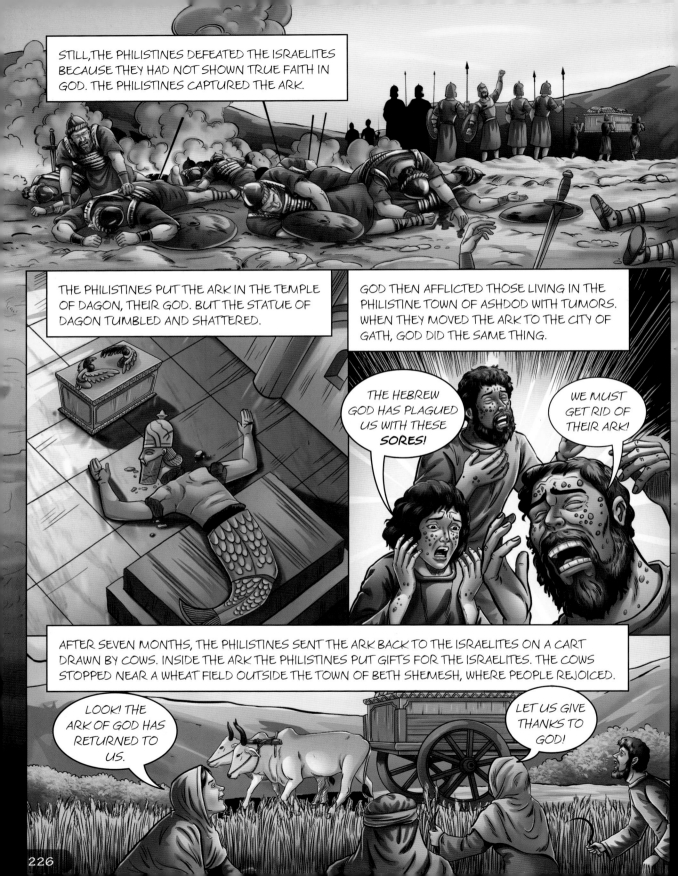

STILL, THE PHILISTINES DEFEATED THE ISRAELITES BECAUSE THEY HAD NOT SHOWN TRUE FAITH IN GOD. THE PHILISTINES CAPTURED THE ARK.

THE PHILISTINES PUT THE ARK IN THE TEMPLE OF DAGON, THEIR GOD. BUT THE STATUE OF DAGON TUMBLED AND SHATTERED.

GOD THEN AFFLICTED THOSE LIVING IN THE PHILISTINE TOWN OF ASHDOD WITH TUMORS. WHEN THEY MOVED THE ARK TO THE CITY OF GATH, GOD DID THE SAME THING.

THE HEBREW GOD HAS PLAGUED US WITH THESE **SORES**!

WE MUST GET RID OF THEIR ARK!

AFTER SEVEN MONTHS, THE PHILISTINES SENT THE ARK BACK TO THE ISRAELITES ON A CART DRAWN BY COWS. INSIDE THE ARK THE PHILISTINES PUT GIFTS FOR THE ISRAELITES. THE COWS STOPPED NEAR A WHEAT FIELD OUTSIDE THE TOWN OF BETH SHEMESH, WHERE PEOPLE REJOICED.

LOOK! THE ARK OF GOD HAS RETURNED TO US.

LET US GIVE THANKS TO GOD!

SAMUEL HEARD THEIR PLEAS AND MADE A SACRIFICE TO GOD.

ON THE BATTLEFIELD OF MIZPAH, GOD SENT THUNDER, WHICH TERRIFIED THE ENEMY. THE HEBREWS RUSHED THE PHILISTINES AND STRUCK THEM DOWN.

THE BATTLE WAS A TURNING POINT. GOD WAS NOW WITH SAMUEL AND THE ISRAELITES IN THEIR FIGHT AGAINST THE PHILISTINES. SAMUEL PLACED A STONE AT THE SITE OF THE BATTLE AS A REMINDER OF GOD'S HELP.

I PLACE THIS STONE HERE. ITS NAME IS EBENEZER, "STONE OF HELP"

THE PHILISTINES WOULD NEVER BOTHER ISRAEL AGAIN ON ISRAEL'S TERRITORY.

Searching for a King

1 Samuel 8–10

WHEN HE BECAME AN OLD MAN, SAMUEL ASKED HIS TWO SONS TO RULE ISRAEL. BUT THE SONS WERE CORRUPT. THEY TOOK BRIBES AND DID NOT FOLLOW THEIR FATHER'S EXAMPLE. THE ELDERS MET WITH SAMUEL AND ASKED HIM TO APPOINT A KING.

SAMUEL CHALLENGED THE ELDERS.

YOU HAVE GOD! WHY DO YOU WANT A KING? A KING WILL TURN YOUR SONS INTO SOLDIERS.

A KING WILL TAKE YOUR BEST FIELDS AND VINEYARDS AND GIVE THEM TO HIS SERVANTS.

A KING WILL FORCE YOUR DAUGHTERS TO BAKE BREAD AND TO COOK.

A KING WILL TAKE YOUR SLAVES AND USE THEM TO DO HIS WORK! NO! YOU DO NOT WANT A KING!

SAMUEL DESPAIRED WHEN THE ELDERS IGNORED HIS ADVICE AND INSISTED THEY WANTED A KING. GOD TOLD SAMUEL TO DO WHAT THE ELDERS SAID. THEY WERE REJECTING GOD, NOT SAMUEL.

Saul's Disobedience

1 Samuel 11–14

WITH SAUL AS KING, THE ISRAELITES WAGED VICTORIOUS WARS ON THEIR ENEMIES, DEFEATING THE AMMONITES, THE KINGS OF ZOBAH, AND THE AMALEKITES. WHEREVER HE TURNED, SAUL WAS SUCCESSFUL.

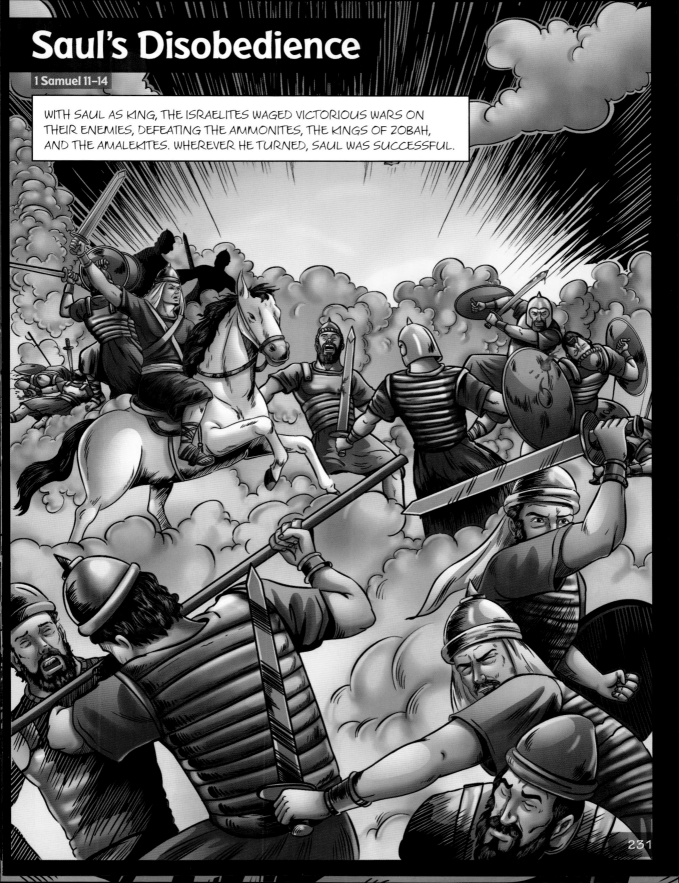

GOLIATH CHARGED AT DAVID...

...BUT DAVID NEVER WAVERED. HE PLACED A SMOOTH STONE IN HIS SLINGSHOT...

...FIRED AT THE MIGHTY WARRIOR...

...AND STRUCK THE GIANT DEAD WITH ONE SHOT.

DAVID CUT OFF GOLIATH'S HEAD TO CLAIM HIS VICTORY AS THE ISRAELITE ARMY CHASED THE PHILISTINES OUT OF THE VALLEY AND PLUNDERED THE ENEMY'S CAMP.

Saul's Jealousy

1 Samuel 18–24

DAVID'S FAME GREW RAPIDLY. THE PEOPLE CHEERED FOR HIM EVERYWHERE HE WENT.

SAUL BECAME ANGRY AND UPSET BECAUSE THE PEOPLE SEEMED TO LOVE AND RESPECT DAVID MORE THAN HIM. DAVID WOULD OFTEN PLAY HIS LYRE TO SOOTH THE KING, BUT ONE DAY AN EVIL SPIRIT SO CONSUMED SAUL THAT HE THREW HIS SPEAR AT HIM. HE MISSED BUT WAS SO JEALOUS OF DAVID THAT HE DECIDED TO SEND HIM AWAY INTO BATTLE TO GET RID OF HIM.

BUT EVERY CHEER FOR DAVID CUT TO THE HEART OF SAUL.

DAVID WAS VERY SUCCESSFUL AS A MILITARY COMMANDER, WHICH ANGERED SAUL EVEN MORE. HE VOWED TO KILL DAVID.

SAUL TOLD DAVID HE WOULD GIVE HIS DAUGHTER, MICHAL, TO HIM AS A BRIDE IF DAVID KILLED 100 PHILISTINES. SAUL HOPED DAVID WOULD DIE IN BATTLE.

DAVID DID KILL THE 100 PLUS MANY MORE. THEN HE MARRIED MICHAL.

JONATHAN WAS CONVINCED THAT HIS FATHER WANTED TO HARM DAVID. JONATHAN AND HIS SERVANT BOY WENT INTO THE FIELD WHERE DAVID WAS HIDING. JONATHAN SHOT HIS ARROWS AS HE AND DAVID HAD PLANNED.

DAVID KNEW HE WAS IN MORTAL DANGER. JONATHAN SENT HIS SERVANT BACK TO THE CITY, AND HE AND DAVID EMBRACED SADLY. THEN DAVID FLED FOR GOOD.

SAUL AND HIS ARMY PURSUED DAVID AND HIS MEN INTO THE WILDERNESS. ONE DAY SAUL CAME CLOSE TO CAPTURING DAVID WHEN HE WAS HIDING IN A CAVE.

KING SAUL! MY MEN TOLD ME TO KILL YOU, BUT I TOOK PITY ON YOU INSTEAD.

HERE IS THE END OF YOUR ROBE THAT I SLICED WHILE YOUR BACK WAS TURNED. BE CONVINCED I WILL NOT HARM YOU.

WHEN SAUL'S BACK WAS TURNED, DAVID CUT OFF A BIT OF HIS ROBE, ALTHOUGH HE COULD HAVE KILLED SAUL INSTEAD.

SAUL HEARD DAVID'S WORDS AND WAS DEEPLY SORRY THAT HE WAS TRYING TO HURT HIM. DAVID WONDERED HOW LONG THE TRUCE WOULD LAST.

David and Abigail

1 Samuel 25

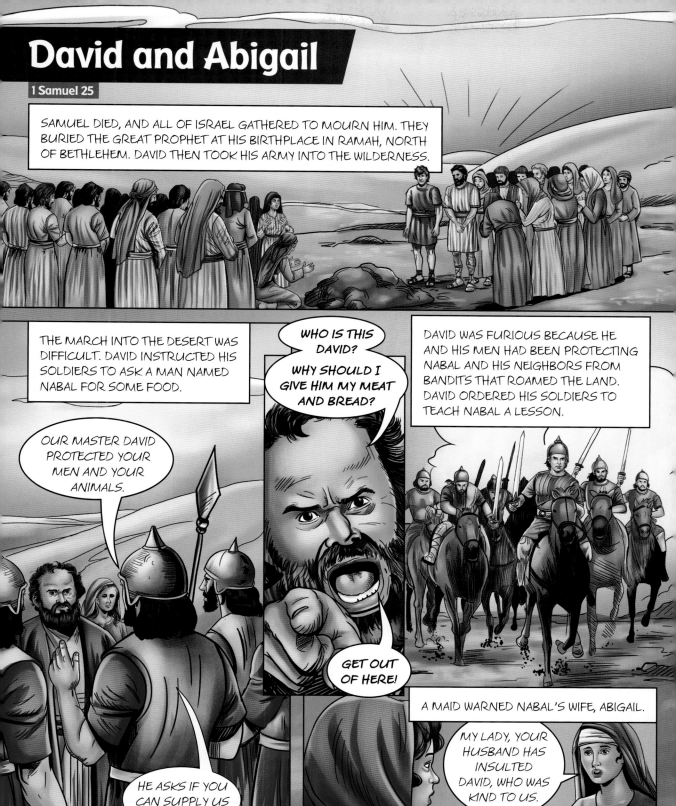

SAMUEL DIED, AND ALL OF ISRAEL GATHERED TO MOURN HIM. THEY BURIED THE GREAT PROPHET AT HIS BIRTHPLACE IN RAMAH, NORTH OF BETHLEHEM. DAVID THEN TOOK HIS ARMY INTO THE WILDERNESS.

THE MARCH INTO THE DESERT WAS DIFFICULT. DAVID INSTRUCTED HIS SOLDIERS TO ASK A MAN NAMED NABAL FOR SOME FOOD.

WHO IS THIS DAVID?

WHY SHOULD I GIVE HIM MY MEAT AND BREAD?

DAVID WAS FURIOUS BECAUSE HE AND HIS MEN HAD BEEN PROTECTING NABAL AND HIS NEIGHBORS FROM BANDITS THAT ROAMED THE LAND. DAVID ORDERED HIS SOLDIERS TO TEACH NABAL A LESSON.

OUR MASTER DAVID PROTECTED YOUR MEN AND YOUR ANIMALS.

GET OUT OF HERE!

HE ASKS IF YOU CAN SUPPLY US WITH FOOD.

A MAID WARNED NABAL'S WIFE, ABIGAIL.

MY LADY, YOUR HUSBAND HAS INSULTED DAVID, WHO WAS KIND TO US.

247

VERY SOON SAMUEL'S WORDS CAME TRUE. THE PHILISTINES DEFEATED ISRAEL.

MOST ALL OF SAUL'S SONS WERE DEAD, INCLUDING JONATHAN. THE KING WAS WOUNDED, AND HIS REMAINING TROOPS WERE ABOUT TO BE OVERRUN. KNOWING HE WOULD BE KILLED BY HIS ENEMIES, SAUL BEGGED A SERVANT TO END HIS LIFE.

KEEP ME FROM MY ENEMIES— END MY LIFE!

I CAN'T! I CAN'T!

WHEN THE SERVANT REFUSED, SAUL PURPOSELY FELL ON HIS OWN SWORD AND DIED.

DAVID WEPT WHEN HE LEARNED OF THE DEATH OF SAUL AND JONATHAN.

WOMEN OF ISRAEL, WEEP OVER SAUL.

I GRIEVE FOR YOU, JONATHAN, MY BROTHER!

King David

2 Samuel 2–6

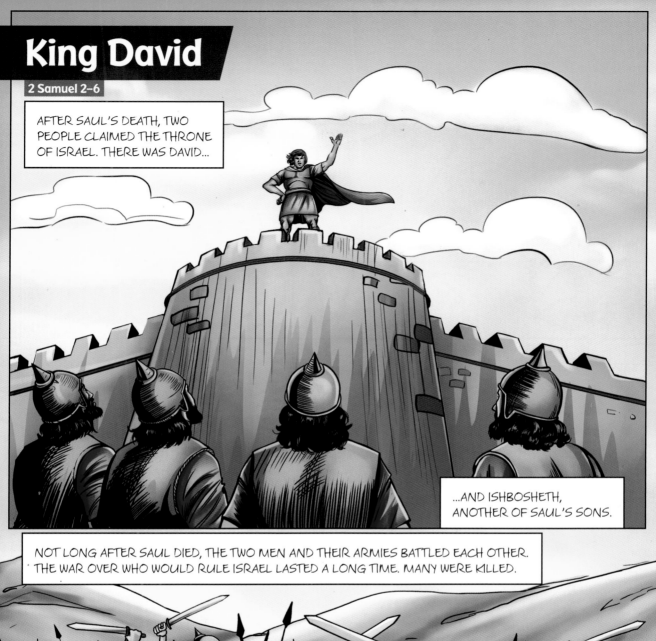

AFTER SAUL'S DEATH, TWO PEOPLE CLAIMED THE THRONE OF ISRAEL. THERE WAS DAVID...

...AND ISHBOSHETH, ANOTHER OF SAUL'S SONS.

NOT LONG AFTER SAUL DIED, THE TWO MEN AND THEIR ARMIES BATTLED EACH OTHER. THE WAR OVER WHO WOULD RULE ISRAEL LASTED A LONG TIME. MANY WERE KILLED.

253

ONE DARK NIGHT ISHBOSHETH WAS SLAIN AS HE LAY IN BED.

DAVID DID NOT CONDONE THE MURDER OF ISHBOSHETH, AND HE SENTENCED THE MURDERERS TO DEATH.

WITH THE LAND RUNNING RED WITH BLOOD, THE ELDERS FROM EACH TRIBE MET WITH DAVID TO PUT A STOP TO THE WAR.

DAVID AGREED TO BECOME KING. HE WAS THIRTY YEARS OLD WHEN HE TOOK THE THRONE. AS WITH SAUL YEARS BEFORE, DAVID WAS ANOINTED WITH OIL.

GOD SAID YOU WOULD BECOME KING WHEN SAUL DIED.

THIS BLOODSHED MUST END.

NOW IS THE TIME.

ONCE DAVID BECAME KING OF ISRAEL, HE DECIDED TO MAKE JERUSALEM HIS CAPITAL. AT THE TIME, THE JEBUSITES INHABITED THE CITY, AND THEY WERE NOT GOING TO GIVE IT UP WITHOUT A FIGHT.

WE WILL SLAUGHTER YOU, DAVID!

YOU WILL NEVER ENTER HERE!

THE ISRAELITES ATTACKED THE CITY BY MARCHING THROUGH A WATER SHAFT.

THE ISRAELITES ROUTED THE JEBUSITES AND SEIZED CONTROL OF JERUSALEM, WHICH BECAME KNOWN AS THE CITY OF DAVID.

DAVID BUILT UP THE CITY ON ALL SIDES, AND HE SAT AS THE EXALTED LEADER OF ISRAEL.

DAVID PICKED 30,000 MEN TO TO BRING THE SACRED ARK OF THE COVENANT TO JERUSALEM.

THE ARK IS NOW IN GOD'S CITY.

DAVID IS A GREAT MAN—A GREAT KING!

255

The Wars of David

2 Samuel 5–10; 1 Chronicles 14–20

DAVID WAS GOD'S WARRIOR.

HE BATTLED THE PHILISTINES AND DEFEATED THEM SEVERAL TIMES.

HE MADE THE MOABITES PAY TRIBUTE TO HIM.

HE DEFEATED THE ARAMEANS, THE EDOMITES, AND OTHER ENEMIES. DAVID FOUGHT BACK HADADEZER, KING OF ZOBAH, AND TOOK THE GOLDEN SHIELDS OF HIS GUARDS.

GOD'S LIGHT AND FAVOR TRULY SHINED ON DAVID.

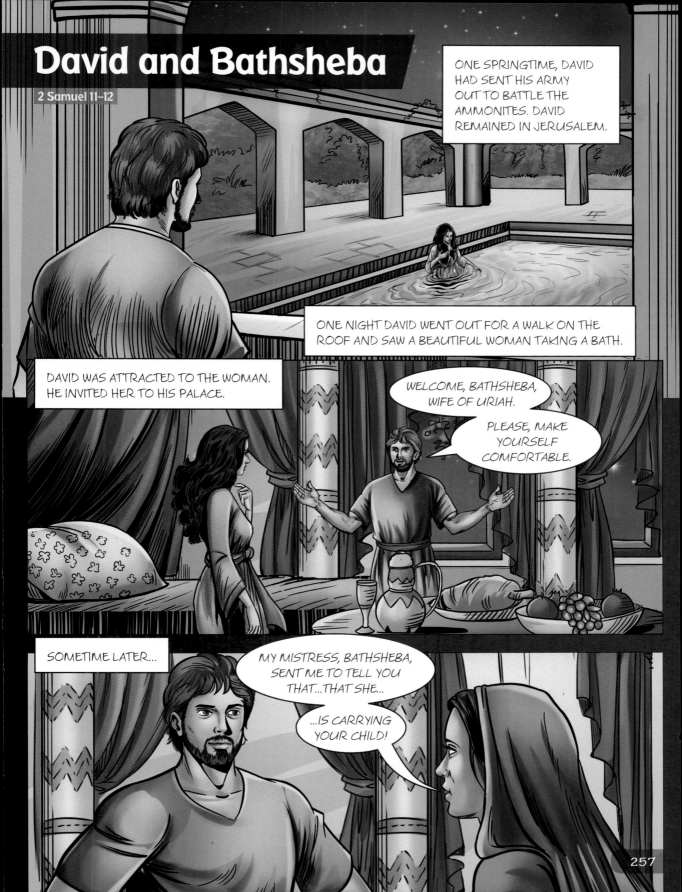

DAVID THOUGHT OF A WAY TO GET BATHSHEBA'S HUSBAND, URIAH, OUT OF HIS WAY. DAVID WROTE A LETTER TO JOAB AND SAID...

I WANT YOU TO PUT URIAH ON THE FRONT LINE IN YOUR NEXT BATTLE.

I HEAR HE IS A STRONG WARRIOR. HE WILL FIGHT WELL FOR YOU!

JOAB FOLLOWED HIS KING'S COMMAND. URIAH WAS PROMPTLY KILLED IN BATTLE.

DAVID HAD SUCCEEDED IN CLEARING THE WAY TO MARRY BATHSHEBA HIMSELF.

AFTER A PERIOD OF MOURNING HAD PASSED, DAVID AND BATHSHEBA WERE MARRIED.

BUT GOD WAS DISPLEASED WITH DAVID. THE KING HAD DONE AN EVIL THING. GOD SENT A MAN NAMED NATHAN TO TALK WITH DAVID.

THE LORD HAS SENT ME TO YOU, DAVID.

I HAVE A STORY TO TELL YOU.

ONCE THERE WERE TWO MEN— A RICH MAN.

...AND A POOR MAN.

THE RICH MAN HAD MANY ANIMALS.

THE POOR MAN ONLY HAD A BABY LAMB, WHICH HE FED AND TOOK CARE OF.

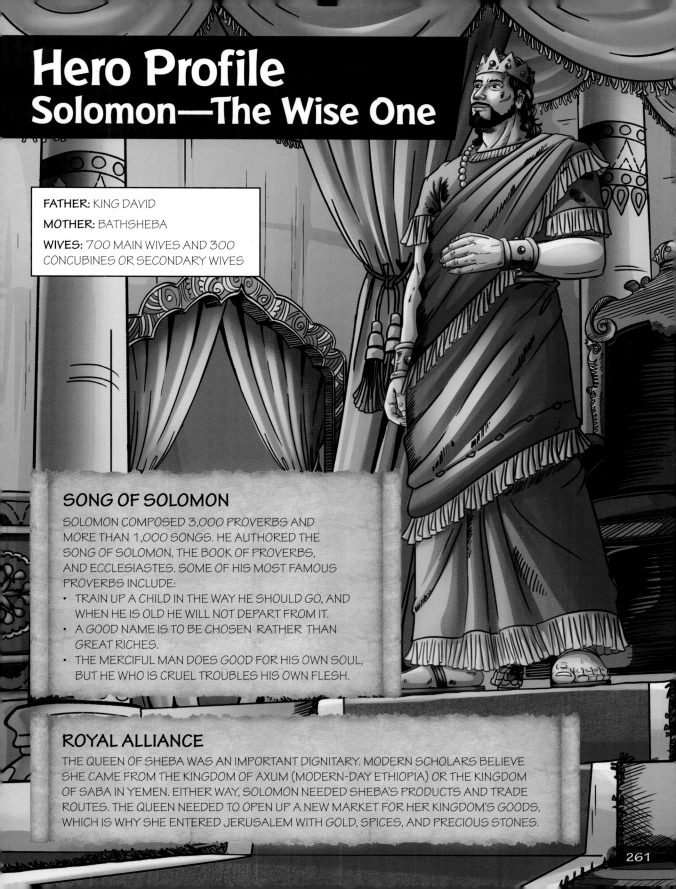

Hero Profile
Solomon—The Wise One

FATHER: KING DAVID

MOTHER: BATHSHEBA

WIVES: 700 MAIN WIVES AND 300 CONCUBINES OR SECONDARY WIVES

SONG OF SOLOMON

SOLOMON COMPOSED 3,000 PROVERBS AND MORE THAN 1,000 SONGS. HE AUTHORED THE SONG OF SOLOMON, THE BOOK OF PROVERBS, AND ECCLESIASTES. SOME OF HIS MOST FAMOUS PROVERBS INCLUDE:

- TRAIN UP A CHILD IN THE WAY HE SHOULD GO, AND WHEN HE IS OLD HE WILL NOT DEPART FROM IT.
- A GOOD NAME IS TO BE CHOSEN RATHER THAN GREAT RICHES.
- THE MERCIFUL MAN DOES GOOD FOR HIS OWN SOUL, BUT HE WHO IS CRUEL TROUBLES HIS OWN FLESH.

ROYAL ALLIANCE

THE QUEEN OF SHEBA WAS AN IMPORTANT DIGNITARY. MODERN SCHOLARS BELIEVE SHE CAME FROM THE KINGDOM OF AXUM (MODERN-DAY ETHIOPIA) OR THE KINGDOM OF SABA IN YEMEN. EITHER WAY, SOLOMON NEEDED SHEBA'S PRODUCTS AND TRADE ROUTES. THE QUEEN NEEDED TO OPEN UP A NEW MARKET FOR HER KINGDOM'S GOODS, WHICH IS WHY SHE ENTERED JERUSALEM WITH GOLD, SPICES, AND PRECIOUS STONES.

The Wisdom of Solomon

1 Kings 2–3

DAVID'S DEATH DREW NEAR. HE BROUGHT SOLOMON INTO HIS BEDCHAMBER AND GAVE THE NEW KING SOME ADVICE.

MY SON, I GROW WEAK. I WILL BE WITH GOD SOON.

REMEMBER WHAT I TELL YOU. BE STRONG AND KEEP GOD CLOSE.

KEEP THE LAW OF MOSES, AND YOUR CHILDREN WILL ALWAYS RULE OVER ISRAEL.

DAVID HAS DIED. FOR FORTY YEARS HE REIGNED.

MAY HE BE WITH THE LORD.

SOON AFTER DAVID'S DEATH, GOD APPEARED TO SOLOMON IN A DREAM AND ASKED HIM WHAT HE WOULD LIKE GOD TO GIVE HIM.

ALL I ASK FROM YOU IS WISDOM SO I MIGHT RULE WELL.

I WILL GIVE YOU WHAT YOU ASKED FOR, AND I WILL GIVE YOU WHAT YOU DID NOT ASK FOR! THERE WILL BE NO KING IN THE WORLD AS GREAT AS YOU!

GOD WAS PLEASED WITH SOLOMON'S ANSWER...

...AND ALONG WITH WISDOM GAVE HIM RICHES, HONOR, GREATNESS, AND LONG LIFE.

SOON AFTER THAT DREAM, TWO WOMEN CAME TO SEE THE KING. BOTH WERE IN GREAT DISTRESS.

MY LORD, THIS WOMAN AND I LIVE IN THE SAME HOUSE.

I GAVE BIRTH TO A CHILD, AS DID SHE.

LAST NIGHT THIS WOMAN'S CHILD DIED. SHE PUT HIM NEXT TO ME.

I WOKE UP, FOUND HER DEAD BOY IN MY BED!

SHE TOOK MY CHILD, THE ONE BEFORE YOUR FEET!

LIES!!! LIES!!! THIS **IS** MY CHILD.

HER CHILD IS DEAD!

265

SOLOMON LISTENED TO THE TWO WOMEN ARGUE. HE OBSERVED THEIR BEHAVIOR.

HE KNEW ONE WOMAN WAS LYING, BUT HOW COULD HE DISCOVER WHICH ONE WAS THE LIAR AND WHICH ONE TOLD THE TRUTH?

SILENCE!

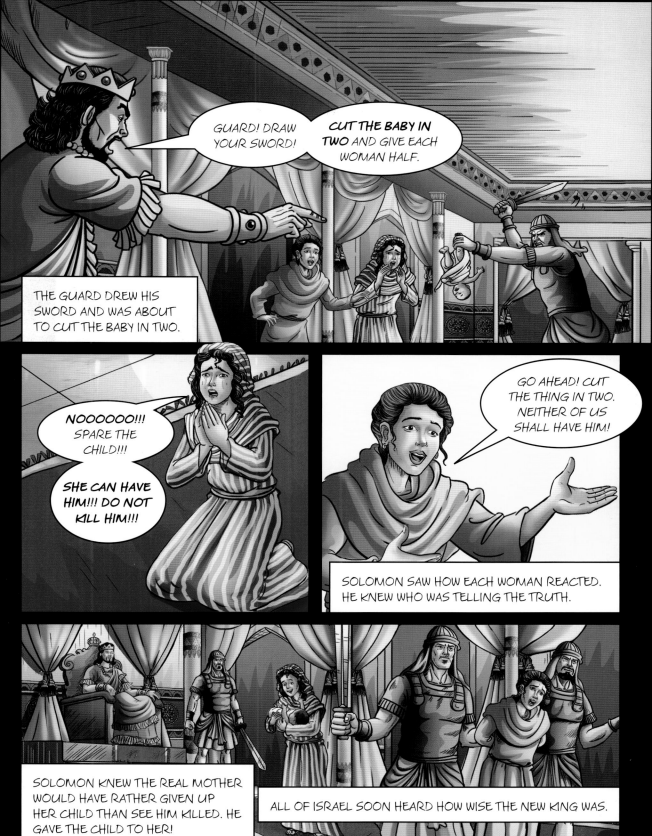

267

Building the Great Temple

BUILDING A GREAT TEMPLE IN JERUSALEM TO HOUSE THE ARK OF THE COVENANT WAS ONE OF DAVID'S DREAMS. BUT GOD HAD DELAYED THE CONSTRUCTION UNTIL ALL THE WARS WERE OVER AND SOLOMON TOOK POWER.

THE KING OF TYRE HAD HIS LABORERS CUT DOWN CEDARS AND CYPRESS FOR THE TEMPLE.

STONE-CUTTERS CHISELED WALLS OUT OF ROCK.

WHEN THE TEMPLE WAS FINISHED, THE INSIDE WAS MAGNIFICENT. THE INTERIOR WAS COVERED IN WOOD FROM FLOOR TO CEILING. IT WAS DECORATED IN CARVED ORNAMENTAL BUDS AND FLOWERS.

SOLOMON THEN HAD THE ARK PLACED INSIDE. KING DAVID'S DREAM HAD FINALLY BEEN REALIZED.

271

The Queen of Sheba

1 Kings 10

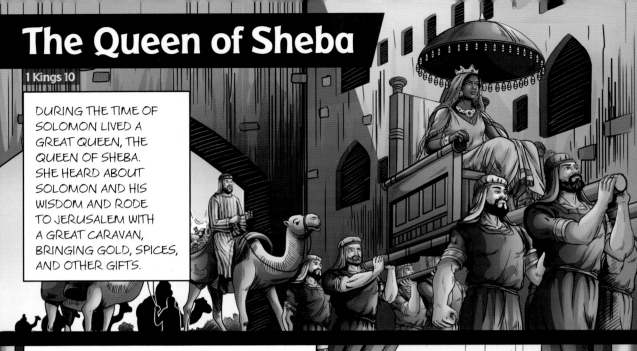

DURING THE TIME OF SOLOMON LIVED A GREAT QUEEN, THE QUEEN OF SHEBA. SHE HEARD ABOUT SOLOMON AND HIS WISDOM AND RODE TO JERUSALEM WITH A GREAT CARAVAN, BRINGING GOLD, SPICES, AND OTHER GIFTS.

SOLOMON THREW THE QUEEN A GREAT FEAST.

THE QUEEN HAD COME TO JERUSALEM SEEKING TRUTH AND WISDOM AND TO TEST SOLOMON'S KNOWLEDGE.

THE STORIES OF YOUR WISDOM ARE LEGENDARY.

I DID NOT BELIEVE THEM...

273

Solomon's Reign Ends

1 Kings 11–12

KING SOLOMON GREW OLD AND LOVED MANY FOREIGN WOMEN. HE MARRIED THE DAUGHTER OF AN EGYPTIAN PHARAOH, A MOABITE, AN AMMONITE, AND OTHERS.

SOLOMON'S WIVES TURNED HIS HEART AWAY FROM GOD. HE BEGAN TO WORSHIP THEIR FALSE GODS.

I WILL TEAR ISRAEL AWAY FROM YOUR SON'S HAND AND GIVE MOST OF IT TO YOUR SERVANT!

I WARNED YOU TO KEEP MY COVENANT.

GOD THEN RAISED UP MEN WHO OPPOSED SOLOMON. THEY PLOTTED AGAINST THE KING.

AMONG SOLOMON'S ADVERSARIES WAS A MAN NAMED JEROBOAM, WHO HAD WORKED FOR THE KING AS A CONSTRUCTION SUPERVISOR.

JEROBOAM, TAKE TEN PIECES FOR YOURSELF.

GOD WILL GIVE YOU TEN OF ISRAEL'S TRIBES. HE WILL LEAVE THE OTHERS TO SOLOMON'S SON.

I WILL DO AS YOU SAY, PROPHET!

ONE DAY, JEROBOAM MET THE PROPHET AHIJAH ON A DUSTY ROAD. THE PROPHET RIPPED OFF HIS ROBE AND TORE IT INTO TWELVE PIECES.

SOLOMON HEARD ALL ABOUT JEROBOAM. THE KING ORDERED THE MAN KILLED. JEROBOAM FLED TO EGYPT.

WHEN SOLOMON DIED, JEROBOAM RETURNED TO ISRAEL. SOLOMON'S SON REHOBOAM THEN BECAME KING.

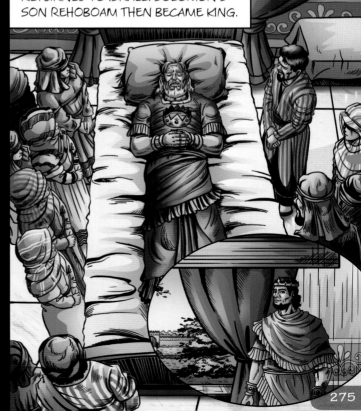

Hero Profile
Elijah—Slayer of Idols

MEANING OF NAME: "MY GOD IS YAHWEH"

HOMETOWN: TISHBE, LOCATED IN UPPER GALILEE

FATHER: UNKNOWN

ELIJAH AND THE PROPHETS OF BAAL

THE KINGS OF ISRAEL WERE EVIL. THEY HAD FORGOTTEN ABOUT GOD AND WORSHIPED A FAKE GOD NAMED BAAL. BUT GOD SENT A BOLD PROPHET, ELIJAH, TO CHALLENGE THE TERRIBLE KING AHAB. GOD GAVE ELIJAH AMAZING POWER TO PERFORM MIRACLES AND BRING THE HEARTS OF THE PEOPLE BACK TO HIM.

WHO TOOK THE ARK?

WHEN BABYLONIAN RULER NEBUCHADNEZZAR DESTROYED SOLOMON'S GRAND TEMPLE, THE ARK OF THE COVENANT VANISHED. SOME PEOPLE BELIEVE IT WAS REMOVED AND TAKEN SOMEWHERE ELSE BEFORE THE DESTRUCTION TO EGYPT. OTHERS SAY NEBUCHADNEZZAR BROUGHT IT TO BABYLON.

The Wicked King and Queen

1 Kings 12, 16–19

BY THE TIME OF SOLOMON'S DEATH, THE PEOPLE OF ISRAEL HAD GROWN TIRED OF PAYING HEAVY TAXES TO SUPPORT THE KING'S ENORMOUS HOUSEHOLD. WHEN THEY ASKED HIS SON, KING REHOBOAM, FOR HELP, THE NEW KING LAUGHED.

MY FATHER MADE YOU WORK HARD. I'LL MAKE YOU WORK HARDER!

ISRAEL SPLIT IN TWO. THE KINGS OF THE NORTH DISOBEYED GOD. THE KINGS OF THE SOUTH STAYED MOSTLY LOYAL TO HIM.

AHAB WAS ONE OF THE MEANEST KINGS OF THE NORTH. HIS QUEEN, JEZEBEL, CAME FROM LEBANON. SHE WAS A FOLLOWER OF BAAL, THE PAGAN GOD OF RAIN.

JEZEBEL ORDERED THE MURDER OF GOD'S PROPHETS.

KILL HIM! THEN GET RID OF HIS BODY!

A TERRIBLE DROUGHT SPREAD THROUGHOUT THE LAND.

WILL THIS DROUGHT EVER END?

GOD IS PUNISHING US FOR OUR KING AND QUEEN'S WICKEDNESS.

IN A WITHERED FIELD EAST OF THE JORDAN RIVER, A PROPHET NAMED ELIJAH WAITED FOR THE LORD TO SPEAK AS RAVENS BROUGHT HIM FOOD.

ELIJAH, WHO LATER FLED TO THE WILDERNESS WHEN JEZEBEL WAS KILLING THE PROPHETS, WOULD SOON CONFRONT THE VILE AHAB AND HIS QUEEN.

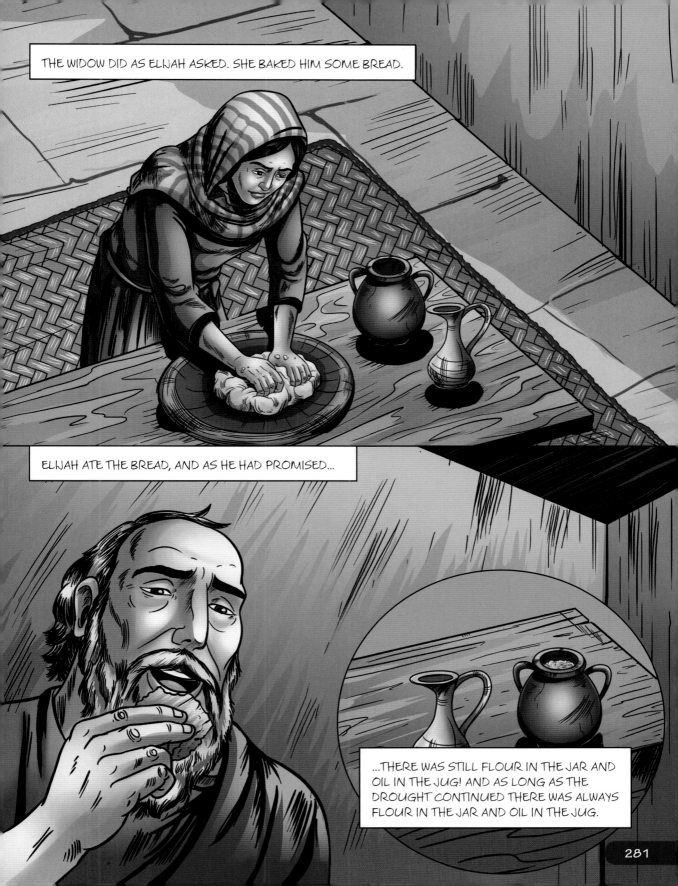

THE WIDOW DID AS ELIJAH ASKED. SHE BAKED HIM SOME BREAD.

ELIJAH ATE THE BREAD, AND AS HE HAD PROMISED...

...THERE WAS STILL FLOUR IN THE JAR AND OIL IN THE JUG! AND AS LONG AS THE DROUGHT CONTINUED THERE WAS ALWAYS FLOUR IN THE JAR AND OIL IN THE JUG.

SOME TIME HAD PASSED, AND THE SON OF THE WIDOW FELL SICK. HE BECAME SO ILL THAT HE STOPPED BREATHING.

WHY HAVE YOU DONE THIS TO ME, MAN OF GOD?

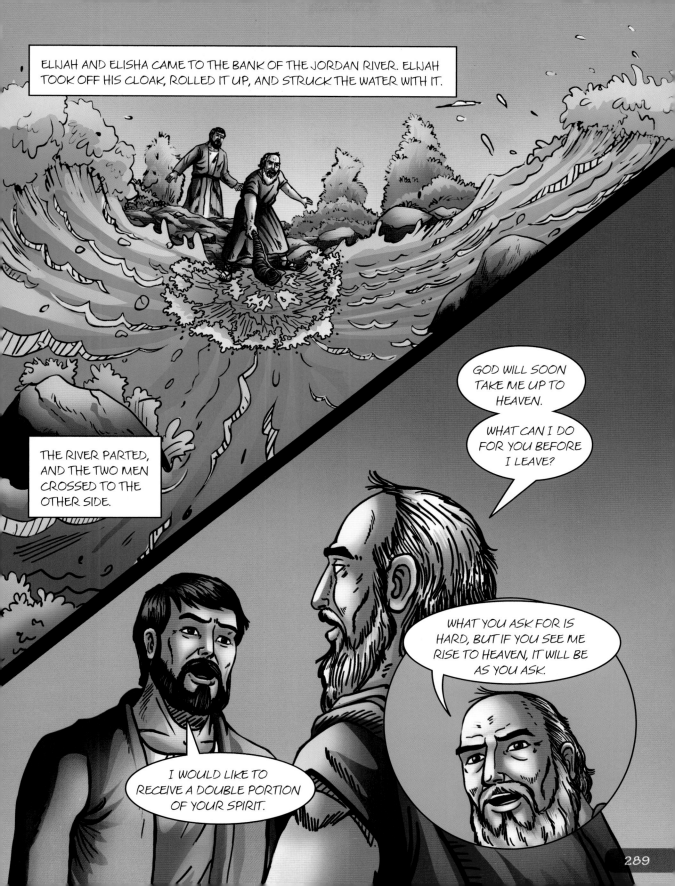

SUDDENLY, A CHARIOT OF FIRE DRAWN BY FIERY HORSES APPEARED AND TOOK ELIJAH UP TO HEAVEN IN A WHIRLWIND. "MY FATHER, MY FATHER!" ELIJAH CRIED OUT, AS THE CHARIOT BROUGHT HIM TO GOD.

ELISHA PICKED UP ELIJAH'S CLOAK FROM WHERE IT LAY ON THE GROUND. HE STRUCK THE RIVER WITH IT AND THEN CROSSED AS THE WATER PARTED BEFORE HIM.

THE ELDERS WATCHED AND BOWED TO ELISHA. "THE SPIRIT OF ELIJAH RESTS IN YOU," THEY SAID.

Jerusalem Is Destroyed

2 Kings 24–25

NEBUCHADNEZZAR, THE GREAT BABYLONIAN KING, WANTED JUDAH FOR HIS VERY OWN. HE ATTACKED JERUSALEM SEVERAL TIMES. EACH TIME, HE TOOK GROUPS OF CAPTIVES AND SENT THEM TO BABYLON.

DURING ONE ATTACK, THE BABYLONIANS FORCED JUDAH'S 18-YEAR-OLD KING, JEHOIACHIN, TO SURRENDER AS HIS MOTHER WATCHED.

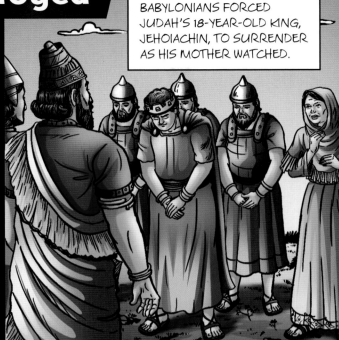

KING NEBUCHADNEZZAR WANTS EVERYONE OUT OF THE CITY!

ALL WARRIORS, ARTISANS AND SMITHS SHALL BE **EXILED**!

AS MORE JUDEANS WERE FORCED TO LEAVE JERUSALEM, NEBUCHADNEZZAR'S SOLDIERS LOOTED THE CITY, INCLUDING SOLOMON'S GRAND TEMPLE.

THE GREAT CITY WAS IN A SHAMBLES. ONLY THE POOR AND UNSKILLED WERE ALLOWED TO STAY.

NEBUCHADNEZZAR THEN INSTALLED ZEDEKIAH AS JUDAH'S PUPPET KING AND MADE HIM SWEAR AN OATH OF ALLEGIANCE. HE WAS 21 YEARS OLD WHEN HE CAME TO THE THRONE. ZEDEKIAH RESTORED THE CITY, BUT AS THE YEARS PASSED, HE BECAME INCREASINGLY DISCONTENT WITH HIS FOREIGN OVERLORD.

LIKE JEHOIACHIN BEFORE HIM, ZEDEKIAH DID NOT PLACE HIS FAITH IN THE LORD. HE LED A REBELLION AGAINST BABYLONIA. NEBUCHADNEZZAR LAUNCHED AN ATTACK ON JERUSALEM AND BATTLED WITHIN THE CITY.

FINALLY, NEBUCHADNEZZAR'S SOLDIERS BREACHED THE CITY'S WALLS.

THEY CAPTURED ZEDEKIAH AND KILLED HIS SONS BEFORE HIS EYES.

THEY CARRIED OFF TREASURES FROM SOLOMON'S TEMPLE.

THE BABYLONIANS THEN SET THE CITY ABLAZE, REDUCING THE TEMPLE TO RUBBLE. AS FOR ZEDEKIAH, THE SOLDIERS BOUND HIM WITH SHACKLES, BLINDED HIM, AND TOOK HIM TO BABYLON, WHERE HE DIED IN PRISON.

Hero Profile
Isaiah—Prophet of Deliverance

MEANING OF NAME: THE LORD HAS SAVED

PLACE OF BIRTH: JUDAH

SONS: SHEAR-JASHUB, MAHER-SHALAL-HASH-BAZ

FATHER: AMOZ

MENTIONING THE MESSIAH
IF YOU READ THE BOOK OF ISAIAH, YOU'LL SEE THAT THE MESSIAH IS MENTIONED MORE IN THIS BOOK THAN IN ANY OTHER OLD TESTAMENT BOOK. IN THE BOOK ARE VIVID DESCRIPTIONS OF JESUS' BIRTH IN BETHLEHEM, ALONG WITH HIS CRUCIFIXION AND RESURRECTION.

BIBLE FACT
EVEN THOUGH ISAIAH LIVED OVER 700 YEARS BEFORE THE BIRTH OF CHRIST, HE WAS A PROPHET WHO GOD INSPIRED TO BOTH WARN THE PEOPLE OF ISRAEL ABOUT THE COMING JUDGMENT OF GOD (CHAPTERS 1–39) AND TELL OF THE PROMISE OF A MESSIAH AND SALVATION (CHAPTERS 40–66).

God Calls Isaiah

Isaiah 6

ABOUT 700 YEARS BEFORE JESUS WAS BORN, GOD CALLED ONE OF HIS GREATEST PROPHETS TO SPEAK FOR HIM. HIS NAME WAS ISAIAH. AT THE TIME, THE ASSYRIAN EMPIRE WAS BEGINNING TO MOVE WEST, THREATENING THE NORTHERN JEWISH NATION OF ISRAEL AND THE SOUTHERN NATION OF JUDAH, WHERE ISAIAH LIVED.

ONE DAY WHILE HE WAS IN THE TEMPLE AT JERUSALEM, ISAIAH SAW THE LORD SEATED ON A LOFTY THRONE. HE WAS SURROUNDED BY SIX ANGELS WHOSE WINGS COVERED THEIR FACES AND FEET. GOD ASKED ISAIAH TO BE HIS PROPHET.

I AM FULL OF SADNESS AND DOOMED! MY EYES HAVE SEEN THE LORD OF HOSTS! I AM A SINNER AND CANNOT BE YOUR VOICE.

Crisis in Judah

Isaiah 7–8

IN THOSE DAYS, SYRIA AND NORTHERN ISRAEL JOINED FORCES AGAINST THE ASSYRIANS TO TRY TO STOP THEIR EXPANSION.

THE KING OF ISRAEL AND THE KING OF SYRIA WANTED JUDAH TO ENTER INTO AN ALLIANCE AGAINST THE ASSYRIANS. KING AHAZ OF JUDAH REFUSED, AND A FORCE OF NORTHERN ISRAEL AND SYRIAN SOLDIERS MARCHED ON HIS KINGDOM.

ISAIAH COUNSELLED THE KING.

TAKE CARE. BE CALM. HAVE NO FEAR. GOD IS WITH YOU.

THE TWO KINGS FROM THE NORTH ARE APPROACHING. ALL IS NOT WELL IN MY KINGDOM.

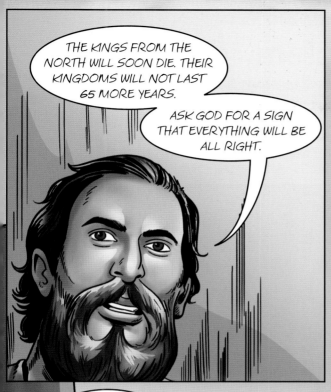

THE KINGS FROM THE NORTH WILL SOON DIE. THEIR KINGDOMS WILL NOT LAST 65 MORE YEARS.

ASK GOD FOR A SIGN THAT EVERYTHING WILL BE ALL RIGHT.

NO. I WILL NOT —CANNOT— TEMPT GOD.

I WILL ASK THE ASSYRIANS FOR HELP.

NO! GOD WILL SEND YOU A SIGN!

A YOUNG WOMAN SHALL BEAR A SON AND WILL NAME HIM IMMANUEL. THIS MEANS "GOD IS WITH US."

BY THE TIME THE BOY KNOWS GOOD FROM EVIL, GOD WILL DEFEAT THE KINGS OF THE NORTH.

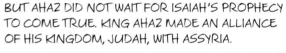

BUT AHAZ DID NOT WAIT FOR ISAIAH'S PROPHECY TO COME TRUE. KING AHAZ MADE AN ALLIANCE OF HIS KINGDOM, JUDAH, WITH ASSYRIA.

THE ASSYRIANS CONQUERED SYRIA, AND TEN YEARS LATER THEY RETURNED TO DESTROY ISRAEL. THE INVADERS SENT THOUSANDS OF HEBREWS TO LIVE ELSEWHERE. JUDAH PAID DEARLY FOR ITS ALLIANCE WITH THE ASSYRIANS INSTEAD OF TRUSTING IN GOD.

The Siege of Jerusalem

2 Kings 18–20; 2 Chronicles 32

THE ASSYRIAN ARMY WAS OUTSIDE THE WALLS OF JERUSALEM. HEZEKIAH WAS NOW KING OF JUDAH. HE WAS A GOOD KING WHO TRUSTED IN GOD. HE HAD LONG KNOWN THAT THIS MOMENT WOULD COME. HE HAD SPENT TIME PLANNING. HE HAD HIS MEN DIG A TUNNEL FROM THE SPRING THROUGH THE ROCK TO ENSURE THAT THE CITY WOULDN'T BE LEFT WITHOUT WATER IN THE EVENT OF A WAR UPON JERUSALEM.

THEY REPAIRED HOLES IN THE CITY'S WALLS AND BUILT TOWERS TO DEFEND AGAINST ATTACK.

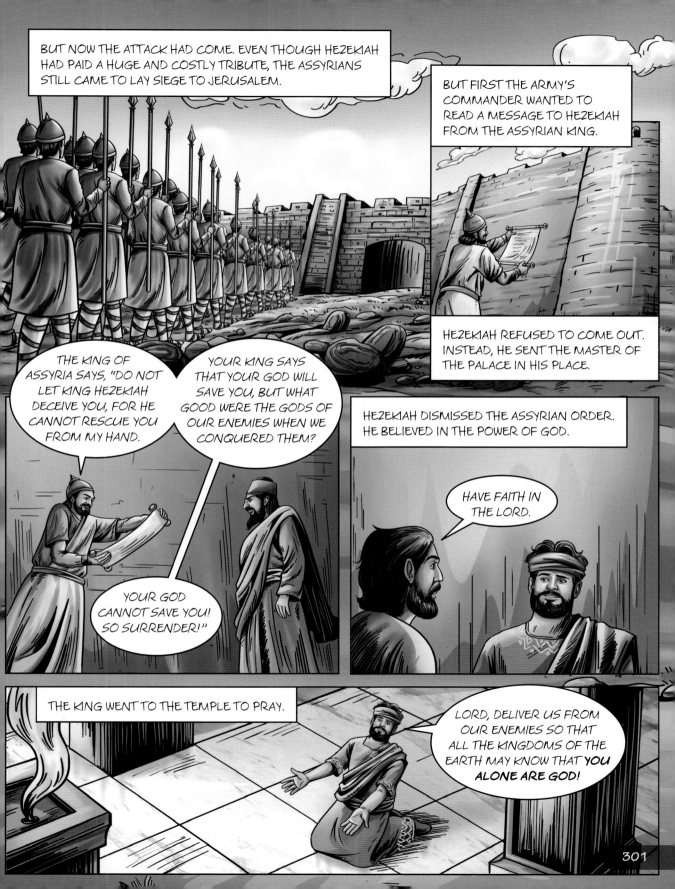

BUT NOW THE ATTACK HAD COME. EVEN THOUGH HEZEKIAH HAD PAID A HUGE AND COSTLY TRIBUTE, THE ASSYRIANS STILL CAME TO LAY SIEGE TO JERUSALEM.

BUT FIRST THE ARMY'S COMMANDER WANTED TO READ A MESSAGE TO HEZEKIAH FROM THE ASSYRIAN KING.

HEZEKIAH REFUSED TO COME OUT. INSTEAD, HE SENT THE MASTER OF THE PALACE IN HIS PLACE.

THE KING OF ASSYRIA SAYS, "DO NOT LET KING HEZEKIAH DECEIVE YOU, FOR HE CANNOT RESCUE YOU FROM MY HAND.

YOUR KING SAYS THAT YOUR GOD WILL SAVE YOU, BUT WHAT GOOD WERE THE GODS OF OUR ENEMIES WHEN WE CONQUERED THEM?

YOUR GOD CANNOT SAVE YOU! SO SURRENDER!"

HEZEKIAH DISMISSED THE ASSYRIAN ORDER. HE BELIEVED IN THE POWER OF GOD.

HAVE FAITH IN THE LORD.

THE KING WENT TO THE TEMPLE TO PRAY.

LORD, DELIVER US FROM OUR ENEMIES SO THAT ALL THE KINGDOMS OF THE EARTH MAY KNOW THAT **YOU ALONE ARE GOD!**

301

THAT NIGHT THE ANGEL OF THE LORD HOVERED OVER THE ASSYRIAN CAMP, KILLING TENS OF THOUSANDS OF TROOPS.

THE ASSYRIANS RETREATED IN DEFEAT, AND JERUSALEM WAS SPARED.

GOD MADE THE SUNLIGHT GO BACKWARD. HEZEKIAH KNEW HE WAS RIGHT WITH THE LORD.

ISAIAH THEN TOLD THE KING TO PUT A MIXTURE OF FIGS ON HIS SORES. HEZEKIAH WAS SOON CURED.

I FEEL BETTER. THE LORD HAS SMILED ON ME.

HE HAS GRANTED ME MORE TIME TO LOOK AFTER MY PEOPLE AND MY CITY.

Hero Profile
Jeremiah—Prophet of Doom

THE WEEPING PROPHET

JEREMIAH'S NAME MEANS "THE LORD LIFTS UP." SOMETIMES HE IS CALLED THE WEEPING PROPHET BECAUSE OF HIS SADNESS FOR THE PEOPLE OF ISRAEL. JEREMIAH BECAME A MESSENGER OF GOD TO WARN THE PEOPLE OF ISRAEL TO TURN AWAY FROM THEIR SINS OR FACE THE SUFFERING THAT WAS ABOUT TO COME FROM THEIR ENEMIES.

IN EXILE!

WHEN THE BABYLONIANS TOOK OVER AN AREA, THEY FORCED PEOPLE TO RESETTLE ELSEWHERE. IT WAS ONE WAY OF DEMONSTRATING THEIR POWER. IT WAS ALSO A WAY TO KEEP REBELLIOUS COMMUNITY LEADERS SEPARATE SO THEY DID NOT STAGE A REVOLT. THESE EXILES COULD THEN BE REUSED AS SOLDIERS, WORKERS, OR FARMERS IN SERVICE TO BABYLON.

The Potter's Wheel

Jeremiah 18–24

JEREMIAH WAS RELUCTANT TO BECOME A PROPHET OF GOD BECAUSE HE FELT HE WAS TOO YOUNG AND DID NOT KNOW WHAT TO SAY. GOD TOLD HIM TO GO TO THE POTTER'S HOUSE. HE PROMISED TO TELL JEREMIAH WHAT TO SAY TO THE PEOPLE OF ISRAEL.

TELL MY PEOPLE THAT I AM LIKE A POTTER. I CAN SHAPE ISRAEL INTO A STRONG NATION.

OR, IF THEY DON'T STOP THEIR EVIL WAYS, I CAN RESHAPE THEM AND START AGAIN.

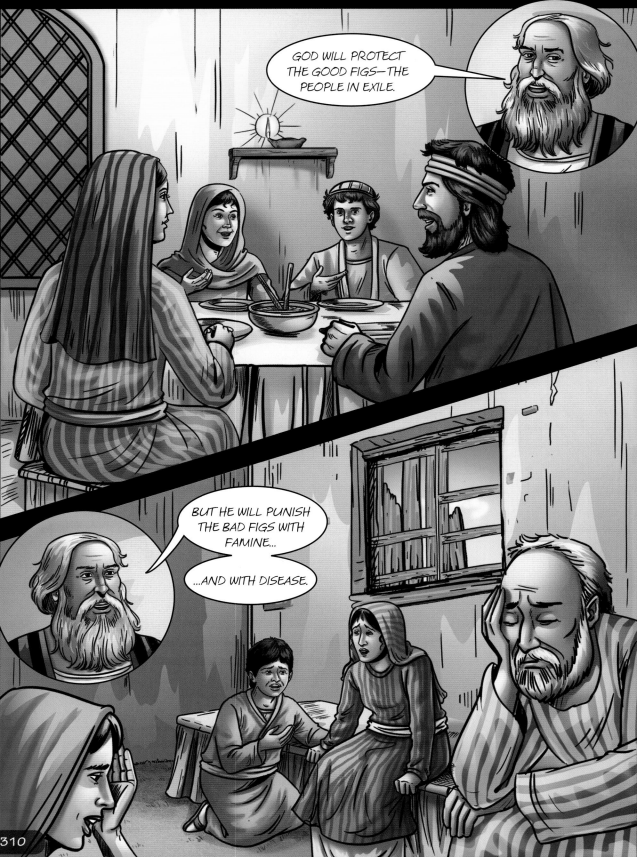

Thrown into a Well

Jeremiah 37–38

WILL YOU PRAY FOR ME, JEREMIAH?

ZEDEKIAH, NEBUCHADNEZZAR'S PUPPET KING, DID NOT PAY MUCH ATTENTION TO JEREMIAH'S PROPHECIES, YET SECRETLY HE RESPECTED HIM.

I WILL, BUT THE BABYLONIANS WILL DESTROY JERUSALEM.

ONLY THOSE WHO SURRENDER WILL BE SAVED.

ONE DAY AS JEREMIAH LEFT THE CITY, HE WAS ARRESTED BY THE CAPTAIN OF THE KING'S GUARD BECAUSE HE BELIEVED JEREMIAH WAS DESERTING TO THE BABYLONIANS.

WHAT HAVE I DONE WRONG? I AM INNOCENT.

WHY SHOULD I BE PUNISHED FOR TELLING THE TRUTH?

IN TIME, THE KING RELEASED JEREMIAH FROM PRISON, BUT HE DIDN'T STAY FREE FOR LONG.

Hero Profile
Ezekiel—Prophet of Hope

MEANING OF NAME: GOD WILL STRENGTHEN

FATHER: BUZI

SENT TO BABYLONIA: AROUND 597 BC

A MAN OF VISIONS: EZEKIEL EXPERIENCED MANY VISIONS OF GOD'S GLORY THROUGHOUT HIS LIFE.

DON'T WORRY
WHEN HE WAS IN EXILE, EZEKIEL BECAME THE COMFORTER OF JEWISH EXILES. THEY LISTENED TO HIM AND TOOK HIS ADVICE.

IN A LAND FAR AWAY
EZEKIEL WAS THE ONLY PROPHET TO MINISTER TO HIS PEOPLE OUTSIDE ISRAEL. HE DID SO IN BABYLONIA, A GREAT KINGDOM IN MESOPOTAMIA. THE RUINS OF THE KINGDOM'S GREATEST CITY, BABYLON, CAN STILL BE SEEN TODAY IN MODERN-DAY IRAQ, SOUTHWEST OF BAGHDAD.

God's Warning

Ezekiel 4–5

BEFORE NEBUCHADNEZZAR'S ARMY LAID SIEGE TO JERUSALEM, A PROPHET NAMED EZEKIEL WARNED THE JEWISH EXILES IN BABYLONIA WHAT THEIR BROTHERS AND SISTERS IN JERUSALEM SHOULD EXPECT.

GOD TOLD EZEKIEL TO TAKE A BLOCK OF CLAY AND DRAW THE CITY ON IT. THEN HE WAS TO LAY SIEGE TO IT, WITH A RAMP, CAMPS, AND BATTERING RAMS.

NEXT GOD TOLD EZEKIEL TO HOLD A PAN BETWEEN HIMSELF AND THE CITY, REPRESENTING AN IRON WALL TO DEFEND AGAINST THE SIEGE.

EZEKIEL, LIE ON YOUR LEFT SIDE AND PUT THE SIN OF THE PEOPLE OF ISRAEL UPON YOURSELF.

An Army of Bones

Ezekiel 37

AFTER THE CAPTIVES IN BABYLONIA SAW WHAT THE FATE OF JERUSALEM WOULD BE, THE SPIRIT OF THE LORD TOOK EZEKIEL TO THE MIDDLE OF A VALLEY FULL OF DRY BONES. EVERYWHERE EZEKIEL LOOKED WERE THE BLEACHED BONES OF DEAD MEN.

DO YOU THINK THESE BONES CAN LIVE AGAIN?

ONLY **YOU** KNOW THAT, LORD!

PROPHESY TO THESE BONES AND SAY TO THEM, 'DRY BONES, HEAR THE WORD OF THE LORD! I WILL MAKE BREATH ENTER YOU, AND YOU WILL COME TO LIFE. THEN YOU WILL KNOW THAT I AM THE LORD."

EZEKIEL BEGAN TO PROPHESY. HE SAW GOD BRING THE DRY BONES TOGETHER. A RATTLING SOUND ECHOED THROUGH THE VALLEY.

EZEKIEL PROPHESIED THAT THE BONES WOULD TAKE A HUMAN SHAPE AND FORM AND BE ALIVE AGAIN. AND HE SAW TENDONS AND FLESH FORM ON THE BONES, AND SKIN BEGAN TO COVER THE BODIES.

GOD TOLD EZEKIEL TO SPEAK TO THE WIND.

THIS IS WHAT THE LORD SAYS: "MAY THE FOUR WINDS BREATHE INTO THESE DEAD BODIES SO THAT THEY WILL LIVE AGAIN!"

AS EZEKIEL PROPHESIED, HE SAW THE BODIES BEGIN TO BREATHE.

THEY CAME TO LIFE AND STOOD UP ON THEIR FEET.

THEY WERE A VAST ARMY. EZEKIEL PREACHED SO THE PEOPLE UNDERSTOOD THAT NO MATTER HOW BAD THINGS GOT, GOD COULD BRING THEM BACK TO LIFE.

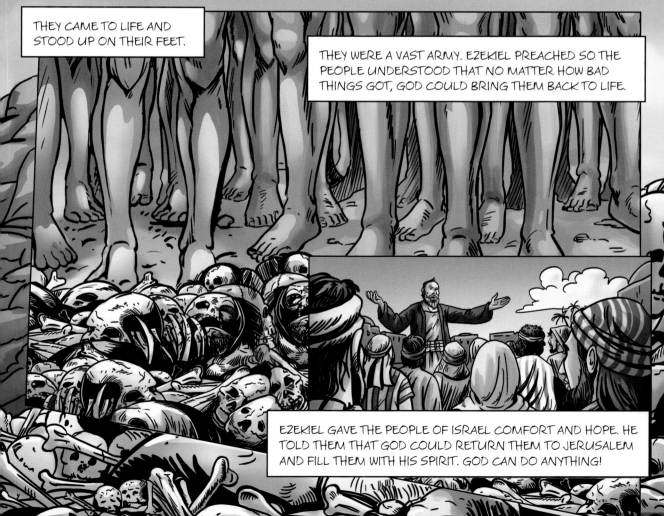

EZEKIEL GAVE THE PEOPLE OF ISRAEL COMFORT AND HOPE. HE TOLD THEM THAT GOD COULD RETURN THEM TO JERUSALEM AND FILL THEM WITH HIS SPIRIT. GOD CAN DO ANYTHING!

Hero Profile
Job—The Sufferer

HOMETOWN: THE LAND OF UZ

LIFESPAN: ABOUT 200 YEARS

MEANING OF NAME:
   HEBREW: "THE PERSECUTED ONE"
   ARABIC: "REPENTANT ONE"

A BOOK OF WISDOM
THE BOOK OF JOB FALLS INTO A CATEGORY OF BIBLICAL WRITING
KNOWN AS WISDOM LITERATURE. IN THE BIBLE, WISDOM IS A WAY OF
LOOKING AT LIFE THROUGH REFLECTION AND OBSERVATION IN THE
HOPES OF GAINING INSIGHT AND UNDERSTANDING.

WHERE CAN IT BE?
NO ONE KNOWS EXACTLY WHERE THE LAND OF UZ WAS LOCATED. SOME EXPERTS SPECULATE IT
WAS IN TODAY'S NORTHWEST SAUDI ARABIA, WHILE OTHERS SAY IT WAS IN WESTERN JORDAN.

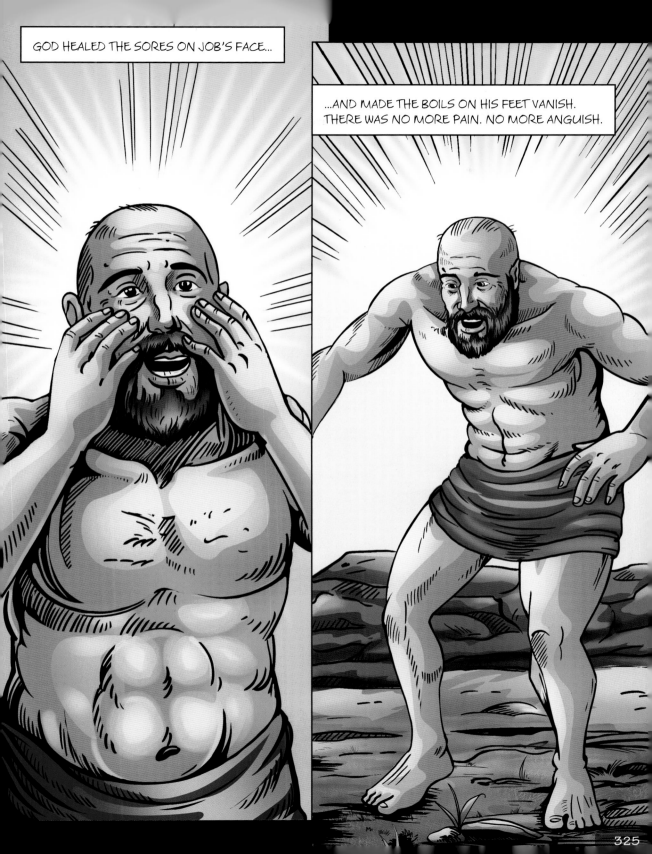

GOD HEALED THE SORES ON JOB'S FACE...

...AND MADE THE BOILS ON HIS FEET VANISH. THERE WAS NO MORE PAIN. NO MORE ANGUISH.

God Blesses Job

Job 42

BECAUSE JOB WAS A GOOD AND FAITHFUL MAN, GOD RESTORED HIS RICHES.

HIS BROTHERS AND SISTER VISITED HIM.

HIS FRIENDS DINED WITH HIM AND CONSOLED HIM FOR ALL THE TRIALS HE HAD ENDURED.

AS JOB GREW OLD, GOD BLESSED HIM WITH 14,000 SHEEP....

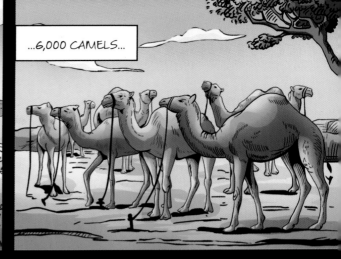

...6,000 CAMELS...

...A THOUSAND YOKE OF OXEN...

...A THOUSAND DONKEYS...

...AND TEN CHILDREN. HIS THREE DAUGHTERS WERE THE MOST BEAUTIFUL IN THE LAND.

THE LORD BLESSED JOB WITH MANY GRANDCHILDREN AND GREAT-GRANDCHILDREN. JOB DIED OLD, CONTENT, AND TRUSTING AND LOVING THE LORD.

327

Hero Profile
Daniel—A Noble Prophet

MEANING OF NAME: GOD IS MY JUDGE
DANIEL TAKEN CAPTIVE: AROUND 605 BC
DANIEL IN THE LIONS' DEN: AROUND 539 BC

WORD WISE

THE OLD SAYING "I COULD SEE THE WRITING ON THE WALL" COMES FROM THE STORY ABOUT TERRIFIED KING BELSHAZZAR WHO SEES A MYSTERIOUS HAND WRITING WORDS ON A WALL DURING A FEAST.

TEEN EXILE

DANIEL WAS A TEENAGER WHEN NEBUCHADNEZZAR FORCED HIM INTO EXILE DURING THE FIRST SIEGE OF JERUSALEM IN 605 BC. ACCORDING TO THE BIBLE, DANIEL SPOKE TO TWO OF GOD'S ARCHANGELS, GABRIEL AND MICHAEL.

Daniel and the King's Food

Daniel 1–2

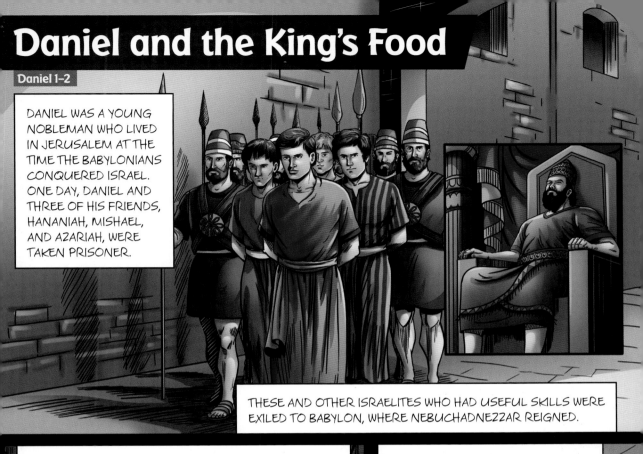

DANIEL WAS A YOUNG NOBLEMAN WHO LIVED IN JERUSALEM AT THE TIME THE BABYLONIANS CONQUERED ISRAEL. ONE DAY, DANIEL AND THREE OF HIS FRIENDS, HANANIAH, MISHAEL, AND AZARIAH, WERE TAKEN PRISONER.

THESE AND OTHER ISRAELITES WHO HAD USEFUL SKILLS WERE EXILED TO BABYLON, WHERE NEBUCHADNEZZAR REIGNED.

DANIEL AND HIS FRIENDS WERE WELL-EDUCATED. THE YOUNG MEN CAME FROM NOBLE FAMILIES IN JERUSALEM. THE KING LOOKED AFTER THEM WELL. HE BROUGHT THEM TO THE PALACE TO LIVE AND LEARN ABOUT BABYLON. THEY WERE ALSO GIVEN THE SAME FOOD AS THE KING, AND THIS CAUSED A PROBLEM.

DANIEL PERSUADED THE STEWARD TO LET THEM EAT VEGETABLES AND WATER FOR TEN DAYS. AT THE END OF THAT TIME, THE STEWARD WAS AMAZED TO FIND THE YOUNG MEN HEALTHIER THAN THOSE WHO ATE THE KING'S FOOD.

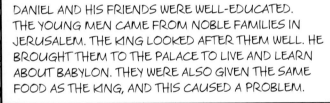

WE CANNOT EAT THIS RICH FOOD OR DRINK THIS WINE.

BUT IF YOU DON'T EAT PROPERLY, YOU WON'T BE FIT AND STRONG, AND THE KING WILL PUNISH ME!

AFTER THREE YEARS, DANIEL AND HIS FRIENDS WERE SELECTED TO ACT AS ADVISORS TO THE KING.

AT THAT TIME, THE KING HAD A STRANGE DREAM. NONE OF NEBUCHADNEZZAR'S MAGICIANS OR ADVISORS COULD INTERPRET THE DREAM—ESPECIALLY AS THE KING WOULDN'T EVEN DESCRIBE IT TO THEM! BUT DANIEL PRAYED TO GOD, AND GOD TOLD HIM HOW TO INTERPRET THE DREAM.

DANIEL EXPLAINED TO THE KING THAT HIS DREAM OF A FALLING STATUE TOLD OF THE FUTURE COLLAPSE OF HIS EMPIRE, AND OF THE ONES TO FOLLOW, AND THEN OF THE KINGDOM OF GOD, WHICH WOULD NEVER END.

NEBUCHADNEZZAR WAS SO IMPRESSED WITH DANIEL THAT HE MADE HIM HIS CHIEF ADVISOR.

The King's Fiery Furnace

Daniel 3

KING NEBUCHADNEZZAR WANTED ALL HIS SUBJECTS TO WORSHIP A HUGE GOLDEN STATUE HE HAD JUST BUILT. HE INVITED MANY NOBLE PEOPLE TO THE UNVEILING, INCLUDING DANIEL'S FRIENDS, WHO HAD BEEN RENAMED SHADRACH, MESHACH, AND ABED-NEGO.

FALL DOWN ON YOUR KNEES AND WORSHIP WHAT IS BEFORE YOU.

DANIEL'S FRIENDS WERE AMONG THE CROWD. THEY REFUSED TO BOW DOWN.

WHAT'S THIS? WHOEVER DOES NOT KNEEL WILL BURN IN THE FIERY FURNACE!

THE FURIOUS KING ORDERED THE MEN INTO HIS FURNACE. THE FLAMES WERE SO HOT THAT THE GUARDS WERE SCORCHED TO DEATH.

THE KING WAS AMAZED.

YOUR GOD IS TRULY GREAT! HE HAS SENT AN ANGEL TO RESCUE HIS SERVANTS. HE SHOULD BE PRAISED!

AS NEBUCHADNEZZAR LOOKED ON, HE COULD SEE THAT THE MEN WERE MOVING FREELY AND UNHARMED AS THE FLAMES LAPPED AT THEIR BODIES. WITH THEM WAS A FOURTH MAN WHO LOOKED LIKE THE SON OF GOD.

Daniel in the Lions' Den

Daniel 6

THE NEW KING, DARIUS, LIKED DANIEL. HE HELPED DARIUS RUN THE COUNTRY.

YOU OUTSHINE ALL THE OTHER MINISTERS, DANIEL. I'M GOING TO PUT YOU IN CHARGE.

THE KING LIKES DANIEL, THE HEBREW.

HIS WORK IS PERFECT. WE MUST STOP HIM, BUT HOW?

WE'LL TRICK THE KING INTO SIGNING A NEW LAW, BUT WHAT WILL IT SAY?

I HAVE AN IDEA. FOR 30 DAYS PEOPLE CAN PRAY ONLY TO THE KING...

...AND TO **NO OTHER GOD**. ANYONE WHO DISOBEYS SHOULD BE THROWN IN THE **LIONS' DEN!**

THE OTHER MINISTERS KNEW THAT DANIEL PRAYED TO GOD EVERY DAY.

KING DARIUS DID NOT WANT DANIEL TO DIE, BUT HIS HANDS WERE TIED. UNDER MEDE LAW, EVERY ROYAL ORDER WAS FINAL. HIS GUARDS THREW DANIEL INTO THE LIONS' DEN.

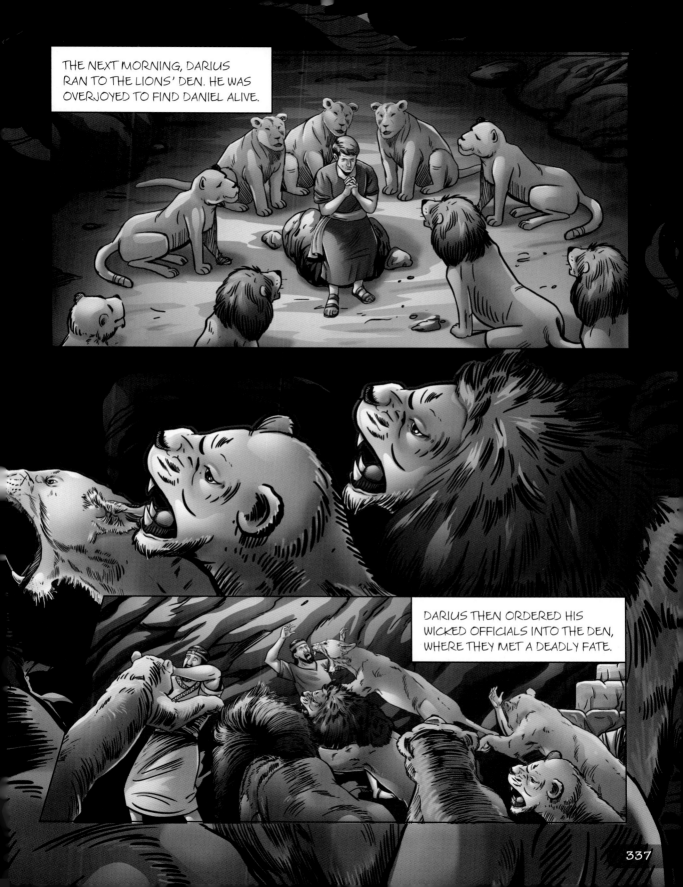

THE NEXT MORNING, DARIUS RAN TO THE LIONS' DEN. HE WAS OVERJOYED TO FIND DANIEL ALIVE.

DARIUS THEN ORDERED HIS WICKED OFFICIALS INTO THE DEN, WHERE THEY MET A DEADLY FATE.

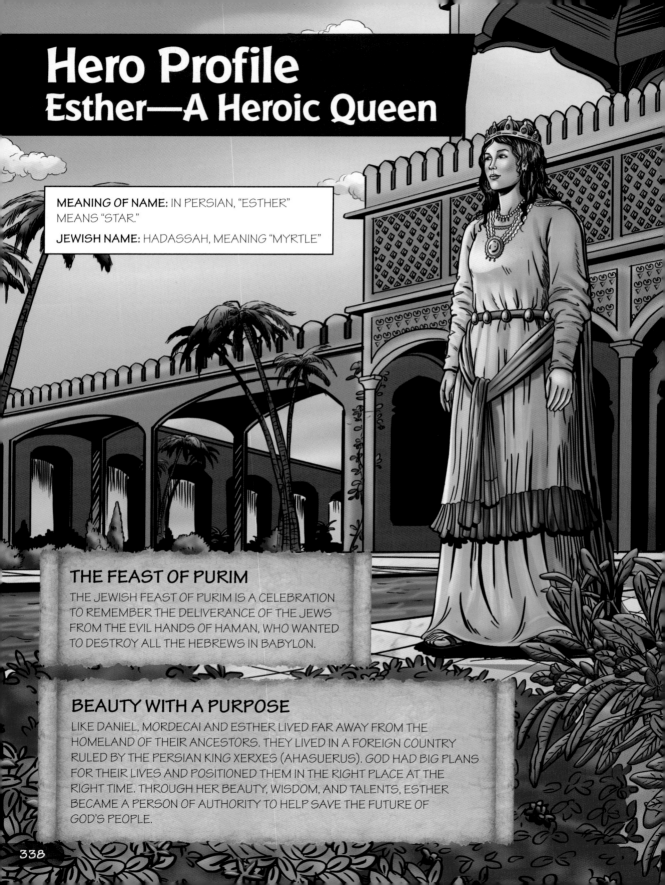

Hero Profile
Esther—A Heroic Queen

MEANING OF NAME: IN PERSIAN, "ESTHER" MEANS "STAR."

JEWISH NAME: HADASSAH, MEANING "MYRTLE"

THE FEAST OF PURIM

THE JEWISH FEAST OF PURIM IS A CELEBRATION TO REMEMBER THE DELIVERANCE OF THE JEWS FROM THE EVIL HANDS OF HAMAN, WHO WANTED TO DESTROY ALL THE HEBREWS IN BABYLON.

BEAUTY WITH A PURPOSE

LIKE DANIEL, MORDECAI AND ESTHER LIVED FAR AWAY FROM THE HOMELAND OF THEIR ANCESTORS. THEY LIVED IN A FOREIGN COUNTRY RULED BY THE PERSIAN KING XERXES (AHASUERUS). GOD HAD BIG PLANS FOR THEIR LIVES AND POSITIONED THEM IN THE RIGHT PLACE AT THE RIGHT TIME. THROUGH HER BEAUTY, WISDOM, AND TALENTS, ESTHER BECAME A PERSON OF AUTHORITY TO HELP SAVE THE FUTURE OF GOD'S PEOPLE.

Esther the Queen

Esther 1–2

KING AHASUERUS OF PERSIA RULED A VAST LAND STRETCHING FROM INDIA TO ETHIOPIA. ONE DAY HE GAVE A GREAT FEAST IN THE PERSIAN CITY OF SHUSHAN, SITE OF THE KINGDOM'S WINTER CAPITAL.

THE KING HAD TOO MUCH TO DRINK.

GUARDS! GO FETCH QUEEN VASHTI. I WANT MY GUESTS TO MARVEL AT HER BEAUTY.

MY QUEEN, THE KING HAS ASKED US TO BRING YOU TO THE CELEBRATION.

I REFUSE TO COME JUST SO HE CAN SHOW ME OFF TO HIS GUESTS!

IN SHUSHAN LIVED A JEWISH MAN NAMED MORDECAI. HE WAS THE COUSIN AND GUARDIAN OF HADASSAH, A BEAUTIFUL YOUNG WOMAN WHOSE PARENTS HAD DIED.

SHE RECEIVED AN ORDER TO PRESENT HERSELF TO KING AHASUERUS.

I WARN YOU, HADASSAH. DO NOT TELL THE KING YOU ARE A HEBREW. DO NOT USE YOUR HEBREW NAME. CALL YOURSELF **ESTHER**.

WHEN AHASUERUS SAW ESTHER, HE FELL IN LOVE. HE MARRIED HER AND MADE HER QUEEN.

Planning the Slaughter

WHEN MORDECAI LEARNED WHAT WAS HAPPENING, HE TORE OFF HIS GARMENTS, PUT ON SACKCLOTH, AND CRIED OUT LOUDLY BEFORE THE ROYAL GATE.

UPON HEARING THE COMMOTION, QUEEN ESTHER GAVE INSTRUCTIONS TO HER SERVANTS.

TAKE THESE CLOTHES TO MORDECAI.

THEN COME BACK AND TELL ME WHAT THIS IS ALL ABOUT.

Esther Saves Her People

Esther 4–9

I MUST PRAY TO GOD FOR HIS GUIDANCE. I AM IN DANGER! MY PEOPLE ARE IN DANGER!

ESTHER WORRIED TERRIBLY FOR HER SAFETY, FOR NO ONE WAS PERMITTED TO VISIT THE KING WITHOUT A ROYAL SUMMONS.

LORD, HELP ME. WE HAVE SINNED, AND YOU DELIVERED US INTO THE HANDS OF OUR ENEMIES!

SHOW ME A WAY TO CONVINCE AHASUERUS THAT HAMAN'S PLAN MUST BE STOPPED.

GIVE ME THE COURAGE TO FACE HIM, FOR I SHALL BE RISKING MY OWN LIFE!

AFTER THE FIRST BANQUET, HAMAN WAS FEELING PLEASED WITH HIMSELF. BUT THEN HE PASSED MORDECAI, WHO AGAIN REFUSED TO BOW TO HIM.

THAT NIGHT AHASUERUS COULD NOT SLEEP, SO HE READ A REPORT OF RECENT EVENTS. HE DISCOVERED THAT MORDECAI HAD PLAYED A ROLE IN STOPPING THE ATTEMPTED ASSASSINATION.

HAMAN WAS FURIOUS. LATER THAT DAY HE DECIDED TO BUILD A GALLOWS TO HANG MORDECAI AND TO GET PERMISSION FROM THE KING TO EXECUTE HIM FOR HIS DISRESPECT.

LATER THAT NIGHT HAMAN VISITED THE KING TO ASK ABOUT MORDECAI. BUT FIRST THE KING ASKED A QUESTION.

WHAT SHOULD I DO TO REWARD SOMEONE TO WHOM I OWE MY LIFE?

HE MUST BE TALKING ABOUT ME!

DRESS HIM IN ROYAL ROBES AND HAVE HIM LED THROUGH THE STREETS ON YOUR HORSE SO THAT ALL CAN SEE HOW YOU VALUE HIM.

I CAN'T BELIEVE HE WAS TALKING ABOUT **MORDECAI!** I CAN'T BELIEVE HE IS GOING TO HONOR HIM!

FINE IDEA. TAKE MY ROBE AND MY HORSE AND **GIVE THEM TO THE JEW,** MORDECAI.

LEAD HIM THROUGH THE STREETS IN HONOR. HE SAVED MY LIFE AND NOTHING WAS DONE TO REPAY HIM.

THINGS ONLY GREW WORSE FOR HAMAN. THE NEXT DAY HE ATTENDED THE QUEEN'S SECOND BANQUET.

WHATEVER YOU ASK QUEEN ESTHER, I SHALL GRANT YOU.

I BEG YOU TO SPARE THE LIVES OF MY PEOPLE, FOR SOMEONE HAS PLOTTED TO WIPE US OUT.

WHO WOULD DO SUCH A THING?

IT IS **HAMAN!**

SPARE MY LIFE!

HOW DARE YOU ASSAULT THE QUEEN! **YOU WILL DIE!**

THE KING'S MINISTERS TOLD HIM ABOUT HAMAN'S PLANS FOR MORDECAI, AND HAMAN WAS EXECUTED ON THE VERY GALLOWS THAT HE HAD BUILT HIMSELF!

AHASUERUS COULD NOT CANCEL THE ORDER TO SLAUGHTER THE JEWS, BUT HE DID ISSUE ANOTHER ORDER ALLOWING THE JEWS TO DEFEND THEMSELVES. THEY DID, AND THE HEBREWS WERE SAVED. EVERY YEAR DURING THE FESTIVAL OF PURIM, JEWS CELEBRATE THE BRAVERY OF ESTHER AND MORDECAI AND THEIR DELIVERANCE FROM DEATH.

Hero Profile
Jonah—A Reluctant Prophet

HOMETOWN: GATH HEPHER, LOCATED JUST NORTH OF NAZARETH AND WEST OF THE SEA OF GALILEE

FOCAL POINT OF HIS MINISTRY: THE ASSYRIAN CITY OF NINEVEH, A CITY THAT IS NOW IN NORTHERN IRAQ

A FISHY STORY

IN THE WELL-KNOWN STORY OF JONAH, THE BIBLE DOES NOT MENTION A WHALE BUT ONLY A "GREAT FISH." THE MODERN EXPRESSION "IN THE BELLY OF THE BEAST" IS A REFERENCE TO THE STORY OF JONAH.

NEW TESTAMENT CONNECTION

JONAH IS THE ONLY PROPHET TO WHOM CHRIST LIKENED HIMSELF IN THE NEW TESTAMENT. ACCORDING TO MATTHEW, JESUS SAID, "FOR AS JONAH WAS THREE DAYS AND THREE NIGHTS IN THE BELLY OF THE GREAT FISH, SO WILL THE SON OF MAN BE THREE DAYS AND THREE NIGHTS IN THE HEART OF THE EARTH."

Jonah and the Whale

Jonah 1–4

A PROPHET NAMED JONAH PREACHED GOD'S WORD TO THE ISRAELITES.

MY FRIENDS, THE LORD SEES ALL, AND KNOWS ALL.

GOD TOLD JONAH TO GO EAST AND DELIVER A MESSAGE TO THE ASSYRIANS.

GO TO NINEVEH AND PREACH TO THEM.

ISRAEL'S ENEMIES ARE IN NINEVEH. I WILL NOT GO. I DON'T WANT TO PREACH TO THEM!

JONAH DEFIED GOD AND BOARDED A SHIP FOR TARSHISH, A CITY IN THE OPPOSITE DIRECTION OF NINEVEH.

ARE YOU HEADING OUR WAY? WELCOME ABOARD.

HOWEVER, GOD SAW JONAH BOARD THE VESSEL.

JONAH TOLD THE STORY OF HOW HE CAME TO BE ON THE BOAT AND HOW HE HAD DEFIED GOD'S COMMAND.

TAKE ME AND **THROW ME IN THE SEA!**

THE STORM WILL SUBSIDE. IT IS THE ONLY WAY TO SAVE YOURSELVES.

AT FIRST THE MEN HESITATED, BUT THEN THEY DID AS JONAH SAID.

GOD FORGIVE US! WE DON'T WANT TO KILL AN INNOCENT MAN, BUT WE WILL DO AS YOU WANT.

AS SOON AS JONAH HIT THE WATER, THE STORM STOPPED, AND THOSE ABOARD THE SHIP WERE FILLED WITH AWE. THEY NOW FEARED AND RESPECTED THE LORD.

AN ENORMOUS FISH THEN APPEARED... **AND SWALLOWED JONAH WHOLE!**

Hero Profile
Nehemiah—The Man Behind the Wall

FATHER: HACHALIAH

CAME FROM: JERUSALEM

MEANING OF NAME: JEHOVAH HAS COMFORTED

NEHEMIAH THE INSPECTOR

UPON ARRIVING IN JERUSALEM, NEHEMIAH UNDERTOOK A SECRET INSPECTION OF THE RUINS. HE THEN ORGANIZED A REBUILDING PARTY OF JEWISH EXILES WHO HAD RETURNED FROM BABYLON.

NEHEMIAH THE GOVERNOR

AFTER NEHEMIAH REBUILT THE WALLS PROTECTING JERUSALEM, HE WENT ON TO BE GOVERNOR OF JUDAH FOR MANY YEARS. HE ENFORCED LAWS THAT PROVIDED CHARITY FOR THE POOR AND STRENGTHENED THE PEOPLE'S OBSERVANCE OF THE SABBATH.

357

Rebuilding Solomon's Temple

Ezra 1–6

FOR MANY YEARS THE JEWS HAD LIVED IN EXILE. BUT AFTER PERSIA DEFEATED BABYLON, PERSIA'S KING CYRUS SAID THE HEBREWS COULD RETURN TO JERUSALEM. MORE THAN 40,000 PEOPLE EMBARKED ON THE JOURNEY.

WHEN THEY ARRIVED, THEY SAW THAT THE TEMPLE HAD BEEN DESTROYED.

KING SOLOMON'S GRAND TEMPLE IS IN RUINS.

WE MUST REBUILD IT!

THE PEOPLE WENT TO WORK AND BEGAN REBUILDING THE TEMPLE'S FOUNDATION.

Walls in Ruin

Nehemiah 1–7

THE WALLS OF THE CITY OF JERUSALEM WERE STILL IN RUINS. MADE FROM HUGE BLOCKS OF STONE, THE WALLS WERE MEANT TO PROTECT THE CITY FROM ATTACK.

THIS CITY OF DAVID IS A SACRED PLACE.

WE ARE DISGRACED!

ONE OF THE JEWISH EXILES IN PERSIA WAS A MAN NAMED NEHEMIAH. HE WAS THE CUPBEARER TO KING ARTAXERXES. HE LEARNED THAT THE EXILES WHO HAD RETURNED TO JERUSALEM WERE IN TROUBLE. WITH THE WALLS OF THE TEMPLE IN RUBBLE, THEY WERE DEFENSELESS AGAINST ENEMY ATTACK.

NEHEMIAH WAS VERY SAD. HE CRIED WHEN HE LEARNED THE NEWS. HE KNEW HE MUST SPEAK TO THE KING, EVEN THOUGH IT MIGHT MAKE HIM ANGRY.

GREAT AND ALMIGHTY GOD, HEAR MY PRAYER.

I WANT TO HELP REBUILD JERUSALEM'S WALLS. LET ME BE SUCCESSFUL WHEN I SPEAK TO THE KING ABOUT WHAT IS IN MY HEART.

WHAT IS WRONG, NEHEMIAH? WHY ARE YOU SO SAD?

MY KING, THE CITY OF MY ANCESTORS IS IN RUIN.

I WANT TO RETURN TO JERUSALEM AND REBUILD IT.

THE KING AGREED, AND NEHEMIAH TRAVELED BACK TO JERUSALEM. THERE HE MADE A SECRET INSPECTION OF THE WALLS.

THE KING HAS GIVEN ME PERMISSION TO REBUILD THE WALLS.

WE WILL START WORK IMMEDIATELY.

WHEN THE WORK BEGAN, WORKERS FIRST CLEARED THE FALLEN STONES AWAY....

...AND REPLACED THEM WITH NEW STONES.

Hero Profile
Ezra—The Priest

FATHER: SERAIAH (DESCENDANT OF AARON, MOSES' BROTHER)

MEANING OF NAME: HELPER

JOBS: PRIEST AND SCRIBE (WROTE AND ORGANIZED BIBLICAL TEXTS)

IGNORING GOD'S LAWS

WHEN EZRA RETURNED FROM EXILE TO JERUSALEM, HE DISCOVERED THAT MANY JEWISH MEN WERE IGNORING GOD'S LAWS ABOUT MARRYING FOREIGN WOMEN. HE ALSO BELIEVED THAT ASSOCIATING WITH NON-JEWS LED TO IDOLATRY. HE FEARED GOD WOULD PUNISH ISRAEL AS HE HAD PUNISHED JUDAH.

ARAMAIC AND HEBREW

THE BOOK OF EZRA IS ONE OF JUST A FEW PARTS OF THE OLD TESTAMENT THAT WAS WRITTEN PARTLY IN ARAMAIC, THE MIDDLE EASTERN LANGUAGE SPOKEN COMMONLY IN ANCIENT TIMES.

Ezra Reads the Law

Ezra 9–10; Malachi 1–4; Nehemiah 8

BEFORE NEHEMIAH RETURNED TO HELP REBUILD JERUSALEM, ANOTHER PROPHET IN EXILE LEARNED THAT THE PEOPLE WHO HAD GONE BACK TO JERUSALEM WERE NOT FOLLOWING GOD'S LAW. THIS MAN WAS EZRA.

I HAVE TRAVELED SUCH A GREAT DISTANCE TO JERUSALEM ONLY TO FIND THAT THE PEOPLE HAVE SINNED. MANY OF OUR MEN HAVE MARRIED FOREIGN WOMEN WHO WORSHIP GODS OTHER THAN OURS!

LORD, I AM SORRY! I APOLOGIZE FOR THE PEOPLE OF JERUSALEM! THEY HAVE SINNED AGAINST YOU!

UPON HEARING EZRA'S PRAYER, THE PEOPLE WEPT TOO. THE MEN PROMISED TO FOLLOW GOD'S COMMAND. THEY WOULD SEND THE FOREIGN WOMEN AWAY. AFTER EZRA SPOKE TO THE LEADERS, THIS IS EXACTLY WHAT HAPPENED.

SOME TIME LATER, AFTER NEHEMIAH HAD OVERSEEN THE REBUILDING OF THE WALLS AND THE PEOPLE HAD MOVED BACK INTO THE CITY, EVERYONE CAME TOGETHER IN ONE OF THE CITY SQUARES. THERE, EZRA READ FROM THE BOOK OF LAW OF MOSES. MANY WERE STILL UPSET BY THEIR SINS.

AND FOR SEVEN DAYS EZRA READ FROM THE BOOK OF LAW. BY THE END OF THE FEAST, EVERYONE RECOMMITTED TO HONOR GOD AND TO KEEP THEIR SIDE OF THE COVENANT.

FRIENDS, DO NOT BE SAD! THIS IS A HOLY DAY—A DAY TO REJOICE!

WE MUST HAVE A FEAST AND MAKE SURE THE POOR HAVE PLENTY TO EAT.

SO THE PEOPLE CELEBRATED.

THE JEWS WERE FILLED WITH GOOD INTENTIONS WHEN THEY COMPLETED THE WALLS, AND JERUSALEM WAS WHOLE ONCE AGAIN. BUT AS THE YEARS PASSED, THEY FELL BACK INTO THEIR OLD WAYS. THEN MALACHI CAME ON THE SCENE—THE LAST OF THE OLD TESTAMENT PROPHETS. HE ENCOURAGED THE PEOPLE TO RETURN TO THEIR COVENANT WITH GOD.

MY PEOPLE, YOU MUST WELCOME GOD BACK INTO YOUR HEARTS!

MALACHI TOLD THE PEOPLE THAT GOD WOULD BE SENDING A MESSENGER—A MIGHTY MESSENGER—TO PREPARE THE WAY FOR THE LORD.

ISRAEL DURING THE
TIME OF JESUS

Damascus

Sidon

SYRIA

Sarepta
(Zarephath)

PANEAS

Mt Hermon

Tyre

Caesarea Philippi

Mediterranean Sea

Ptolemais

Capernaum
Bethsaida/Julias

Cana
GALILEE
Gennesaret

Tiberias

Sea of Galilee

Nazareth

Caesarea

Pella

Salim

Mt Ebal

SAMARIA
Sychar

River Jordan

Mt Gerizim

Alexandrium

PEREA

Ephraim

Joppa

Jericho

Emmaus

Jerusalem
Bethany

JUDAH

Ashkelon

Bethlehem

Wilderness of Judah

Dead Sea

Callirrhoe

Gaza

NABATEA

Hebron

En-gedi

IDUMEA
Masada

Areopolis

Malatha

Zoar

Kadesh-Barnea

The New Testament

"For God so loved the world that he gave his one and only Son, that whoever believes in him shall not perish but have eternal life."

John 3:16

Hero Profile
John the Baptist

RELATION TO JESUS: COUSIN
FATHER: ZACHARIAS
MOTHER: ELIZABETH

LOCUSTS AND HONEY
WHEN JOHN THE BAPTIST WAS IN THE WILDERNESS PREACHING, HE ATE LOCUSTS AND HONEY. PEOPLE STILL EAT LOCUSTS TODAY IN MANY AFRICAN, MIDDLE EASTERN, AND ASIAN COUNTRIES. THE BUGS ARE CONSIDERED A DELICACY.

GOD'S MESSENGERS
ANGELS ARE HEAVENLY BEINGS—GOD'S MESSENGERS ON EARTH. THE WORD "ANGEL" COMES FROM THE GREEK WORD "AGGELOS," WHICH MEANS "MESSENGER." WHEN GOD WANTS TO COMMUNICATE WITH HUMANS, HE OFTEN SENDS HIS ANGELS. THE ANGEL GABRIEL PLAYS AN IMPORTANT ROLE AS THE NEW TESTAMENT BEGINS, AS HE IS THE ONE WHO FORETELLS THE BIRTH OF JOHN THE BAPTIST.

MARY LEFT HER HOME IN NAZARETH AND WENT TO SEE ELIZABETH. WHEN ELIZABETH GREETED MARY, THE BABY IN ELIZABETH'S WOMB JUMPED. ELIZABETH SMILED AND WAS FILLED WITH THE HOLY SPIRIT.

MOST BLESSED ARE YOU AMONG WOMEN, AND BLESSED IS THE FRUIT OF YOUR WOMB.

WHEN I HEARD THE SOUND OF YOUR VOICE, THE CHILD IN MY WOMB LEAPED FOR JOY.

GOD IS GREAT. HE SHOWS MERCY TO THOSE THAT HONOR HIM.

ELIZABETH LATER GAVE BIRTH TO A SON, JUST AS GABRIEL HAD PROMISED. WHEN PEOPLE ASKED WHAT THE CHILD WAS TO BE CALLED, ZACHARIAS WROTE ON A SLATE, "HIS NAME IS JOHN." FROM THEN ON, HE COULD SPEAK AGAIN. PEOPLE WERE FILLED WITH WONDER.

The Ultimate Hero
Jesus Christ—The Son of God

MOTHER: MARY

EARTHLY FATHER: JOSEPH

BORN: BETHLEHEM

DIED: JERUSALEM

MEANING OF NAME: "GOD SAVES"
(IN HEBREW)

HERE COMES THE MESSIAH

JESUS IS GOD'S SON IN A HUMAN BODY AND IS THE MESSIAH THAT THE OLD TESTAMENT PROPHETS PREDICTED. THERE ARE MANY PROPHECIES IN THE OLD TESTAMENT ABOUT THE COMING OF THE MESSIAH, BUT THE MOST SPECIFIC COMES FROM ISAIAH. "THEREFORE THE LORD HIMSELF WILL GIVE YOU A SIGN: BEHOLD, THE VIRGIN SHALL CONCEIVE AND BEAR A SON, AND SHALL CALL HIS NAME IMMANUEL." ISAIAH ALSO FORETOLD JESUS' DEATH.

FAMILY MATTERS

JESUS WAS A DESCENDANT OF ABRAHAM AND KING DAVID. HE BEGAN TEACHING WHEN HE WAS ABOUT 30 YEARS OLD AND WAS CRUCIFIED ABOUT THREE YEARS LATER.

The Birth of Christ

BORN IN A STABLE?

THE TRADITIONAL NATIVITY STORY HAS JESUS' BIRTH IN A STABLE BECAUSE THERE WAS NO ROOM AT THE INN. WE DON'T KNOW EXACTLY THE TYPE OF STRUCTURE WHERE HE WAS BORN, BUT WE DO KNOW THAT ANIMALS WERE BEING CARED FOR THERE. THE BIBLE SAYS JESUS WAS PLACED IN A MANGER, THE FEEDING BOX WHERE ANIMALS WOULD EAT THEIR FOOD.

OUT OF WEDLOCK

AN UNMARRIED GIRL WHO GAVE BIRTH TO A CHILD MIGHT HAVE BEEN REJECTED BY HER FAMILY OR EVEN FORCED TO LEAVE HER VILLAGE. THE BIBLE TELLS US THAT JOSEPH MARRIED MARY AFTER AN ANGEL OF THE LORD SPOKE TO HIM.

WHILE MARY WAS IN THE STABLE, SHE GAVE BIRTH TO A SON. SHE WRAPPED HIM IN SWADDLING CLOTHS AND LAID HIM IN A MANGER.

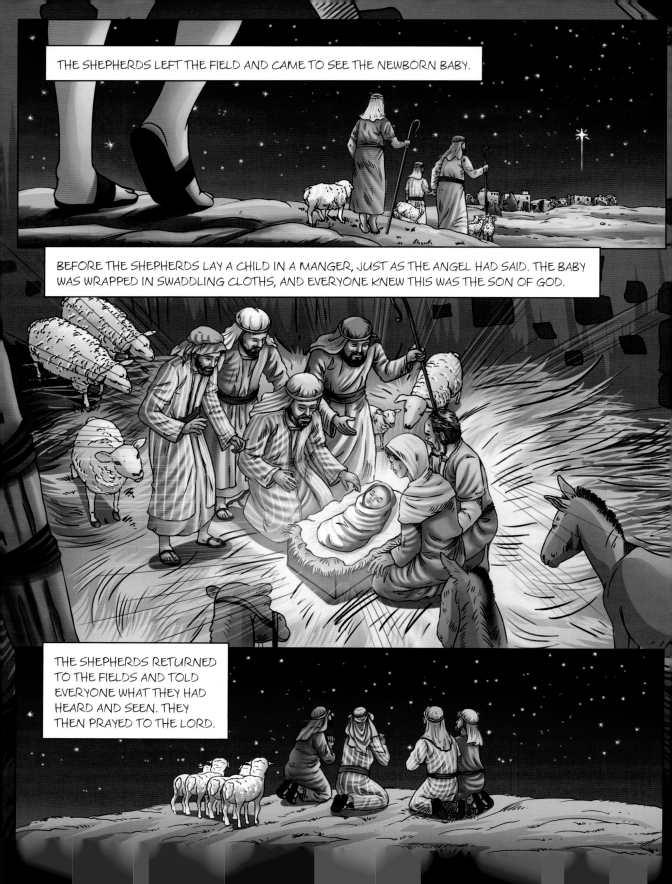

THE SHEPHERDS LEFT THE FIELD AND CAME TO SEE THE NEWBORN BABY.

BEFORE THE SHEPHERDS LAY A CHILD IN A MANGER, JUST AS THE ANGEL HAD SAID. THE BABY WAS WRAPPED IN SWADDLING CLOTHS, AND EVERYONE KNEW THIS WAS THE SON OF GOD.

THE SHEPHERDS RETURNED TO THE FIELDS AND TOLD EVERYONE WHAT THEY HAD HEARD AND SEEN. THEY THEN PRAYED TO THE LORD.

The Wise Men

Matthew 2

AS JESUS WAS BORN IN BETHLEHEM, A BRIGHT STAR APPEARED IN THE SKY. FROM THE EAST, SOME WISE MEN LOOKED UP AND SAW THE SAME BURNING LIGHT.

EACH OF THE WISE MEN SET OUT FOR ISRAEL, THE STAR GUIDING THEM WITH EACH STEP.

THE WISE MEN WENT TO JERUSALEM, WHERE THEY ASKED ABOUT THE NEWBORN KING OF THE JEWS. WHEN HEROD LEARNED OF THIS, HE CALLED THE CHIEF PRIESTS AND TEACHERS TO HIM.

WHO IS THIS KING? WHERE HAS HE BEEN BORN?

THE PROPHET SAID, "AND YOU, BETHLEHEM, FROM YOU SHALL COME A RULER WHO WILL SHEPHERD MY PEOPLE ISRAEL."

AS THE WISE MEN SLEPT, AN ANGEL WARNED THEM NOT TO RETURN TO HEROD.

SO THEY PACKED UP THEIR BELONGINGS AND LEFT FOR THEIR OWN COUNTRIES BY A DIFFERENT ROUTE.

Jesus in the Temple

Luke 2

WHEN JOSEPH AND HIS FAMILY RETURNED FROM EGYPT, THEY WENT BACK TO LIVE IN NAZARETH. JESUS GREW UP STRONG, WISE, AND HEALTHY.

WHEN JESUS WAS TWELVE, THE FAMILY WENT TO JERUSALEM TO CELEBRATE PASSOVER JUST AS THEY HAD DONE EVERY YEAR.

WHEN THE CELEBRATION WAS OVER, MARY AND JOSEPH LEFT FOR HOME, BUT THEY DIDN'T REALIZE UNTIL THEY WERE WELL ON THEIR JOURNEY THAT JESUS WAS NOT WITH THEM.

WHERE IS JESUS?

I CAN'T FIND HIM ANYWHERE! HE'S NOT HERE!

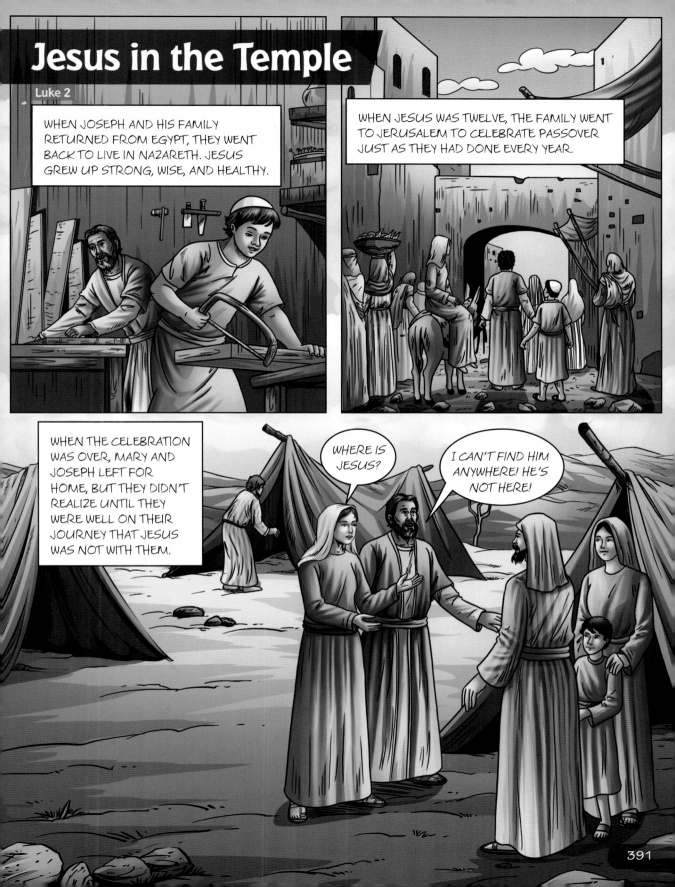

MARY AND JOSEPH RETURNED TO JERUSALEM. THEY SEARCHED EVERYWHERE FOR JESUS.

HAVE YOU SEEN MY SON? HE'S TWELVE YEARS OLD, AND WE CANNOT FIND HIM.

NO, I HAVE NOT SEEN YOUR BOY.

MARY AND JOSEPH THEN CAME TO THE TEMPLE.

WHY ARE ALL THOSE PEOPLE LOOKING INSIDE?

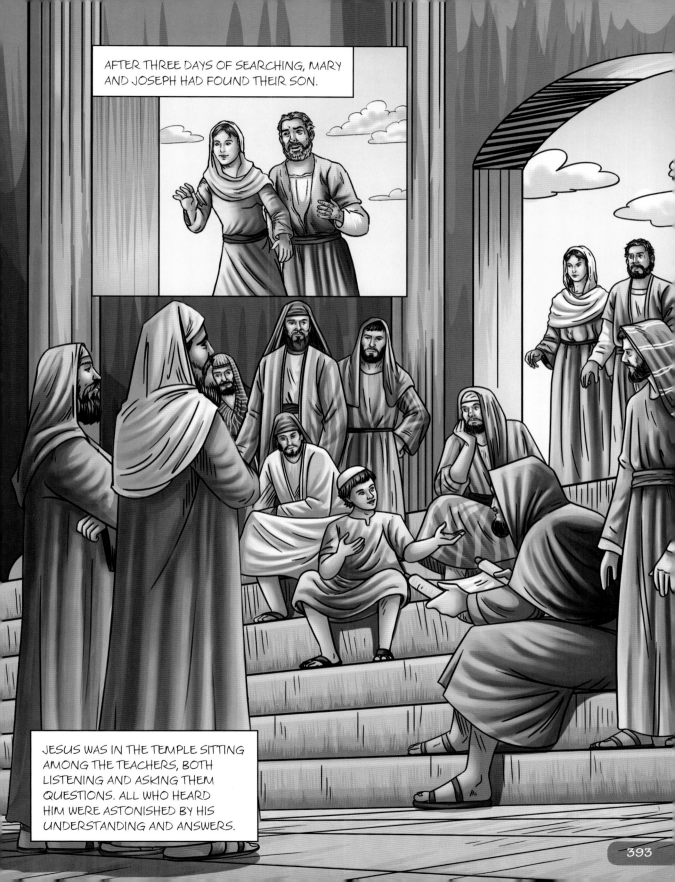

AFTER THREE DAYS OF SEARCHING, MARY AND JOSEPH HAD FOUND THEIR SON.

JESUS WAS IN THE TEMPLE SITTING AMONG THE TEACHERS, BOTH LISTENING AND ASKING THEM QUESTIONS. ALL WHO HEARD HIM WERE ASTONISHED BY HIS UNDERSTANDING AND ANSWERS.

The Ministry of Jesus

POLITICS OF THE TIME

JESUS LIVED IN A TIME OF TERRIBLE POLITICAL STRIFE. CAESAR AUGUSTUS RULED THE REGION FROM ROME. HIS SOLDIERS KEPT ORDER AND UNIFIED THE MEDITERRANEAN WORLD UNDER ONE GOVERNMENT.

THREAT OF THE PHARISEES

AT THE SAME TIME, JESUS ANGERED THE JEWISH PHARISEES. THEY SAW JESUS AS A THREAT. THE PHARISEES WERE A JEWISH RELIGIOUS GROUP WHO FOLLOWED THE RELIGIOUS LAWS AND CUSTOMS VERY STRICTLY. JESUS OFTEN CRITICIZED THE PHARISEES FOR DISTORTING GOD'S LAW AND NOT UNDERSTANDING THE TRUE MESSAGE.

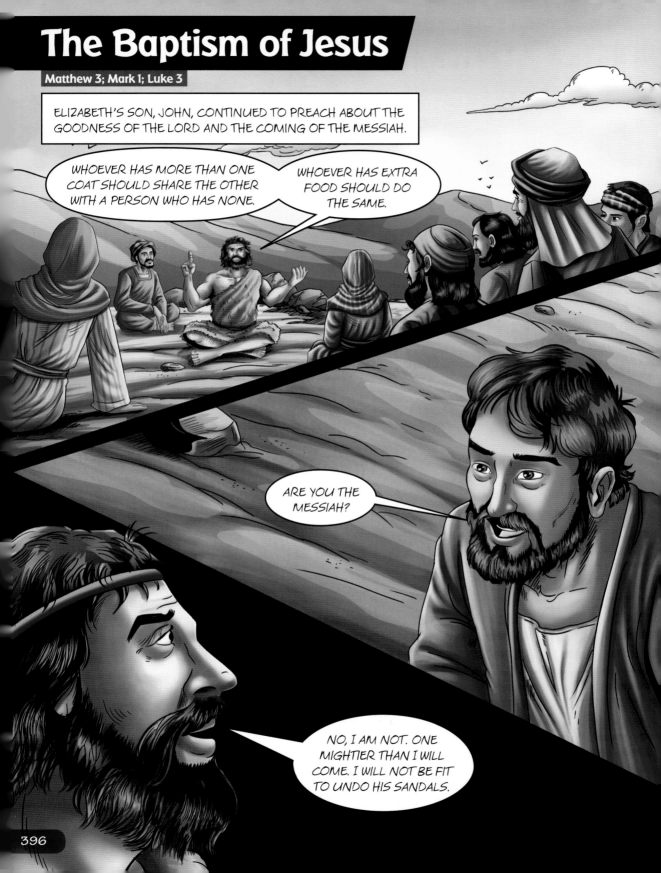

JOHN CONTINUED TO BAPTIZE PEOPLE. ONE DAY A STRANGER CAME TO HIM.

I HAVE COME HERE TO BE BAPTIZED.

MASTER, YOU SHOULD BE BAPTIZING ME!

IT IS WHAT GOD WANTS.

JOHN BAPTIZED JESUS IN THE JORDAN RIVER, AND THE HEAVENS OPENED UP. A VOICE FROM ABOVE SAID, "THIS IS MY BELOVED SON, IN WHOM I AM WELL PLEASED."

Temptation in the Desert

Matthew 4; Mark 1; Luke 4

AFTER HIS BAPTISM, JESUS WAS FILLED WITH THE HOLY SPIRT. HE LEFT JOHN AND WALKED FROM THE JORDAN RIVER INTO THE WILDERNESS.

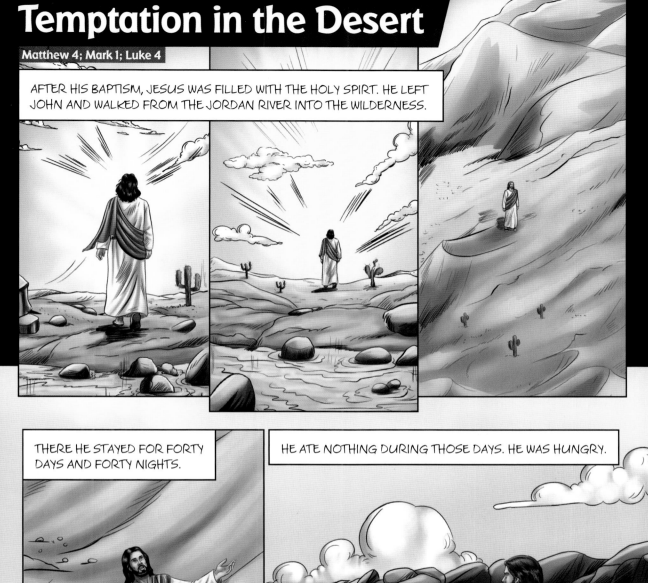

THERE HE STAYED FOR FORTY DAYS AND FORTY NIGHTS.

HE ATE NOTHING DURING THOSE DAYS. HE WAS HUNGRY.

A Prophet in His Hometown

Luke 4

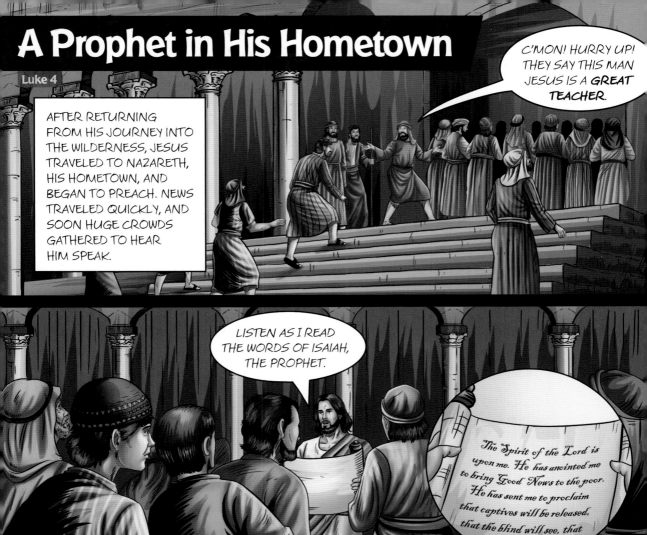

C'MON! HURRY UP! THEY SAY THIS MAN JESUS IS A **GREAT TEACHER**.

AFTER RETURNING FROM HIS JOURNEY INTO THE WILDERNESS, JESUS TRAVELED TO NAZARETH, HIS HOMETOWN, AND BEGAN TO PREACH. NEWS TRAVELED QUICKLY, AND SOON HUGE CROWDS GATHERED TO HEAR HIM SPEAK.

LISTEN AS I READ THE WORDS OF ISAIAH, THE PROPHET.

The Spirit of the Lord is upon me. He has anointed me to bring Good News to the poor. He has sent me to proclaim that captives will be released, that the blind will see, that oppressed will be set free.

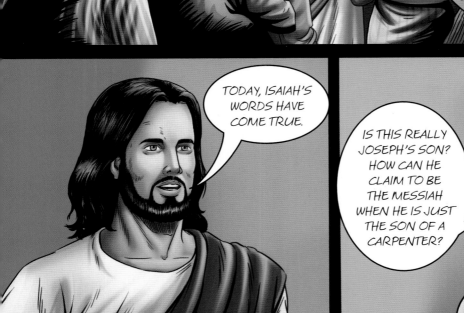

TODAY, ISAIAH'S WORDS HAVE COME TRUE.

IS THIS REALLY JOSEPH'S SON? HOW CAN HE CLAIM TO BE THE MESSIAH WHEN HE IS JUST THE SON OF A CARPENTER?

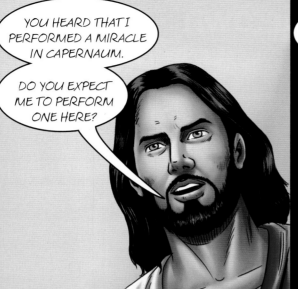

YOU HEARD THAT I PERFORMED A MIRACLE IN CAPERNAUM.

DO YOU EXPECT ME TO PERFORM ONE HERE?

NO PROPHET HAS EVER BEEN WELCOMED IN HIS OWN HOMETOWN.

ELIJAH DID NOT GO TO HIS OWN PEOPLE BUT TO A WIDOW FROM ANOTHER LAND.

THE PEOPLE WERE SO ENRAGED WHEN THEY HEARD JESUS SPEAK THESE WORDS THAT THEY FORCED HIM FROM THE SYNAGOGUE AND INTO THE STREET.

THE CROWD LED HIM TO THE EDGE OF TOWN TO THROW HIM OFF A CLIFF. BUT JESUS JUST WALKED CALMLY THROUGH THE MOB AND WENT ON HIS WAY.

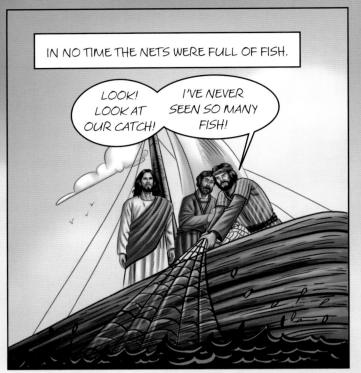

IN NO TIME THE NETS WERE FULL OF FISH.

LOOK! LOOK AT OUR CATCH!

I'VE NEVER SEEN SO MANY FISH!

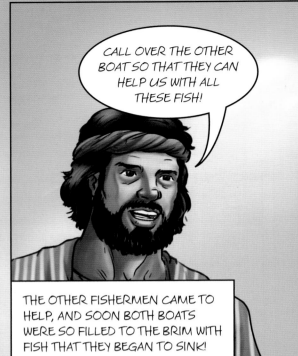

CALL OVER THE OTHER BOAT SO THAT THEY CAN HELP US WITH ALL THESE FISH!

THE OTHER FISHERMEN CAME TO HELP, AND SOON BOTH BOATS WERE SO FILLED TO THE BRIM WITH FISH THAT THEY BEGAN TO SINK!

LORD, YOU SHOULD LEAVE ME, FOR I AM A SINFUL MAN!

DON'T BE AFRAID. FROM THIS DAY ON, YOU WILL BE CALLED PETER. YOU WILL BE A FISHER OF MEN.

SIMON LEFT HIS NETS BEHIND THAT VERY DAY TO FOLLOW JESUS, AND SO TOO DID HIS FELLOW FISHERMEN ANDREW, JAMES, AND JOHN.

ONE NIGHT JESUS WENT UP TO THE TOP OF A MOUNTAIN TO PRAY. WHEN HE CAME DOWN, HE ASSEMBLED THE MEN WHO BECAME HIS SPECIAL DISCIPLES. THEY AGREED TO TRAVEL WITH HIM AND HELP SPREAD THE WORD OF GOD.

WHEN JESUS BEGAN HIS MINISTRY, HE CALLED ON TWELVE MEN TO FOLLOW HIM. KNOWN AS HIS DISCIPLES, THESE MEN CAME FROM EVERY WALK OF LIFE. TWO OF THE TWELVE—MATTHEW AND JOHN—WOULD EACH WRITE A GOSPEL, A RECORDING OF JESUS' TEACHINGS AND THE EVENTS IN HIS LIFE. THE GOSPELS WERE NOT MEANT TO BE A MOMENT-BY-MOMENT ACCOUNT OF JESUS' LIFE. IN FACT, JOHN WROTE, "THERE ARE ALSO MANY OTHER THINGS THAT JESUS DID . . . THAT EVEN THE WORLD ITSELF COULD NOT CONTAIN THE BOOKS THAT WOULD BE WRITTEN." TWO OTHERS WOULD ALSO WRITE GOSPELS: LUKE, A DOCTOR, AND A YOUNG MAN NAMED MARK, WHO IS BELIEVED TO HAVE BEEN A COMPANION AND INTERPRETER OF THE DISCIPLE PETER.

Simon Peter

SIMON WAS A FISHERMAN WHO JESUS NAMED PETER. HE WAS MARRIED. BORN IN GALILEE, PETER'S FATHER WAS NAMED JONAH. REFERRING TO PETER, JESUS SAID, "UPON THIS ROCK I WILL BUILD MY CHURCH". IN GREEK, PETER'S NAME WAS PETROS, AND THE WORD FOR "ROCK" IN GREEK IS PETRA.

James the Greater

JAMES THE GREATER WAS THE SON OF ZEBEDEE AND SALOME. HE WAS THE BROTHER OF ANOTHER DISCIPLE, JOHN. FISHERMEN BY TRADE, HE AND JOHN WERE SEEMINGLY NEVER APART.

Andrew

ANDREW WAS PETER'S BROTHER. HE WAS ORIGINALLY A DISCIPLE OF JOHN THE BAPTIST, AND ACCORDING TO SOME ACCOUNTS, WAS THE PERSON WHO INTRODUCED PETER TO JESUS.

John

JOHN WAS A FISHERMAN FROM GALILEE AND WAS POSSIBLY THE YOUNGER BROTHER OF JAMES THE GREATER. A MEMBER OF JESUS' INNER CIRCLE, JOHN WAS "THE DISCIPLE WHOM JESUS LOVED." MANY BELIEVE HE WROTE ONE OF THE GOSPELS, ALTHOUGH SOME EXPERTS DISPUTE THIS. SOME SCHOLARS BELIEVE THE NEW TESTAMENT REFERS TO THREE SEPARATE JOHNS: JOHN THE APOSTLE, JOHN THE EVANGELIST, AND JOHN OF PATMOS (TO WHOM THE BOOK OF REVELATION IS TRADITIONALLY ATTRIBUTED).

Simon the Zealot

NOT MUCH IS KNOWN ABOUT SIMON, ONLY THAT HE WAS A ZEALOT—A FANATIC WHO HATED THE RULING ROMANS.

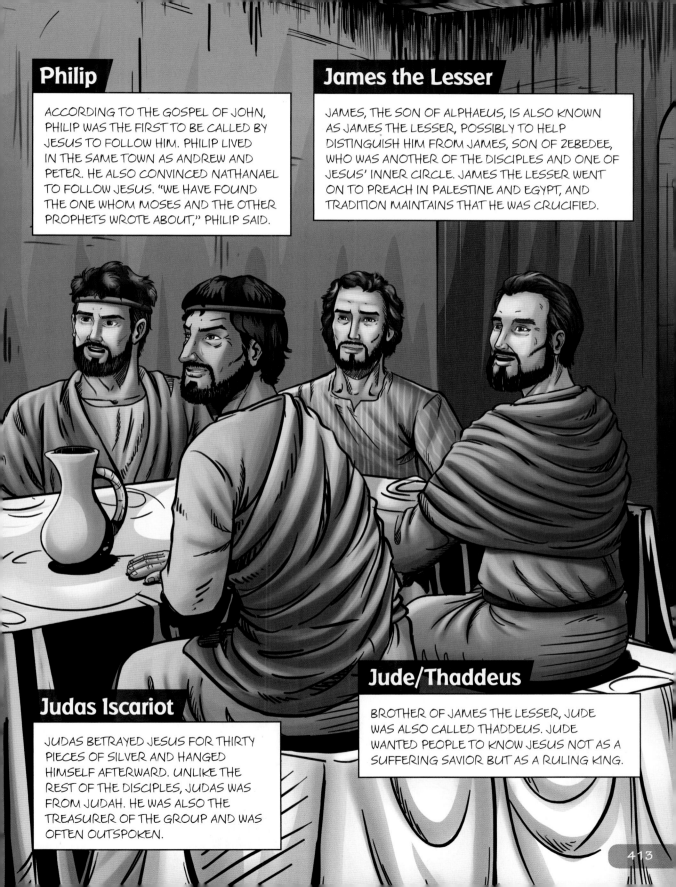

Philip

ACCORDING TO THE GOSPEL OF JOHN, PHILIP WAS THE FIRST TO BE CALLED BY JESUS TO FOLLOW HIM. PHILIP LIVED IN THE SAME TOWN AS ANDREW AND PETER. HE ALSO CONVINCED NATHANAEL TO FOLLOW JESUS. "WE HAVE FOUND THE ONE WHOM MOSES AND THE OTHER PROPHETS WROTE ABOUT," PHILIP SAID.

James the Lesser

JAMES, THE SON OF ALPHAEUS, IS ALSO KNOWN AS JAMES THE LESSER, POSSIBLY TO HELP DISTINGUISH HIM FROM JAMES, SON OF ZEBEDEE, WHO WAS ANOTHER OF THE DISCIPLES AND ONE OF JESUS' INNER CIRCLE. JAMES THE LESSER WENT ON TO PREACH IN PALESTINE AND EGYPT, AND TRADITION MAINTAINS THAT HE WAS CRUCIFIED.

Judas Iscariot

JUDAS BETRAYED JESUS FOR THIRTY PIECES OF SILVER AND HANGED HIMSELF AFTERWARD. UNLIKE THE REST OF THE DISCIPLES, JUDAS WAS FROM JUDAH. HE WAS ALSO THE TREASURER OF THE GROUP AND WAS OFTEN OUTSPOKEN.

Jude/Thaddeus

BROTHER OF JAMES THE LESSER, JUDE WAS ALSO CALLED THADDEUS. JUDE WANTED PEOPLE TO KNOW JESUS NOT AS A SUFFERING SAVIOR BUT AS A RULING KING.

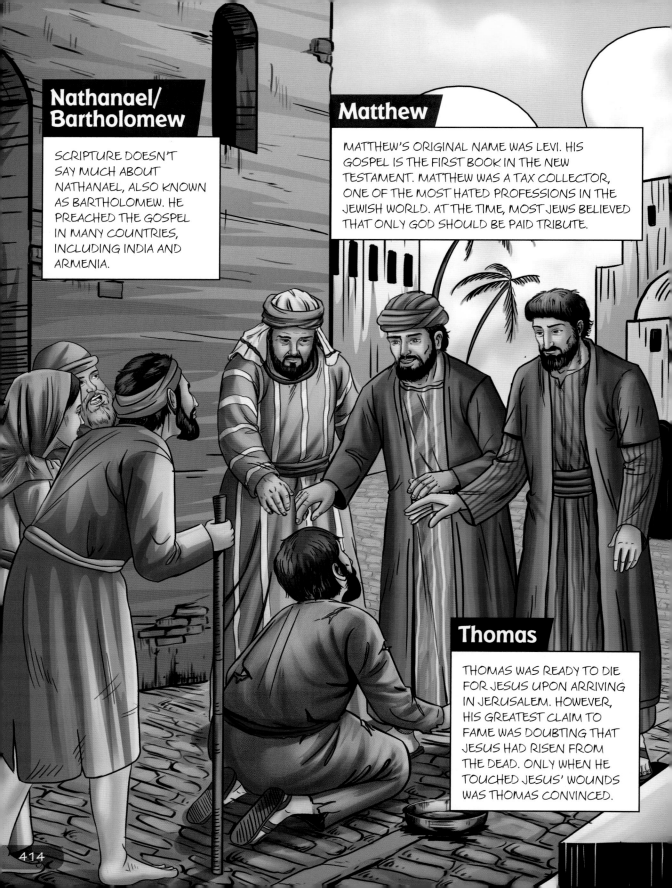

Nathanael/Bartholomew

SCRIPTURE DOESN'T SAY MUCH ABOUT NATHANAEL, ALSO KNOWN AS BARTHOLOMEW. HE PREACHED THE GOSPEL IN MANY COUNTRIES, INCLUDING INDIA AND ARMENIA.

Matthew

MATTHEW'S ORIGINAL NAME WAS LEVI. HIS GOSPEL IS THE FIRST BOOK IN THE NEW TESTAMENT. MATTHEW WAS A TAX COLLECTOR, ONE OF THE MOST HATED PROFESSIONS IN THE JEWISH WORLD. AT THE TIME, MOST JEWS BELIEVED THAT ONLY GOD SHOULD BE PAID TRIBUTE.

Thomas

THOMAS WAS READY TO DIE FOR JESUS UPON ARRIVING IN JERUSALEM. HOWEVER, HIS GREATEST CLAIM TO FAME WAS DOUBTING THAT JESUS HAD RISEN FROM THE DEAD. ONLY WHEN HE TOUCHED JESUS' WOUNDS WAS THOMAS CONVINCED.

THE SERVANT DID AS MARY ASKED. NEARBY WERE SIX STONE JARS THAT PEOPLE USED TO WASH THEMSELVES DURING CEREMONIES. EACH JAR HELD PERHAPS 20 TO 30 GALLONS OF WATER.

FILL THE JARS WITH WATER.

THEN DRAW SOME OUT AND BRING IT TO THE HEAD WAITER.

THE SERVANTS DID WHAT JESUS WANTED.

The Samaritan Woman

John 4

ONE DAY JESUS WAS WALKING THROUGH SAMARIA. HE WAS NEAR A PLACE CALLED SYCHAR, WHERE JACOB HAD GIVEN HIS SON JOSEPH A PLOT OF LAND. JESUS SAT BY A WELL. IT WAS A BLAZING HOT DAY.

AS HE SAT, A SAMARITAN WOMAN CAME TO THE WELL.

WOMAN, MAY I HAVE A DRINK?

YOU ARE A JEW. JEWS ARE NOT SUPPOSED TO TALK TO SAMARITANS.

HOW CAN YOU ASK ME FOR A DRINK?

Jesus Cures the First Leper

Matthew 8; Mark 1; Luke 5

PEOPLE FEARED AND SCORNED PEOPLE WITH LEPROSY.

IN JESUS' TIME, THE DISEASE OF LEPROSY WAS BELIEVED TO BE A CURSE FROM GOD. THE DISEASE DISFIGURED PEOPLE'S FACES AND LIMBS.

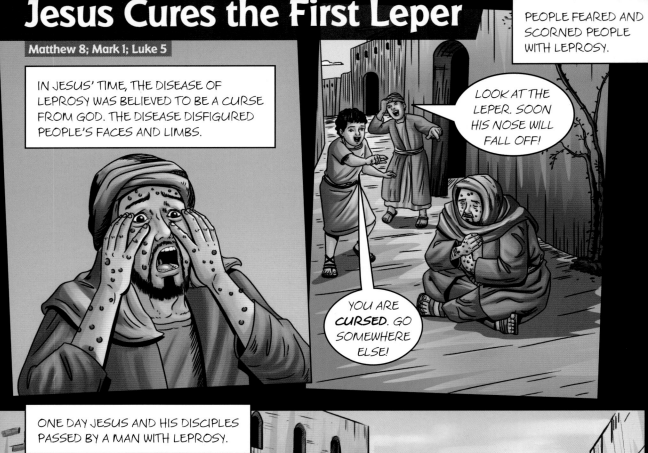

LOOK AT THE LEPER. SOON HIS NOSE WILL FALL OFF!

YOU ARE **CURSED**. GO SOMEWHERE ELSE!

ONE DAY JESUS AND HIS DISCIPLES PASSED BY A MAN WITH LEPROSY.

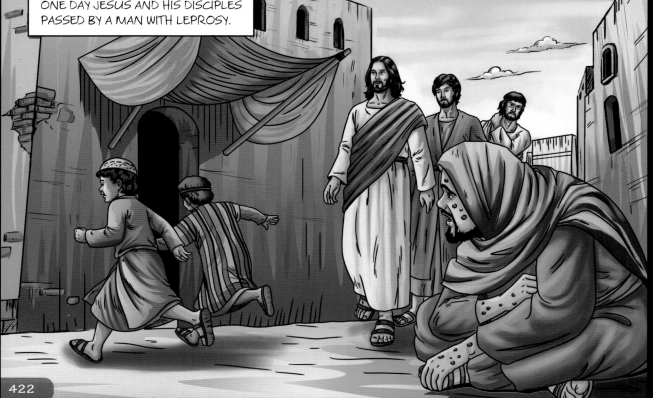

The Roman Centurion

JESUS ENTERED CAPERNAUM, A TOWN NEAR NAZARETH. A ROMAN CENTURION, A MILITARY OFFICER IN THE TOWN, CAME TO SEE JESUS. HE WAS A FRIEND OF THE JEWS. HE HELPED THEM BUILD THE SYNAGOGUE.

LORD, MY SERVANT IS LYING AT HOME, PARALYZED, SUFFERING DREADFULLY. CAN YOU HELP HIM?

I WILL COME AND CURE HIM.

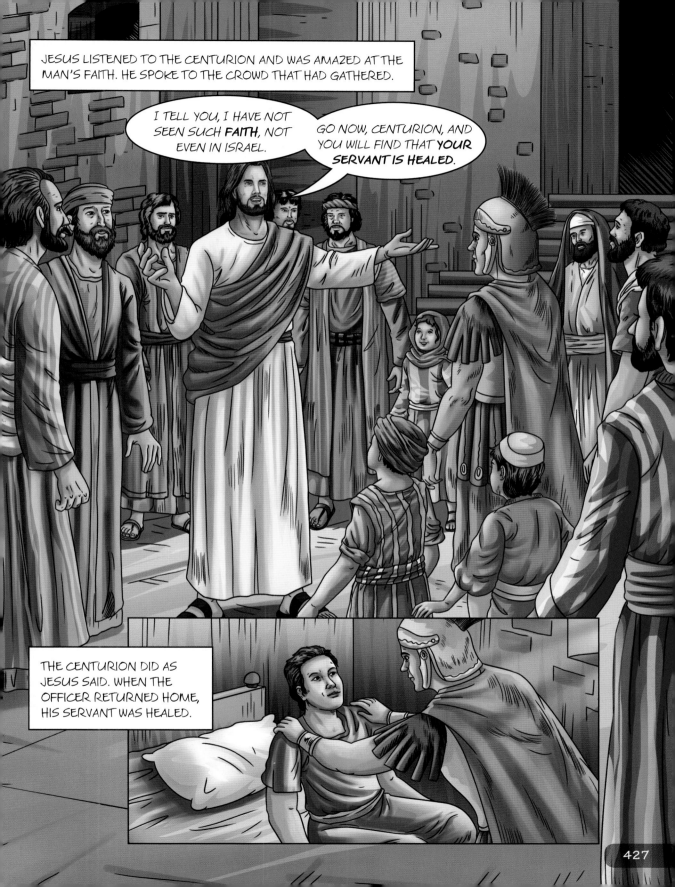

Sermon on the Mount

Matthew 5–7; Luke 6, 11

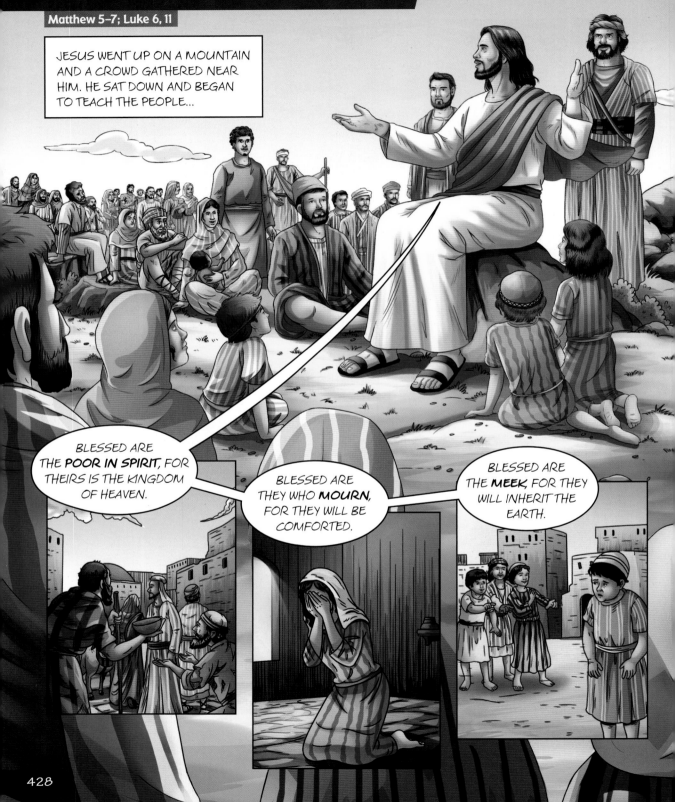

JESUS WENT UP ON A MOUNTAIN AND A CROWD GATHERED NEAR HIM. HE SAT DOWN AND BEGAN TO TEACH THE PEOPLE...

BLESSED ARE THE **POOR IN SPIRIT**, FOR THEIRS IS THE KINGDOM OF HEAVEN.

BLESSED ARE THEY WHO **MOURN**, FOR THEY WILL BE COMFORTED.

BLESSED ARE THE **MEEK**, FOR THEY WILL INHERIT THE EARTH.

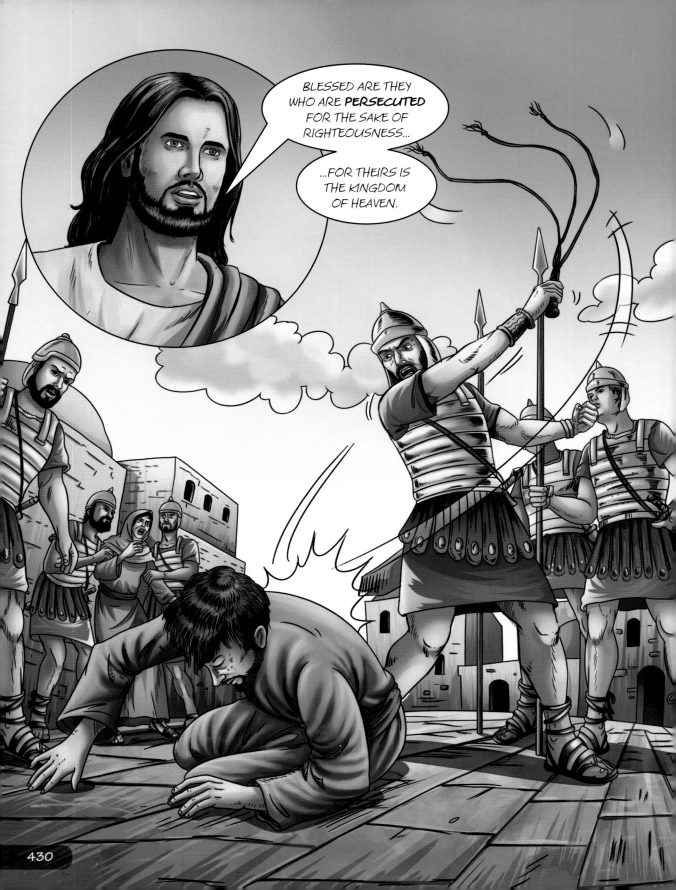

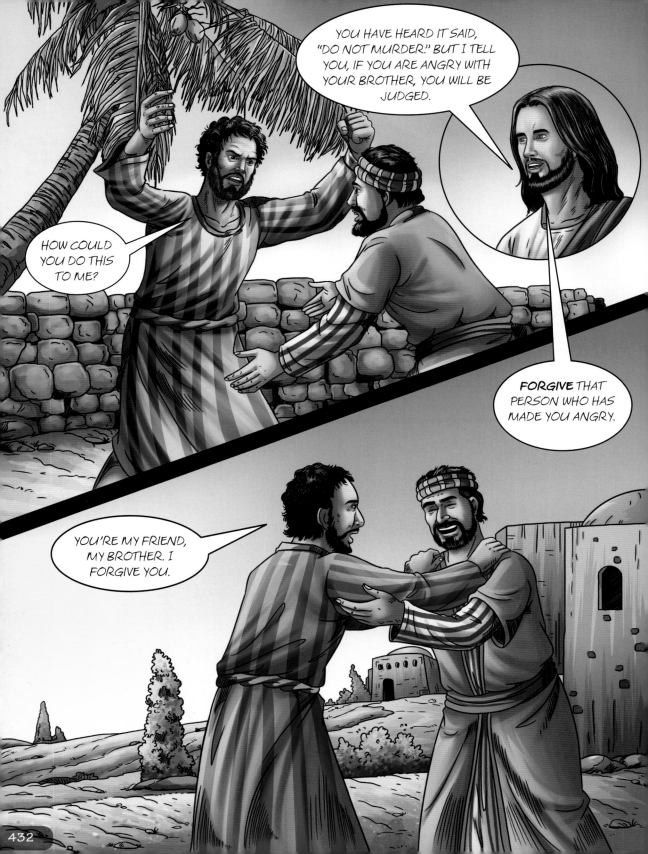

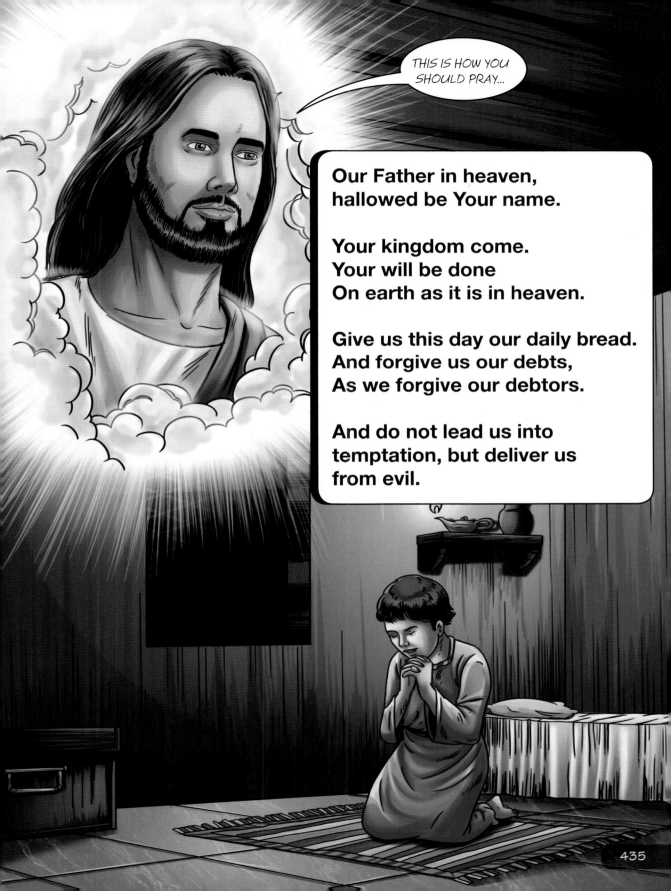

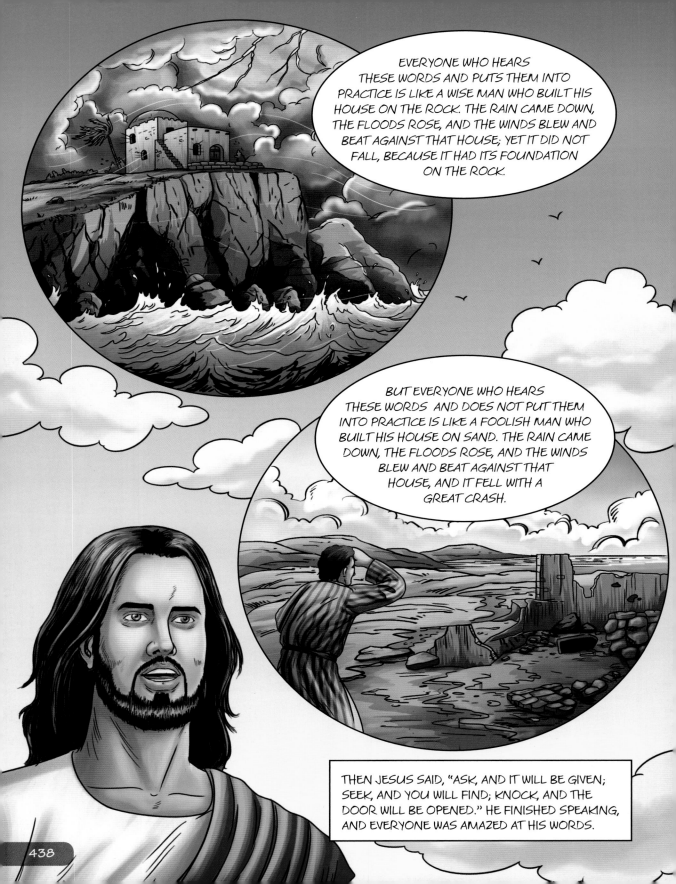

Jesus and the Children

Matthew 19; Mark 10; Luke 18

EVERYWHERE JESUS WENT, PEOPLE WOULD BRING THEIR CHILDREN TO HIM SO THAT HE COULD PRAY FOR THEM. JESUS LOVED THE CHILDREN DEARLY.

BUT ONE TIME, SOME OF HIS DISCIPLES TOLD THE PEOPLE TO LEAVE JESUS ALONE, SAYING THAT HE WAS TOO BUSY TO SPEAK TO THE CHILDREN. JESUS TOLD HIS DISCIPLES FIRMLY, "LET THE LITTLE CHILDREN COME TO ME, AND DON'T STOP THEM, FOR THE KINGDOM OF HEAVEN BELONGS TO SUCH AS THESE. THE TRUTH IS, ANYONE WHO WILL NOT RECEIVE THE KINGDOM OF GOD LIKE A LITTLE CHILD WILL NEVER ENTER IT."

The Parable of the Sower

Matthew 13; Luke 8

JESUS OFTEN TALKED IN PARABLES, WHICH ARE SIMPLE STORIES THAT HELP PEOPLE UNDERSTAND LARGER IDEAS OR TEACH IMPORTANT LESSONS. MANY OF THE PEOPLE WERE FARMERS OR GREW THEIR OWN FOOD. JESUS USED LANGUAGE AND IMAGES THAT THEY COULD UNDERSTAND AND RELATE TO.

JESUS TOLD A STORY. ONCE THERE WAS A FARMER WHO WENT OUT TO SOW SOME SEEDS.

SOME OF THE SEEDS FELL ON THE PATH AND WERE EATEN BY THE BIRDS.

SOME FELL ON ROCKY GROUND. A PLANT SPROUTED, BUT IT HAD NO MOISTURE. IT SHRIVELED IN THE HOT SUN.

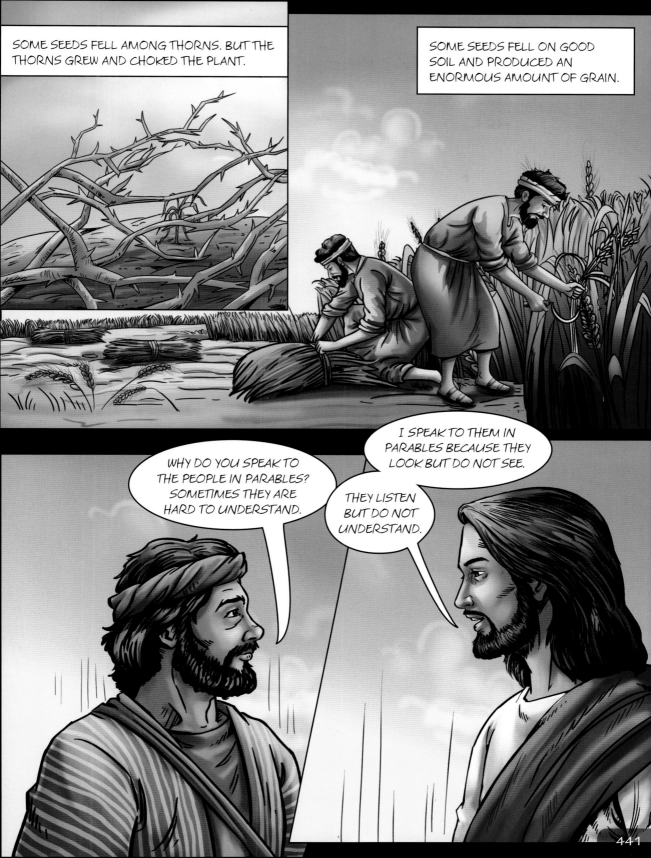

LOOK AT THE PARABLE OF THE SOWER AND SEEDS, FOR EXAMPLE.

THE SEED ON THE PATH IS LIKE A PERSON WHO HEARS GOD'S WORD BUT DOESN'T UNDERSTAND IT. THE DEVIL, THE EVIL ONE, COMES AND TAKES AWAY WHAT WAS SOWN IN THAT PERSON'S HEART.

THE SEED BETWEEN THE ROCKS IS LIKE A PERSON WHO HEARS GOD'S WORD AND RECEIVES IT WITH GREAT JOY. BUT HIS FAITH HAS NO ROOTS, AND IT LASTS ONLY FOR A SHORT TIME.

THE SEED AMONG THE THORNS IS LIKE A PERSON WHO HEARS GOD'S WORD, BUT THE WORRIES OF THIS LIFE AND THE LURE OF RICHES CHOKE HIM AND HE BEARS NO FRUIT.

BUT THE SEED SOWN ON RICH SOIL IS LIKE A PERSON WHO HEARS GOD'S WORD, UNDERSTANDS IT, AND LETS IT GROW AND BEAR FRUIT.

The Parable of Weeds and Wheat

Matthew 13

JESUS THEN TOLD ANOTHER PARABLE.

A MAN'S ENEMIES SCATTERED WEEDS OVER A FIELD OF WHEAT. THE WHEAT GREW, AS DID THE WEEDS.

I MUST TELL MY MASTER THAT HIS WHEAT FIELD IS RUINED.

MASTER, WHERE DID THESE WEEDS COME FROM?

SHALL I PULL THEM UP?

NO. IF YOU DO, YOU'LL PULL UP THE WHEAT TOO. LET THEM GROW TOGETHER. WE'LL HARVEST THE WEEDS FIRST AND THEN THE WHEAT.

THE STORY CONFOUNDED JESUS' DISICIPLES.

PLEASE EXPLAIN WHAT THAT PARABLE MEANS, MASTER.

WE DON'T UNDERSTAND.

JESUS TOLD HIS DISCIPLES, "THE PERSON WHO SOWS THE SEEDS IS THE SON OF MAN. THE FIELD IS THE WORLD, AND THE SEEDS OF WHEAT ARE THE CHILDREN OF GOD."

The Parable of the Lost Sheep

Luke 15

THE PHARISEES DID NOT LIKE THAT JESUS ASSOCIATED HIMSELF WITH SINNERS.

JESUS HEARD THE PHARISEES TALKING ABOUT HIM. JESUS ASKED WHO AMONG THEM WOULD NOT LEAVE 99 SHEEP IN THE FIELD TO FIND THE ONE SHEEP THAT WAS LOST.

THIS MAN, JESUS, SITS WITH TAX COLLECTORS AND SINNERS.

HE EATS WITH THEM. HE WELCOMES THEM.

ONCE THE SHEEP WAS FOUND, JESUS SAID, WHO WOULD NOT CALL HIS FRIENDS TO CELEBRATE AND SAY, "I HAVE FOUND MY LOST SHEEP"?

THERE WILL BE MORE JOY IN HEAVEN OVER ONE SINNER WHO REPENTS...

...THAN OVER THE 99 RIGHTEOUS PEOPLE WHO DO NOT NEED TO REPENT.

The Parable of the Lost Coin

Luke 15

JESUS CONTINUED HIS STORIES.

A WOMAN HAD 10 COINS BUT LOST ONE.

SHE LIT HER LAMP AND SWEPT EVERY CORNER OF HER HOUSE SEARCHING FOR THE COIN.

WHEN SHE DID FIND IT, SHE CELEBRATED WITH HER FRIENDS...

...THE SAME WAY ANGELS WOULD REJOICE OVER ONE SINNER WHO REPENTS.

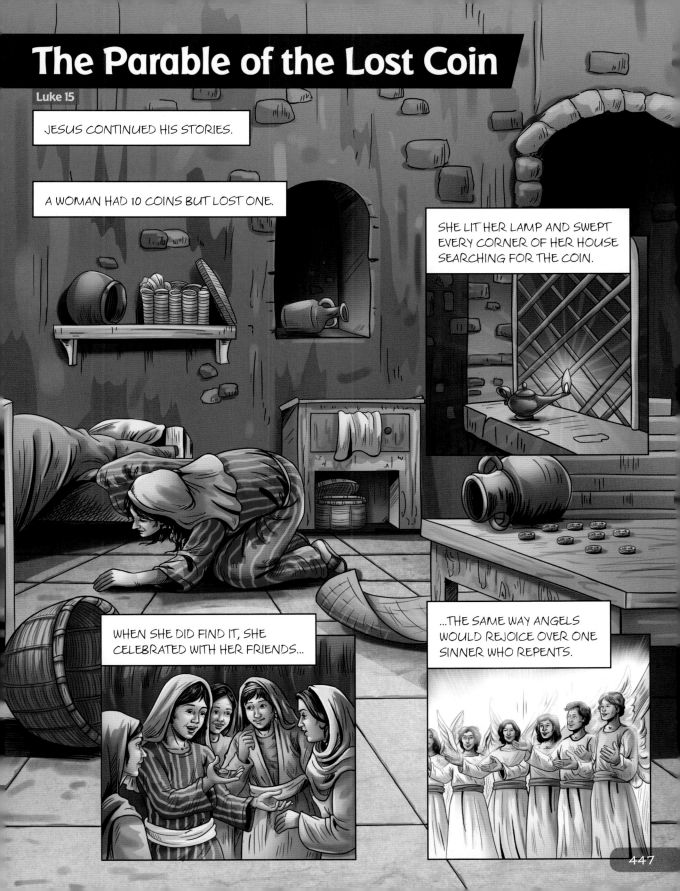

447

The Parable of the Good Samaritan

Luke 10

A TEACHER OF LAW WANTED TO TEST JESUS. THE MAN STOOD UP AND CONFRONTED HIM.

WHAT DOES THE LAW SAY?

LOVE THE LORD WITH ALL YOUR HEART, WITH ALL YOUR STRENGTH, AND WITH ALL YOUR MIND, AND LOVE YOUR NEIGHBOR AS YOURSELF.

TEACHER, WHAT MUST I DO TO INHERIT ETERNAL LIFE?

BUT THE MAN WANTED TO SHOW HOW RIGHTEOUS HE WAS.

BUT WHO EXACTLY IS MY NEIGHBOR?

THEN JESUS TOLD THIS PARABLE.

THERE WAS ONCE A MAN WHO WAS TRAVELING FROM JERUSALEM TO JERICHO. AS HE WALKED, A GROUP OF ROBBERS ATTACKED HIM.

THE ROBBERS STRIPPED THE MAN OF HIS CLOTHES...

...AND LEFT HIM ON THE ROAD TO DIE.

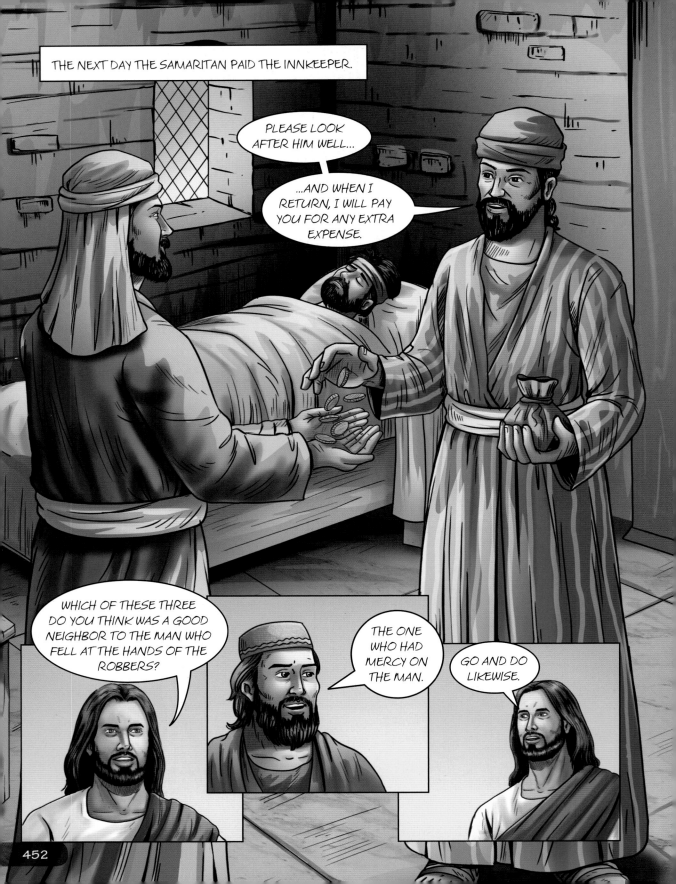

The Parable of the Wise and Foolish Girls

Matthew 25

JESUS TOLD ANOTHER PARABLE.

THE KINGDOM OF HEAVEN WILL BE LIKE TEN YOUNG WOMEN WHO TOOK THEIR LAMPS TO MEET A BRIDEGROOM. FIVE WERE FOOLISH, BECAUSE THEY BROUGHT NO OIL FOR THEIR LAMPS...

...AND FIVE WERE WISE BECAUSE THEY BROUGHT OIL WITH THEM.

THE BRIDEGROOM WAS LATE, BUT AT AROUND MIDNIGHT HE WAS SPOTTED.
HERE COMES THE GROOM!
PLEASE GIVE US SOME OF YOUR OIL. OUR LAMPS ARE GOING OUT!
WE CANNOT GIVE YOU ANY OIL. THERE ISN'T ENOUGH FOR ALL OF US.
GO TO THE MERCHANT AND BUY SOME OIL YOURSELVES.

THE BRIDEGROOM FINALLY ARRIVED. THE FIVE WISE GIRLS FOLLOWED HIM INTO THE BANQUET HALL.

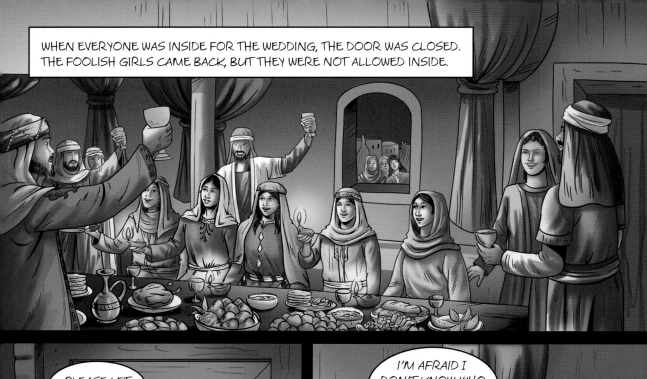

WHEN EVERYONE WAS INSIDE FOR THE WEDDING, THE DOOR WAS CLOSED. THE FOOLISH GIRLS CAME BACK, BUT THEY WERE NOT ALLOWED INSIDE.

PLEASE LET US IN!

I'M AFRAID I DON'T KNOW WHO YOU ARE. YOU'RE TOO LATE!

SO STAY AWAKE, FOR YOU DO NOT KNOW THE DAY OR THE HOUR WHEN THE SON OF MAN IS COMING.

The Parable of the Lost Son

Luke 15

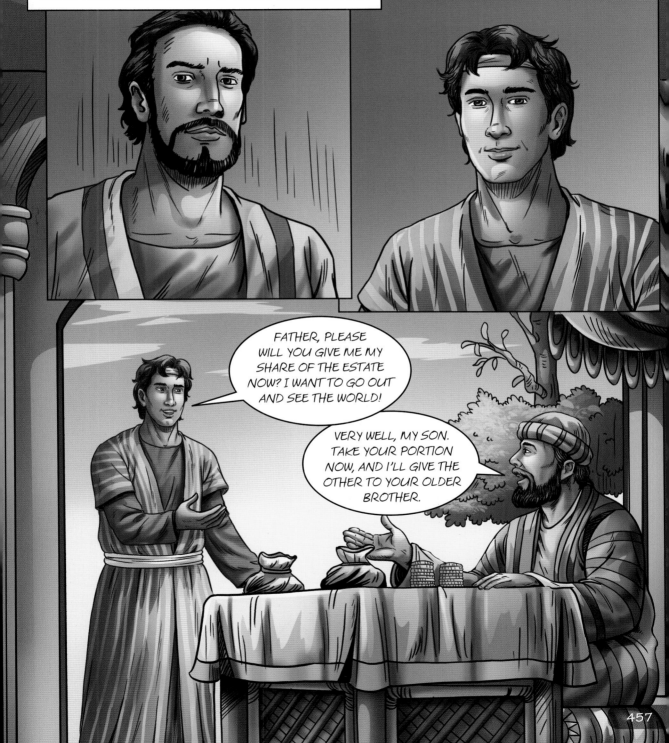

JESUS TOLD ANOTHER STORY OF A MAN WITH TWO SONS.

FATHER, PLEASE WILL YOU GIVE ME MY SHARE OF THE ESTATE NOW? I WANT TO GO OUT AND SEE THE WORLD!

VERY WELL, MY SON. TAKE YOUR PORTION NOW, AND I'LL GIVE THE OTHER TO YOUR OLDER BROTHER.

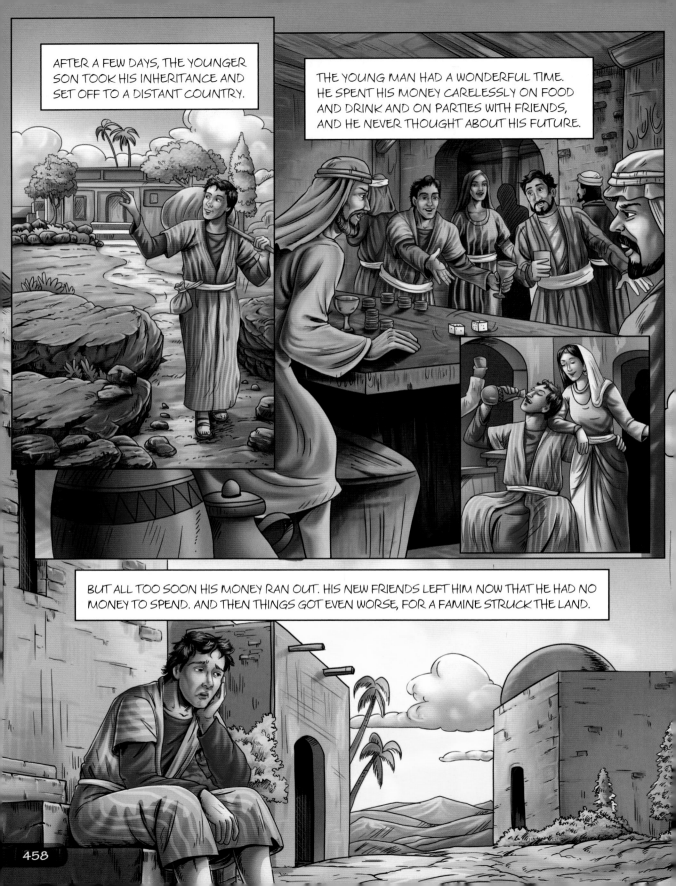

AFTER A FEW DAYS, THE YOUNGER SON TOOK HIS INHERITANCE AND SET OFF TO A DISTANT COUNTRY.

THE YOUNG MAN HAD A WONDERFUL TIME. HE SPENT HIS MONEY CARELESSLY ON FOOD AND DRINK AND ON PARTIES WITH FRIENDS, AND HE NEVER THOUGHT ABOUT HIS FUTURE.

BUT ALL TOO SOON HIS MONEY RAN OUT. HIS NEW FRIENDS LEFT HIM NOW THAT HE HAD NO MONEY TO SPEND. AND THEN THINGS GOT EVEN WORSE, FOR A FAMINE STRUCK THE LAND.

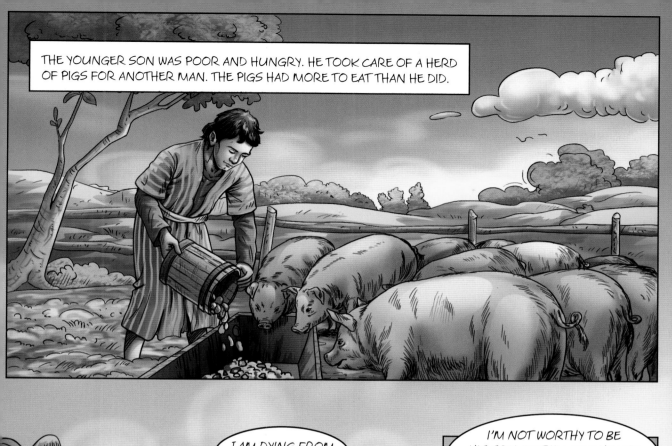

THE YOUNGER SON WAS POOR AND HUNGRY. HE TOOK CARE OF A HERD OF PIGS FOR ANOTHER MAN. THE PIGS HAD MORE TO EAT THAN HE DID.

I AM DYING FROM HUNGER.

I'LL GO SEE MY FATHER AND TELL HIM I HAVE SINNED.

I'M NOT WORTHY TO BE HIS SON, BUT I'LL BEG HIM TO TREAT ME AS HE WOULD ONE OF HIS WORKERS.

SOME TIME HAD PASSED. THE FATHER LOOKED OUT ACROSS THE FIELD AND SAW HIS YOUNGER SON COMING DOWN THE ROAD.

THE FATHER RAN TO HIS SON AND EMBRACED AND KISSED HIM.

FATHER, I HAVE SINNED AGAINST HEAVEN AND AGAINST YOU. I'M NOT WORTHY TO BE CALLED YOUR SON!

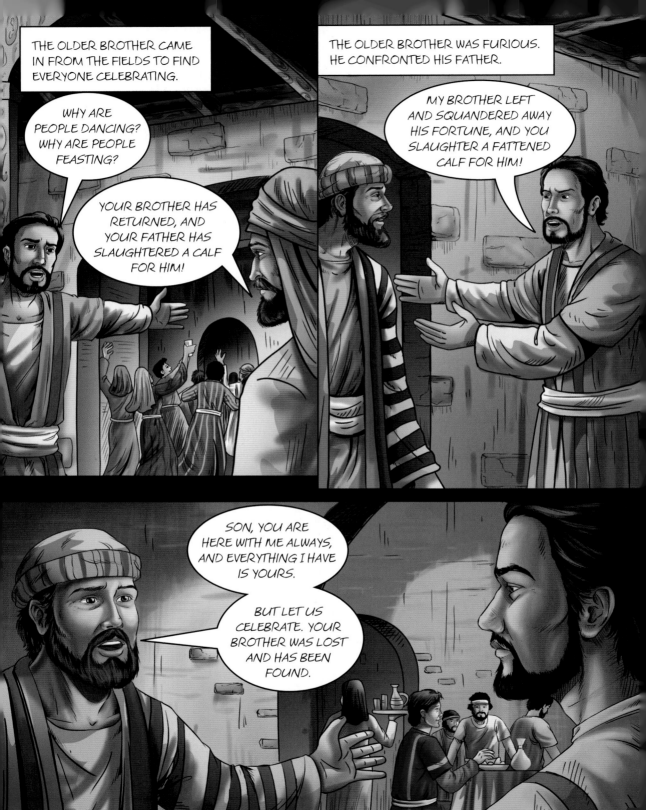

A Hole in the Roof

Mark 2; Luke 5

JESUS PERFORMED MANY DIFFERENT MIRACLES OVER HIS LIFE. HE HEALED THE SICK, RAISED THE DEAD, AND CAST OUT EVIL SPIRITS. PEOPLE FLOCKED TO JESUS, HOPING HE WOULD PERFORM AN ACT OF HEALING OR CAST OUT A DEMON. ONCE, SOME MEN BROUGHT THEIR PARALYZED FRIEND TO JESUS WHEN HE WAS STAYING IN A HOUSE IN CAPERNAUM. BUT THE HOUSE WAS SO PACKED THAT THEY COULDN'T GET ANYWHERE NEAR IT.

PLEASE MOVE ASIDE! OUR FRIEND CANNOT WALK! HE NEEDS THE HELP OF JESUS!

I HAVE AN IDEA. WE CAN CUT A HOLE THROUGH THE ROOF AND LOWER OUR FRIEND INSIDE SO HE CAN BE HEALED BY THE TEACHER.

THE MAN'S FRIENDS CLIMBED ONTO THE HOUSE AND BEGAN CUTTING A HOLE THROUGH THE ROOF. INSIDE...

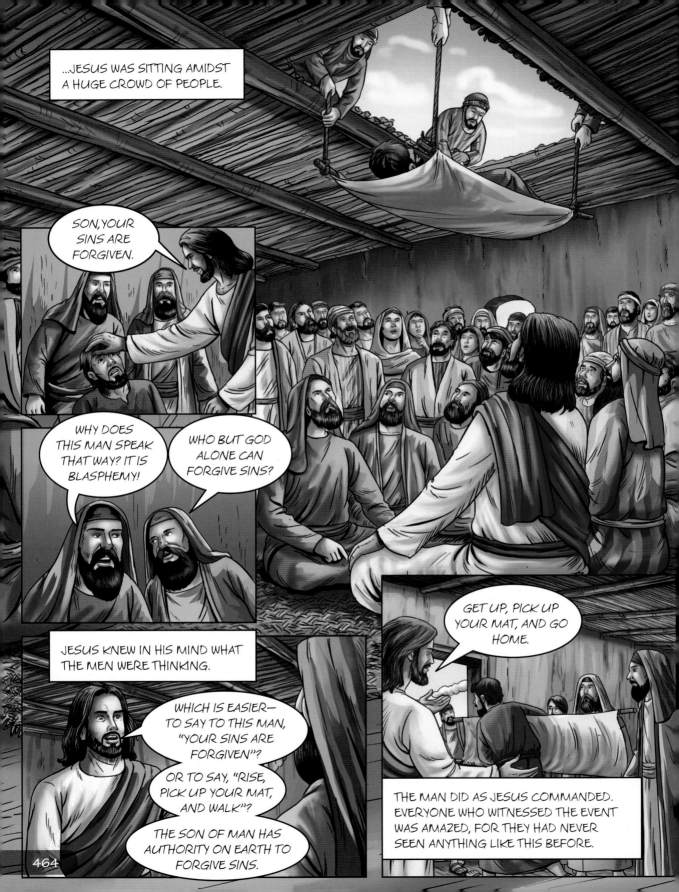

465

DO NOT WEEP ANY LONGER. SHE IS NOT DEAD, ONLY SLEEPING.

CHILD, ARISE!

IN THAT INSTANT, THE GIRL BEGAN TO BREATHE AGAIN.

JESUS TOLD HER PARENTS TO FEED THE CHILD. HE THEN INSTRUCTED JAIRUS AND HIS WIFE NOT TO TELL PEOPLE WHAT HAD JUST HAPPENED.

Calming the Storm

Matthew 8; Mark 4; Luke 8

MASTER, WAKE UP! WE'RE ALL GOING TO DROWN!

JESUS NOT ONLY HEALED THE SICK AND THE POSSESSED, BUT HE ALSO CONTROLLED THE FORCES OF NATURE. ONE DAY, HE AND HIS DISCIPLES WERE SAILING TO THE OTHER SIDE OF THE LAKE. JESUS LAY SLEEPING WHEN A DREADFUL STORM ROSE UP. THE WINDS HOWLED, AND HUGE WAVES TOSSED THE BOAT DANGEROUSLY.

THE DISCIPLES WERE TERRIFIED. THEY WOKE JESUS UP AND BEGGED HIM TO SAVE THEM. JESUS STOOD UP CALMLY AND COMMANDED THE WINDS AND WAVES TO BE STILL. AND AT ONCE, ALL WAS CALM.

BE STILL.

WHY ARE YOU SO AFRAID? DO YOU STILL HAVE NO FAITH?

WHO IS THIS MAN?

EVEN THE WINDS AND WAVES OBEY HIM!

The Head of John the Baptist

Matthew 11, 14; Mark 6; Luke 7

AS JESUS PERFORMED HIS MIRACLES, JOHN THE BAPTIST CONTINUED TO SPEAK HIS MIND. HE WAS BLUNT AND CRITICAL. SOME OF THE PHARISEES DID NOT LIKE WHAT HE HAD TO SAY.

IT'S TIME TO BEGIN ANEW.

A NEW BEGINNING IS COMING. TURN BACK TO GOD.

WHEN JOHN HEARD THAT KING HEROD HAD MARRIED HERODIAS, HIS OWN BROTHER'S WIFE, JOHN WAS UPSET.

IT IS AGAINST GOD'S LAW FOR YOU TO HAVE HER.

HOW DARE YOU TELL ME WHAT I CAN AND CANNOT DO!

HEROD WAS ANGRY. HE COULD HAVE HAD HIM KILLED, BUT INSTEAD HE THREW HIM IN PRISON BECAUSE HE FEARED JOHN'S FOLLOWERS.

IT WAS HEROD'S BIRTHDAY, AND A GRAND FEAST WAS UNDERWAY. THE DAUGHTER OF HERODIAS DANCED FOR THEM.

KING HEROD WAS PLEASED BY THE DANCE.

YOU CAN HAVE ANYTHING YOU WISH!

MOTHER, WHAT SHALL I ASK FOR?

I SHALL TELL YOU.

Feeding the Crowd

Matthew 14; Mark 6; Luke 9; John 6

JESUS WANTED TO BE ALONE, BUT HE WAS FOLLOWED BY A HUGE CROWD. THOUSANDS OF PEOPLE CAME TO LISTEN TO HIM. ALL HAD HEARD ABOUT THE MIRACLES HE HAD PERFORMED. JESUS TOOK PITY ON THEM AND DID NOT SEND THEM AWAY.

THE PEOPLE CROWDED AROUND JESUS AND LISTENED. HE SPOKE TO THEM UNTIL THE SUN BEGAN TO SET.

PHILIP, WHERE CAN WE BUY ENOUGH FOOD FOR THEM TO EAT?

MASTER, WE DON'T HAVE NEARLY ENOUGH MONEY TO FEED THEM!

LORD, SEND THESE PEOPLE TO THE VILLAGE SO THEY CAN FIND FOOD TO EAT.

473

A WHILE LATER, ANDREW, THE BROTHER OF SIMON PETER, BROUGHT A SMALL BOY TO JESUS.

THIS BOY HAS FIVE BARLEY LOAVES AND TWO FISH. BUT I DON'T KNOW HOW MUCH USE THEY WILL BE WITH SO MANY PEOPLE!

JESUS TOOK THE BOY'S FISH AND BREAD AND PRAYED OVER THEM. HE THEN BROKE THE FOOD INTO PIECES. HIS DISCIPLES BEGAN GIVING FOOD TO THE PEOPLE.

THE DISCIPLES KEPT ON HANDING OUT FOOD. THERE WAS ALWAYS MORE BREAD AND FISH TO REFILL THE BASKETS. WHEN EVERYONE HAD EATEN, JESUS' DISCIPLES COLLECTED WHAT WAS LEFT. THE BITS AND PIECES OF FOOD FILLED TWELVE BASKETS.

Jesus Walks on Water

Matthew 14

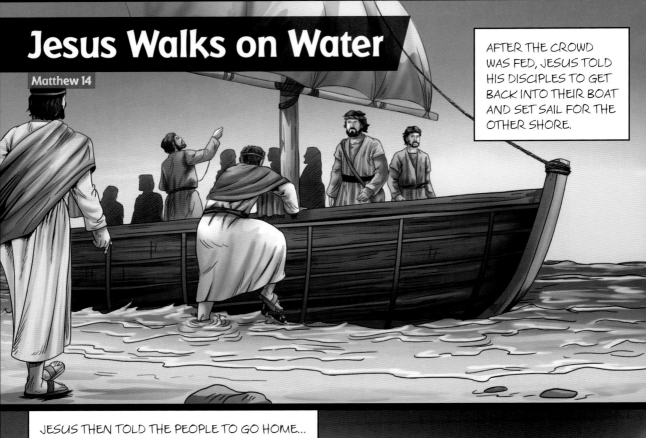

AFTER THE CROWD WAS FED, JESUS TOLD HIS DISCIPLES TO GET BACK INTO THEIR BOAT AND SET SAIL FOR THE OTHER SHORE.

JESUS THEN TOLD THE PEOPLE TO GO HOME...

...AND HE WALKED UP THE SIDE OF THE MOUNTAIN TO PRAY.

477

A Woman of Great Faith

Matthew 15; Mark 7

JESUS AND HIS DISCIPLES TRAVELED TO THE AREA OF TYRE AND SIDON. THEY STAYED IN A HOUSE, HOPING TO BE ALONE. ONE DAY, A GREEK WOMAN KNOCKED AT THE DOOR AND CALLED OUT.

HAVE PITY ON ME, LORD, SON OF DAVID! A DEMON TORMENTS MY DAUGHTER!

JESUS DID NOT SAY A WORD, BUT THE WOMAN DIDN'T GO AWAY.

LORD, SEND HER AWAY. SHE KEEPS CRYING OUT AND WON'T LEAVE US ALONE.

I WAS SENT ONLY TO HELP THE LOST SHEEP OF THE HOUSE OF ISRAEL.

The Transfiguration of Jesus Christ

Mark 9; Luke 9

ONE DAY JESUS LED PETER, JOHN, AND JAMES UP TO A HIGH MOUNTAIN.

ONCE THEY REACHED THE SUMMIT, JESUS' FACE SHONE LIKE THE SUN.

HIS CLOTHES BECAME AS WHITE AS LIGHT.

IN THAT INSTANT, MOSES AND ELIJAH APPEARED AND SPOKE WITH JESUS.

PETER, JOHN, AND JAMES HAD FALLEN ASLEEP. WHEN THEY AWOKE, THEY SAW JESUS WITH THE GREAT PROPHETS. THEY WERE AMAZED AT WHAT THEY WERE WITNESSING.

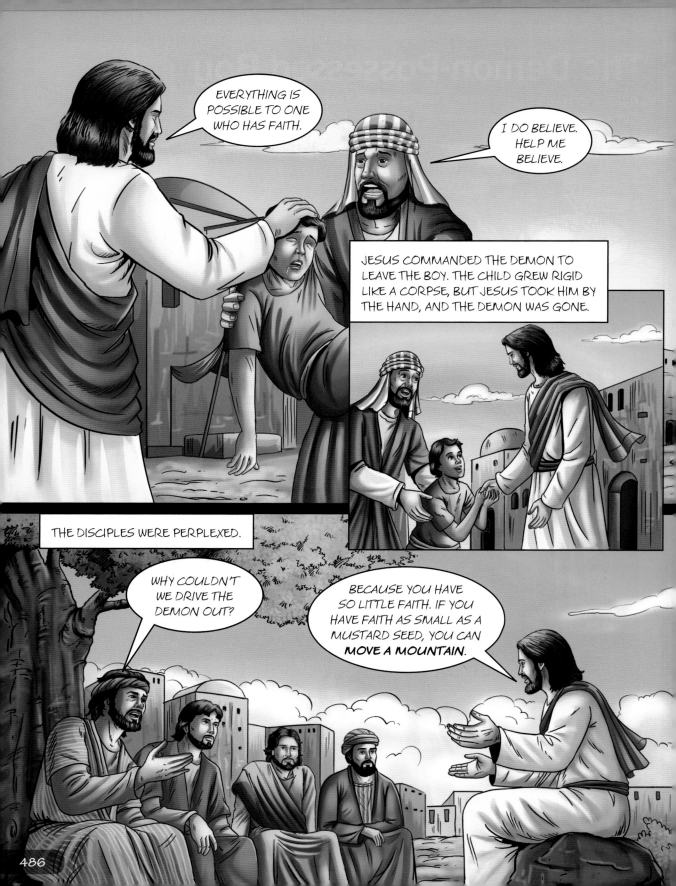

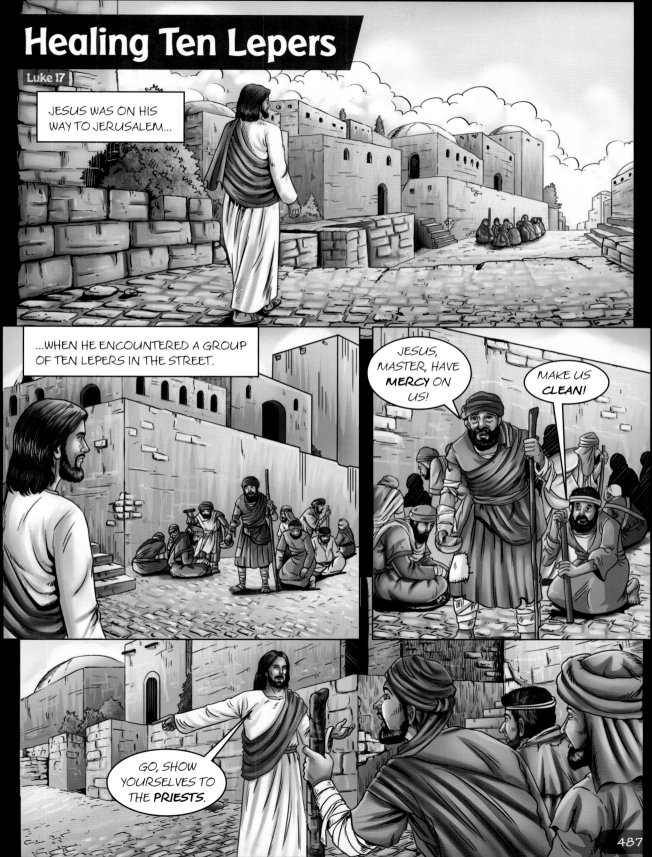

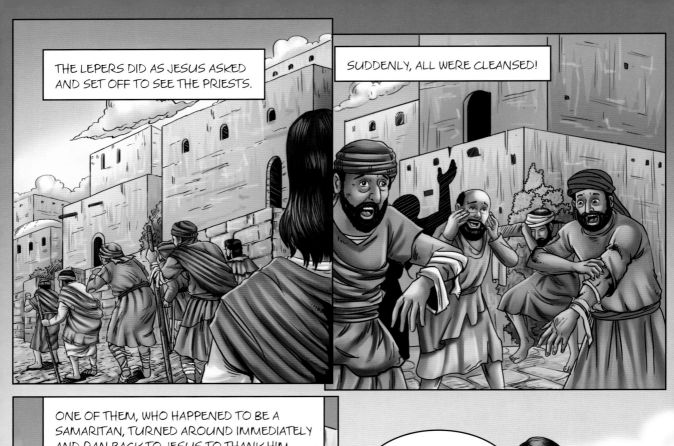

THE LEPERS DID AS JESUS ASKED AND SET OFF TO SEE THE PRIESTS.

SUDDENLY, ALL WERE CLEANSED!

ONE OF THEM, WHO HAPPENED TO BE A SAMARITAN, TURNED AROUND IMMEDIATELY AND RAN BACK TO JESUS TO THANK HIM.

I GIVE PRAISE TO THE LORD! I AM CLEANSED! THANK YOU! THANK YOU!

TEN WERE CLEANSED AND ONLY YOU RETURNED TO GIVE THANKS?

STAND UP. YOUR **FAITH** HAS SAVED YOU.

JESUS RESTORED THE BEGGAR'S SIGHT. WHEN THE PEOPLE SAW THIS, THEY GAVE PRAISE TO GOD.

THE MAN THEN FOLLOWED JESUS AS HE CONTINUED ON HIS JOURNEY.

Zacchaeus the Tax Collector

Luke 19

A MAN NAMED ZACCHAEUS WANTED TO SEE JESUS AS HE PASSED. ZACCHAEUS, WHO WAS A WEALTHY TAX COLLECTOR, WAS TOO SHORT TO SEE ABOVE EVERYONE'S HEAD.

HE CLIMBED A SYCAMORE TREE TO GET A BETTER LOOK.

ZACCHAEUS, COME DOWN FROM THAT TREE.

TODAY I WILL STAY AT YOUR HOUSE.

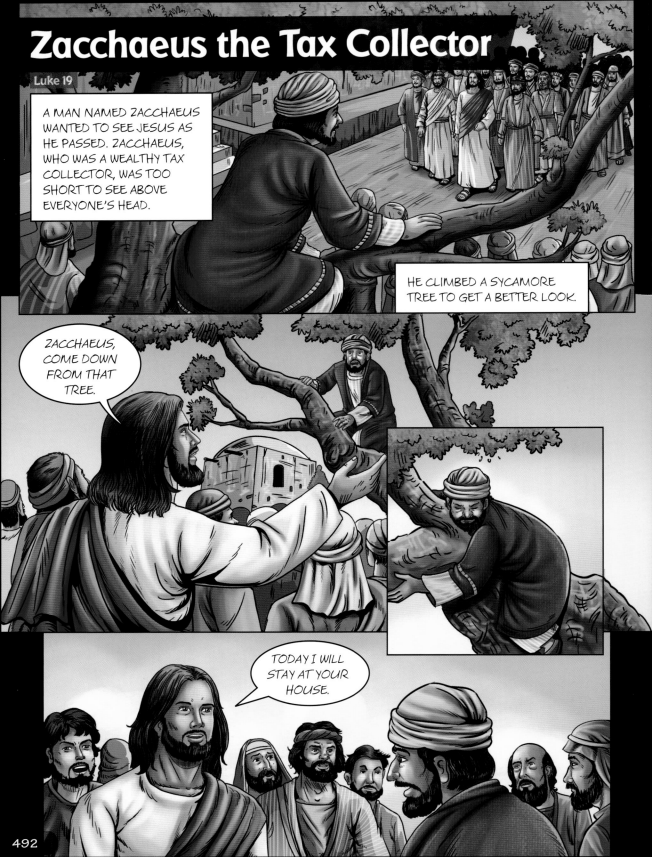

Luke 10

JESUS WAS FRIENDS WITH TWO SISTERS, MARTHA AND MARY. ONE DAY JESUS AND HIS DISCIPLES STOPPED TO VISIT.

MARTHA RUSHED AROUND TRYING TO PREPARE THE ROOM AND GET FOOD READY FOR ALL THE MEN, BUT MARY DROPPED EVERYTHING TO SIT BY JESUS' FEET AND LISTEN TO HIS EVERY WORD.

WHY SHOULD MARY GET AWAY WITH SITTING AROUND WHILE I DO ALL THE WORK!

MARTHA, MARTHA, YOU ARE WORRYING ABOUT LOTS OF THINGS, BUT ONLY ONE THING IS IMPORTANT. MARY HAS CHOSEN WHAT IS BETTER, AND IT WON'T BE TAKEN AWAY FROM HER.

MARTHA WAS ANGRY THAT HER SISTER WASN'T HELPING HER.

Raising Lazarus from the Dead

John 11

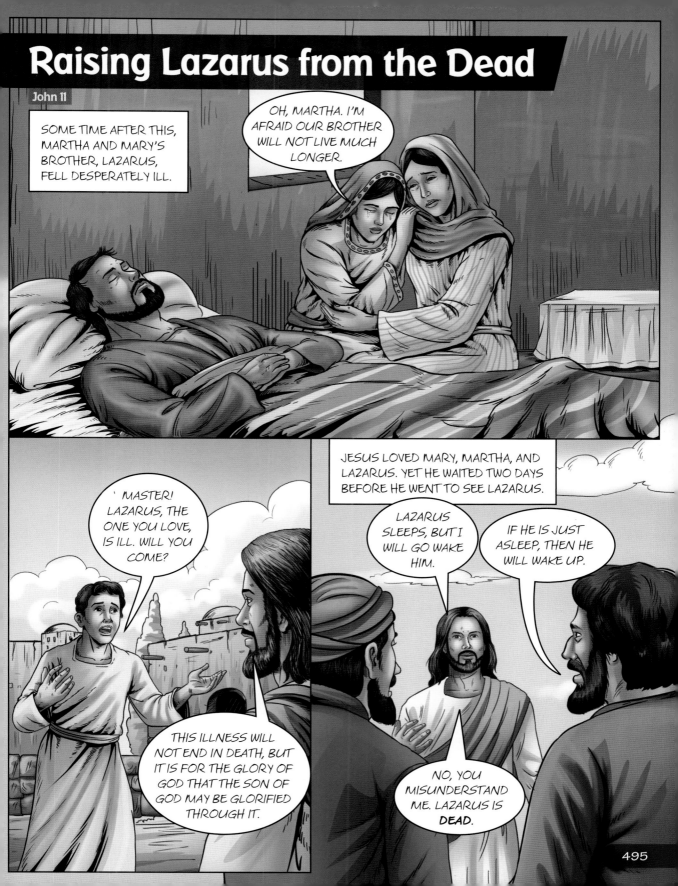

SOME TIME AFTER THIS, MARTHA AND MARY'S BROTHER, LAZARUS, FELL DESPERATELY ILL.

OH, MARTHA. I'M AFRAID OUR BROTHER WILL NOT LIVE MUCH LONGER.

MASTER! LAZARUS, THE ONE YOU LOVE, IS ILL. WILL YOU COME?

THIS ILLNESS WILL NOT END IN DEATH, BUT IT IS FOR THE GLORY OF GOD THAT THE SON OF GOD MAY BE GLORIFIED THROUGH IT.

JESUS LOVED MARY, MARTHA, AND LAZARUS. YET HE WAITED TWO DAYS BEFORE HE WENT TO SEE LAZARUS.

LAZARUS SLEEPS, BUT I WILL GO WAKE HIM.

IF HE IS JUST ASLEEP, THEN HE WILL WAKE UP.

NO, YOU MISUNDERSTAND ME. LAZARUS IS **DEAD**.

FINALLY, JESUS LEFT FOR MARY AND MARTHA'S HOUSE WITH THOMAS. MARTHA RUSHED OUT TO MEET JESUS WHILE MARY STAYED AT HOME.

LORD, IF YOU HAD BEEN HERE, MY BROTHER WOULD STILL BE ALIVE!

I KNOW THAT WHATEVER YOU ASK OF GOD, GOD WILL GIVE YOU.

YOUR BROTHER WILL RISE AGAIN.

I KNOW HE WILL RISE WHEN HE IS **RESURRECTED** ON THE LAST DAY.

I AM THE RESURRECTION AND THE LIFE. WHOEVER **BELIEVES** IN ME, EVEN IF HE DIES, WILL **LIVE**.

496

Peter the Rock

Matthew 16

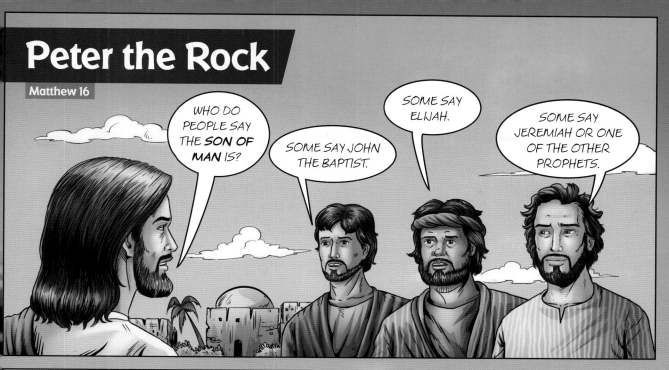

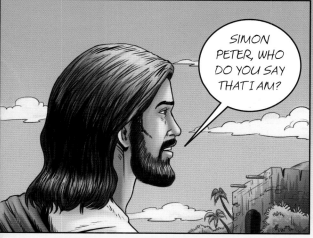

JESUS TRAVELED TO JERUSALEM KNOWING HE WOULD MEET HIS DEATH. HE TRIED TO PREPARE HIS DISCIPLES:

"ALL THINGS THAT ARE WRITTEN BY THE PROPHETS CONCERNING THE SON OF MAN WILL BE ACCOMPLISHED. FOR HE WILL BE DELIVERED TO THE GENTILES AND WILL BE MOCKED AND INSULTED AND SPIT UPON. THEY WILL SCOURGE HIM AND KILL HIM. AND THE THIRD DAY HE WILL RISE AGAIN."

JERUSALEM AT THE TIME OF JESUS

AT THE TIME OF JESUS, JERUSALEM WAS A BUSTLING CITY OF ABOUT 30,000 PEOPLE AND WAS UNDER ROMAN CONTROL. INSIDE ITS GATES, DUSTY STREETS AND ALLEYWAYS RAN IN EVERY DIRECTION. THE CITY'S ARTISANS, CRAFTSMEN, WEAVERS, BAKERS, AND CARPENTERS SAT IN OPEN-AIR SHOPS WORKING AND TRYING TO MAKE A LIVING.

A HUGE CROWD GATHERED AS JESUS ENTERED JERUSALEM. SOME WAVED PALM BRANCHES IN THE AIR, WHILE OTHERS PUT THEIR CLOAKS ON THE ROAD AS JESUS PASSED.

HOSANNA TO THE SON OF DAVID!

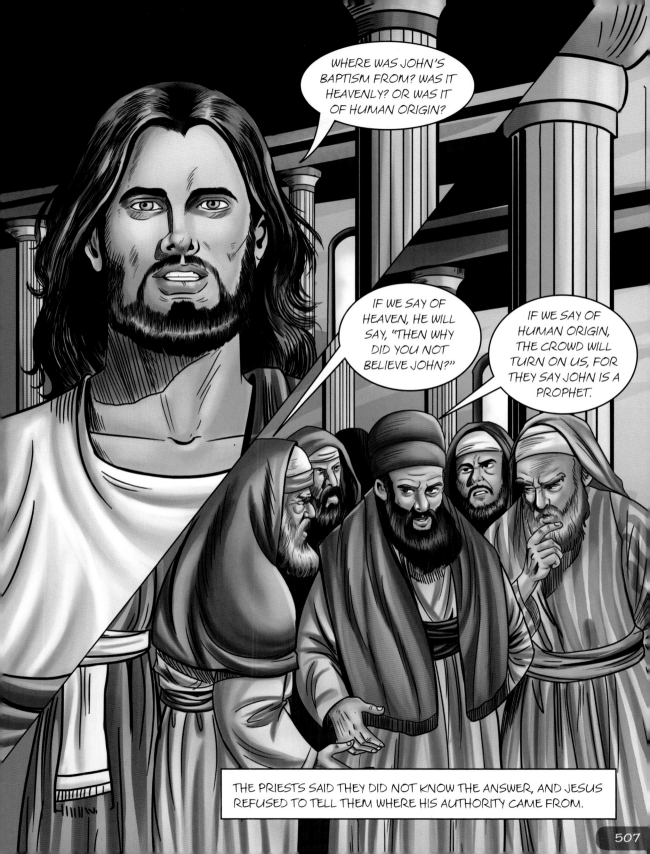

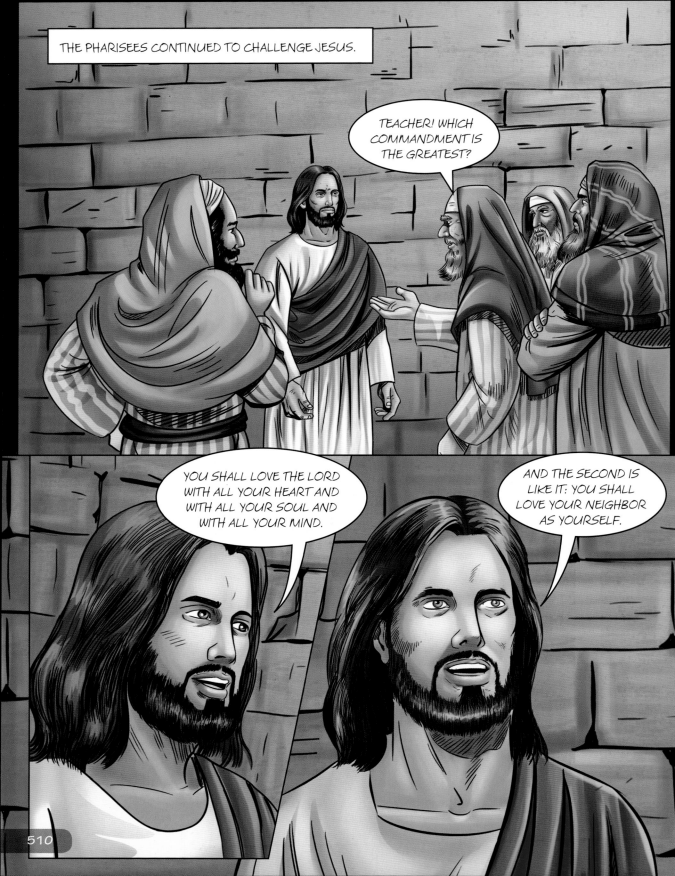

511

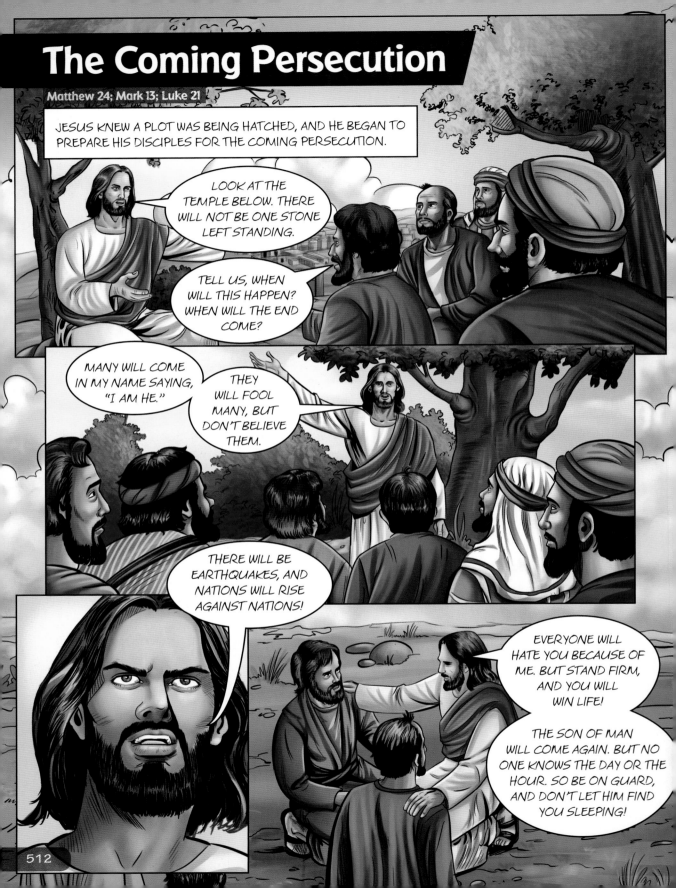

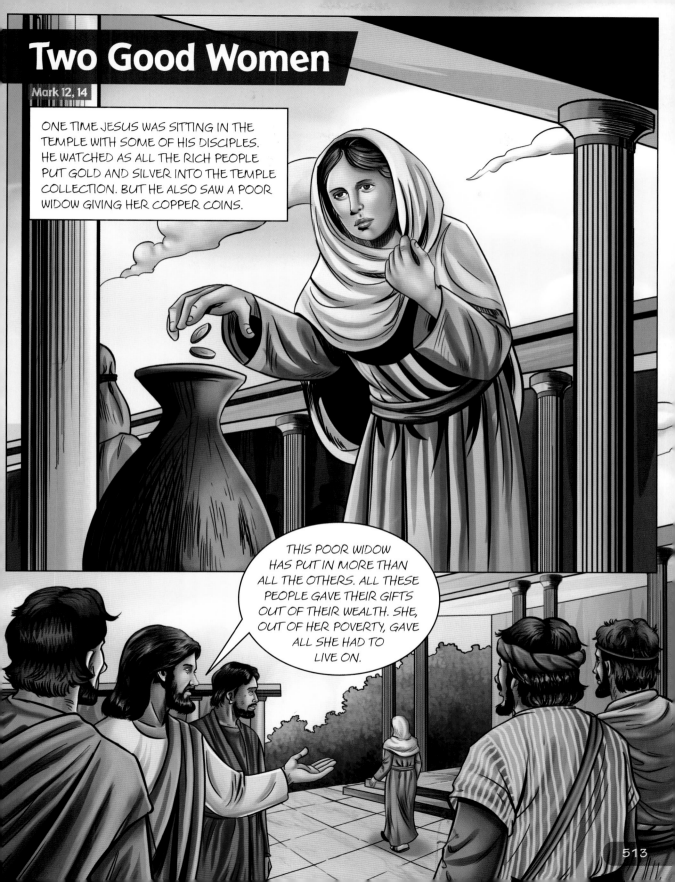

Two Good Women

Mark 12, 14

ONE TIME JESUS WAS SITTING IN THE TEMPLE WITH SOME OF HIS DISCIPLES. HE WATCHED AS ALL THE RICH PEOPLE PUT GOLD AND SILVER INTO THE TEMPLE COLLECTION. BUT HE ALSO SAW A POOR WIDOW GIVING HER COPPER COINS.

THIS POOR WIDOW HAS PUT IN MORE THAN ALL THE OTHERS. ALL THESE PEOPLE GAVE THEIR GIFTS OUT OF THEIR WEALTH. SHE, OUT OF HER POVERTY, GAVE ALL SHE HAD TO LIVE ON.

Preparing for Passover

Luke 22

WHEN PASSOVER ARRIVED, JESUS SENT PETER AND JOHN OUT TO MAKE PREPARATIONS FOR THE GREAT FEAST. THEY WERE TO GO INTO JERUSALEM AND FOLLOW A MAN CARRYING A WATER JAR.

FOLLOW ME. THERE IS A GUEST ROOM WHERE THE MASTER AND HIS DISCIPLES MAY FEAST.

PETER AND JOHN THEN FOUND EVERYTHING THEY NEEDED FOR THE CELEBRATION AND PREPARED EVERYTHING JUST AS JESUS HAD REQUESTED.

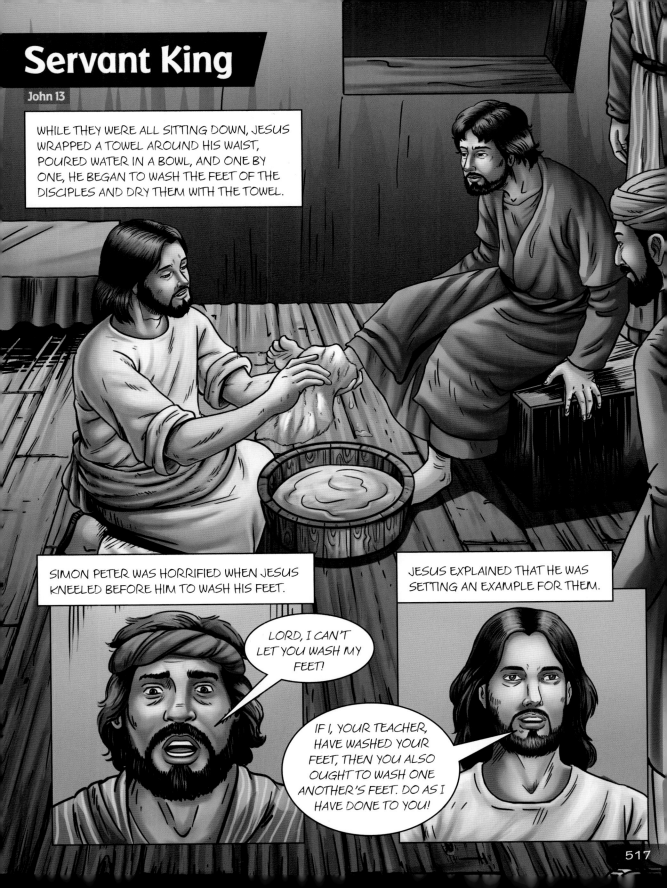

The Last Supper

Matthew 26; Mark 14; Luke 22

JESUS MADE AN ANNOUNCEMENT THAT SHOCKED HIS FOLLOWERS.

ONE OF YOU WILL **BETRAY** ME!

SURELY YOU DON'T MEAN ME, LORD?

SURELY YOU DON'T MEAN ME?

NOR ME?

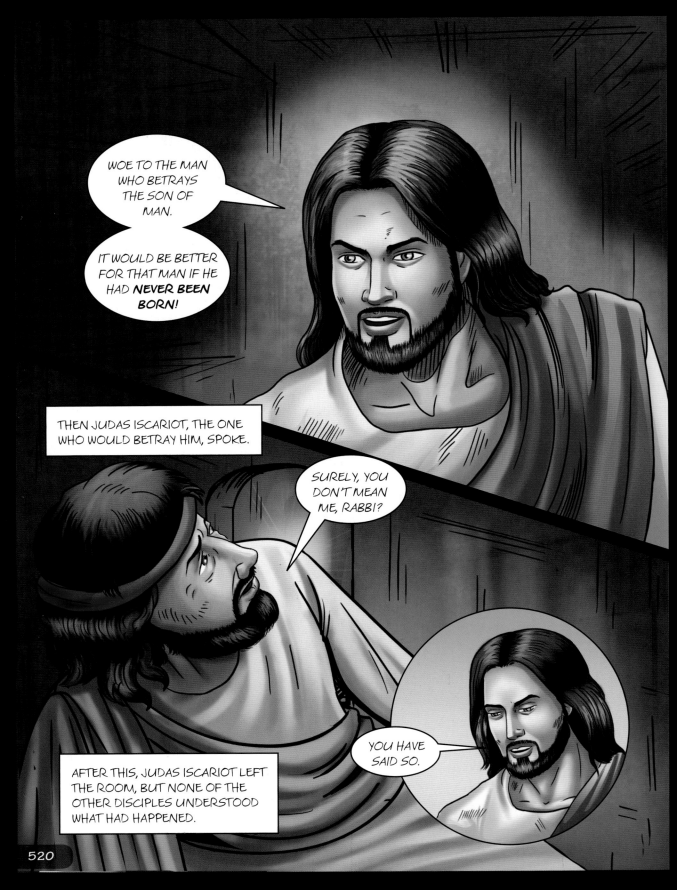

Betrayed with a Kiss

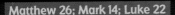

Matthew 26; Mark 14; Luke 22

AFTER SUPPER, JESUS AND THE OTHERS WALKED TOWARD THE MOUNT OF OLIVES. HE TOLD HIS FOLLOWERS THAT THEY WOULD HAVE THEIR FAITH TESTED IN THE COMING HOURS.

I TELL YOU, PETER, BEFORE THE ROOSTER CROWS, YOU WILL DENY THAT YOU KNOW ME THREE TIMES.

ALL OF YOU WILL LEAVE ME.

LORD, I WOULD NEVER LEAVE YOU. I WOULD FOLLOW YOU ANYWHERE, EVEN TO DEATH!

NO MATTER WHAT HAPPENS, I WOULD NEVER DENY THAT I KNEW YOU, LORD!

THEN JESUS AND THREE OF HIS DISCIPLES—INCLUDING PETER—WALKED TO THE GARDEN OF GETHSEMANE. JESUS BECAME SAD BECAUSE HE KNEW HIS LIFE ON EARTH WOULD SOON BE OVER.

STAY HERE WHILE I GO AND PRAY.

KEEP WATCH FOR ME.

AFTER PETER DENIED JESUS THE THIRD TIME, A ROOSTER CROWED IN THE DISTANCE. PETER REMEMBERED WHAT JESUS HAD SAID AND BEGAN TO WEEP BITTERLY.

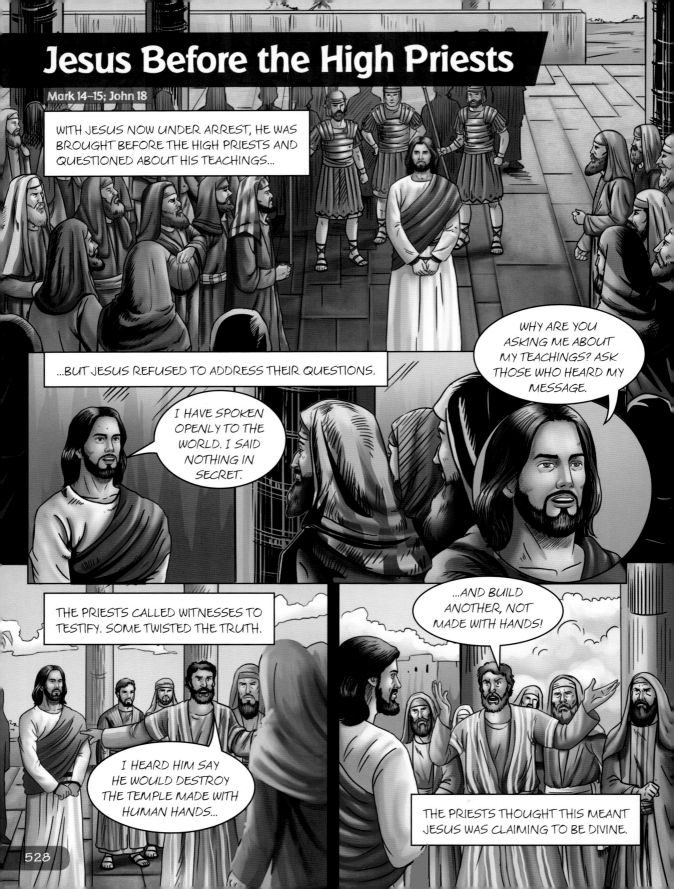

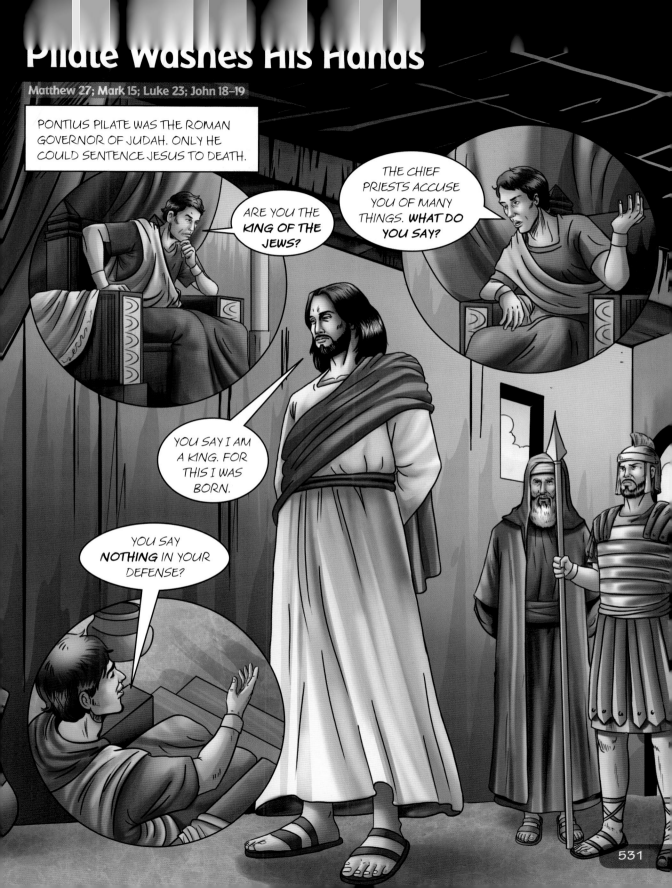

Pilate Washes His Hands

Matthew 27; Mark 15; Luke 23; John 18–19

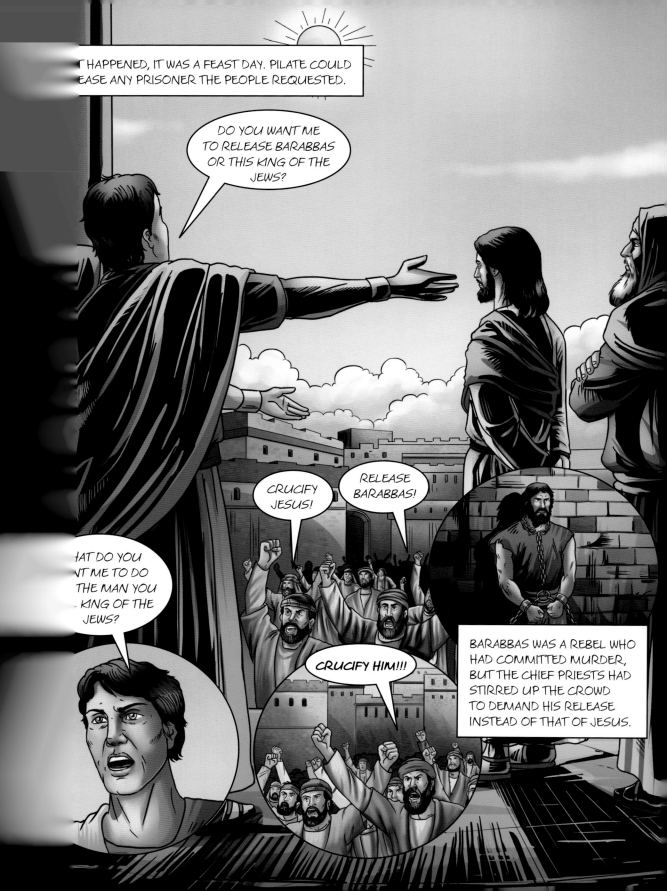

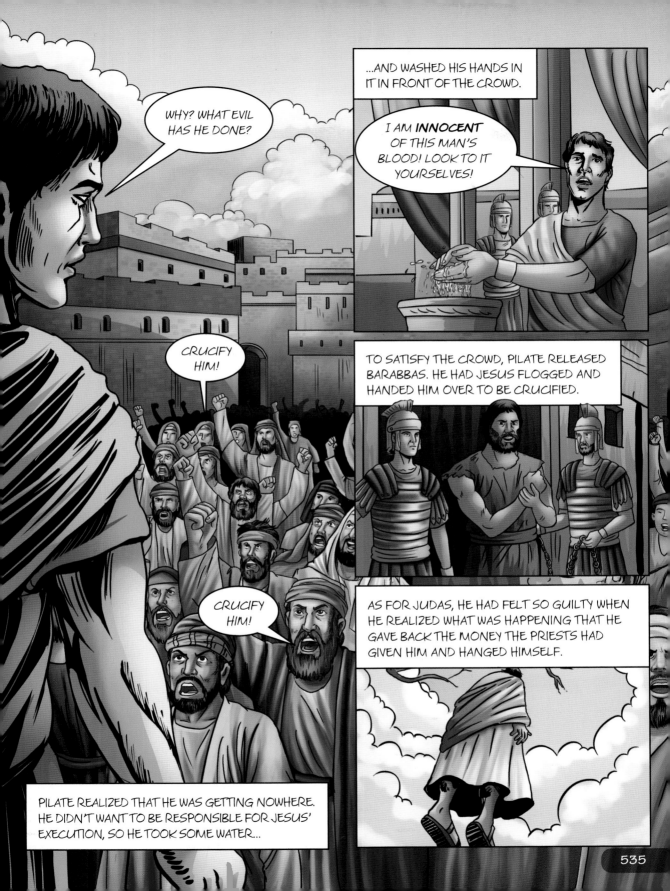

THE SOLDIERS FORCED JESUS TO CARRY THE CROSS ON WHICH HE WOULD BE CRUCIFIED OUT OF THE CITY TO A HILL CALLED GOLGOTHA, THE PLACE OF THE SKULL.

FINALLY, JESUS ARRIVED AT THE SITE OF HIS DEATH.

THE SOLDIERS OFFERED JESUS SOUR WINE TO DRINK, BUT HE REFUSED.

AND WHEN THEY CRUCIFIED HIM, THEY DIVIDED HIS CLOTHES BY CASTING LOTS.

THE SOLDIERS NAILED JESUS TO THE CROSS AND STOOD IT ON THE HILL NEAR TWO OTHERS WHO WERE ALSO BEING CRUCIFIED. ABOVE JESUS' HEAD WAS A SIGN THAT READ "THE KING OF THE JEWS."

The Resurrection

ACCORDING TO THE APOSTLE PAUL (1 CORINTHIANS 15:1–8), THE RESURRECTION OF JESUS WAS WITNESSED BY MORE THAN 500 PEOPLE. THE WRITERS OF THE GOSPELS SPECIFICALLY MENTION THE WOMEN WHO WENT TO THE TOMB, THE CHOSEN DISCIPLES, AND CLEOPAS AND HIS FRIEND WHO WERE TRAVELING TO EMMAUS.

A MOVABLE FEAST

THE DATE OF EASTER SUNDAY VARIES FROM YEAR TO YEAR BECAUSE IT IS BASED ON THE LUNAR CALENDAR. IT IS CELEBRATED ON THE FIRST SUNDAY AFTER THE FULL MOON, ON OR AFTER MARCH 21.

THE ULTIMATE SACRIFICE

EASTER IS THE MOST IMPORTANT FESTIVAL IN THE CHRISTIAN CALENDAR AND THE STARTING POINT FOR CHRISTIAN FAITH. IT CELEBRATES GOD RAISING HIS SON JESUS FROM THE DEAD AS WELL AS THE DESTRUCTION OF THE POWER OF SIN AND DEATH FOREVER. JESUS' SACRIFICE ENDED THE SEPARATION BETWEEN MAN AND GOD THAT SIN HAD CREATED.

Jesus Rises

Matthew 27–28; Mark 15–16; Luke 23–24; John 19–20

JOSEPH OF ARIMATHEA WAS A MEMBER OF THE COUNCIL BUT WAS SECRETLY A FOLLOWER OF JESUS. AFTER JESUS DIED, JOSEPH ASKED PILATE IF HE COULD PREPARE JESUS' BODY FOR BURIAL.

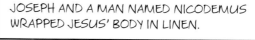

JOSEPH AND A MAN NAMED NICODEMUS WRAPPED JESUS' BODY IN LINEN.

THEY THEN BROUGHT JESUS TO A TOMB, PLACED THE BODY INSIDE, AND ROLLED A STONE OVER THE GRAVE'S OPENING.

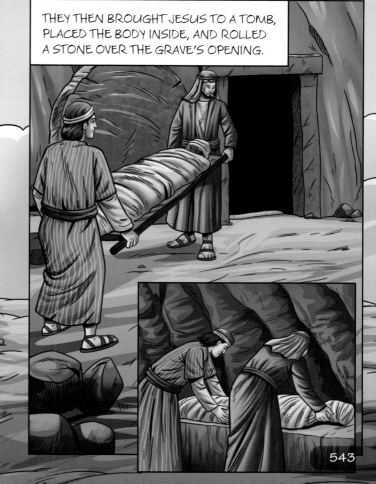

AS THEY APPROACHED THE TOMB, THE GROUND BEGAN TO SHAKE. THE WOMEN WERE SHOCKED TO SEE THAT THE STONE TO THE TOMB HAD BEEN PUSHED ASIDE.

WHY IS THE TOMB OPEN?

IT SEEMS STRANGE, DOESN'T IT?

THE WOMEN DID NOT KNOW THAT AN ANGEL OF THE LORD HAD COME DOWN FROM HEAVEN AND ROLLED BACK THE STONE. THE GUARDS WERE SO FEARFUL WHEN THEY SAW HIM THAT THEY BECAME LIKE DEAD MEN.

MEANWHILE, MARY RUSHED TO TELL PETER AND JOHN ABOUT THE EMPTY TOMB.

COME QUICKLY!

PETER AND JOHN RUSHED TO THE TOMB. INSIDE THEY FOUND ONLY THE DISCARDED CLOTH THAT HAD BEEN USED TO WRAP JESUS' BODY. THE TOMB WAS EMPTY!

THE DISCIPLES WERE FILLED WITH AWE.

551

...AND THE THREE MEN SAT DOWN TO EAT.

AS THE STRANGER BROKE BREAD, CLEOPAS AND HIS FRIEND REALIZED WHO THE STRANGER WAS.

MY LORD, IT IS YOU!

JESUS VANISHED AS SOON AS CLEOPAS AND HIS FRIEND RECOGNIZED HIM.

CLEOPAS AND HIS FRIEND RACED TO JERUSALEM TO TELL THE OTHERS WHAT THEY HAD SEEN.

WHEN HE SPOKE TO US, IT WAS AS IF OUR HEARTS WERE ON FIRE!

THE LORD IS RISEN INDEED!

559

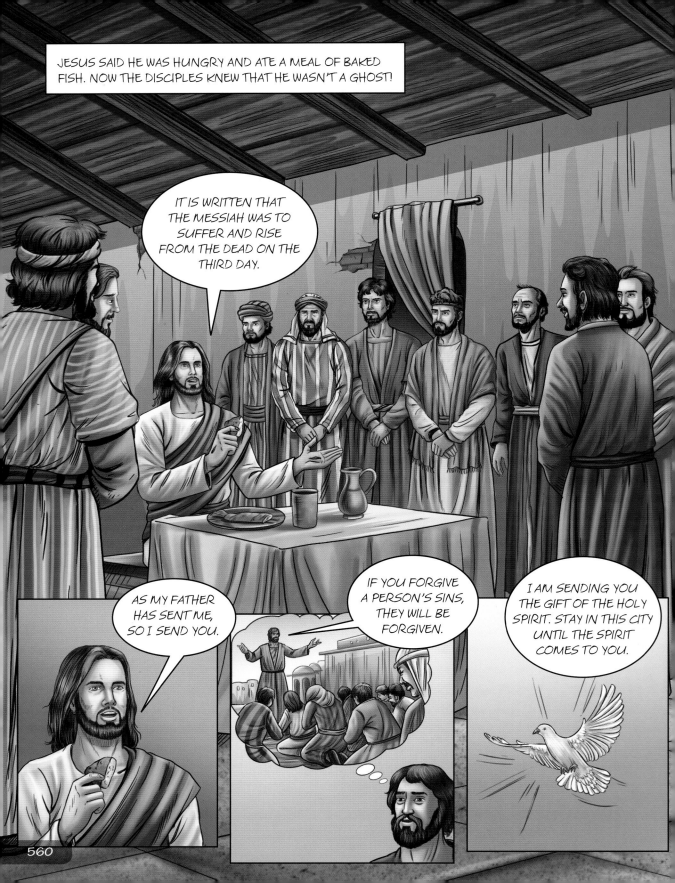

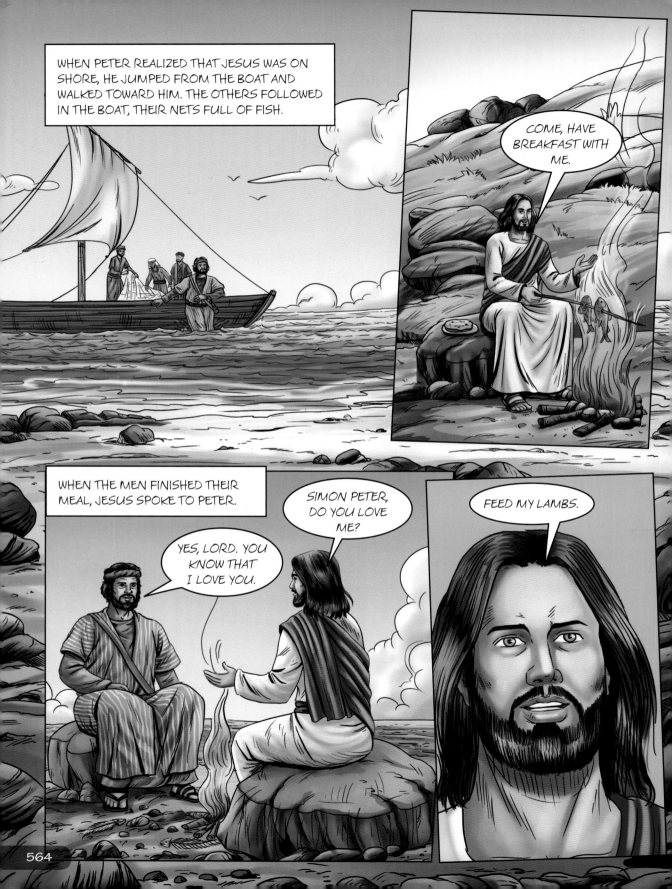

WHEN PETER REALIZED THAT JESUS WAS ON SHORE, HE JUMPED FROM THE BOAT AND WALKED TOWARD HIM. THE OTHERS FOLLOWED IN THE BOAT, THEIR NETS FULL OF FISH.

COME, HAVE BREAKFAST WITH ME.

WHEN THE MEN FINISHED THEIR MEAL, JESUS SPOKE TO PETER.

SIMON PETER, DO YOU LOVE ME?

YES, LORD. YOU KNOW THAT I LOVE YOU.

FEED MY LAMBS.

The Good News

AUTHOR OF BOOK OF ACTS: LUKE

WRITTEN: AROUND AD 60–65

CHRONICLES: GROWTH AND EXPANSION OF THE CHURCH AND IMPORTANT EVENTS IN THE LIVES OF SOME OF THE KEY APOSTLES, IN PARTICULAR PETER AND PAUL

FILLING THE GAP

AT THE BEGINNING OF THE BOOK OF ACTS WE ARE TOLD THAT THE DISCIPLES CHOSE ANOTHER MAN TO TAKE THE PLACE OF JUDAS ISCARIOT (WHO HAD HANGED HIMSELF FOLLOWING HIS BETRAYAL OF JESUS). THE MAN CHOSEN WAS MATTHIAS, WHO HAD BEEN A FOLLOWER OF JESUS SINCE HIS BAPTISM BY JOHN, BUT WE KNOW LITTLE ELSE ABOUT HIM FOR CERTAIN.

MESSENGERS

THE TWELVE DISCIPLES OF JESUS (WITH THE EXCEPTION OF JUDAS ISCARIOT WHO WAS LATER REPLACED BY MATTHIAS) WENT ON TO BECOME APOSTLES. THE WORD "APOSTLE" COMES FROM THE GREEK "APOSTOLOS" MEANING "MESSENGER," WHICH IS ITSELF DERIVED FROM THE GREEK WORD "APOSTELLEIN" MEANING "TO SEND FORTH." THESE MEN WERE SENT BY JESUS TO PASS ON THE GOOD NEWS. OTHER APOSTLES ARE MENTIONED IN THE NEW TESTAMENT, MOST NOTABLY SAUL OF TARSUS, WHO BECAME KNOWN AS PAUL AFTER HIS CONVERSION.

The Coming of the Holy Spirit

Acts 2

PENTECOST, THE JEWISH HARVEST FESTIVAL, HAD ARRIVED. JEWISH PEOPLE FROM DIFFERENT REGIONS GATHERED IN JERUSALEM TO CELEBRATE.

THE CITY IS CROWDED THIS YEAR.

YES, THE HARVEST WAS GOOD.

THE DISCIPLES WERE GATHERED TOGETHER IN A ROOM, STILL WAITING FOR THE GIFT THAT JESUS HAD PROMISED GOD WOULD SEND THEM. A FEW DAYS HAD PASSED SINCE JESUS HAD ASCENDED TO HEAVEN.

THEY HEARD A GREAT NOISE AS IF A HOWLING WIND WAS BLOWING THROUGH THE HOUSE. THEN BEFORE THEM THEY SAW WHAT SEEMED TO BE A TONGUE OF FIRE THAT SEPARATED AND CAME TO REST ON EACH OF THEM.

THEY WERE FILLED WITH THE POWER OF THE HOLY SPIRIT.

AND THEY BEGAN TO PRAISE GOD IN LANGUAGES THEY HAD NEVER SPOKEN BEFORE!

THE PEOPLE FELT DREADFUL WHEN THEY HEARD PETER'S WORDS.

WHAT ARE WE TO DO?

TELL GOD YOU ARE SORRY FOR YOUR SINS! BE BAPTIZED IN THE NAME OF JESUS CHRIST!

GOD WILL FORGIVE YOU, AND THE HOLY SPIRIT WILL COME UPON YOU.

THAT DAY, THREE THOUSAND PEOPLE WERE BAPTIZED. THEY JOINED FOLLOWERS OF JESUS AND BECAME THE FIRST CHRISTIANS.

Peter Heals the Beggar

Acts 3–4

ONE DAY, JOHN AND PETER WERE GOING TO THE TEMPLE TO PRAY. BY THE STEPS WAS A MAN WHO HAD BEEN CRIPPLED ALL HIS LIFE.

SIR, ALMS FOR A POOR BEGGAR?

EVERY DAY, HIS FRIENDS CARRIED HIM TO THE TEMPLE SO THAT HE COULD BEG FOR MONEY.

FRIENDS, CAN YOU SPARE SOME COIN FOR ONE CRIPPLED AT BIRTH?

I HAVE NEITHER SILVER NOR GOLD. BUT WHAT I DO HAVE IS THE NAME OF JESUS CHRIST.

578

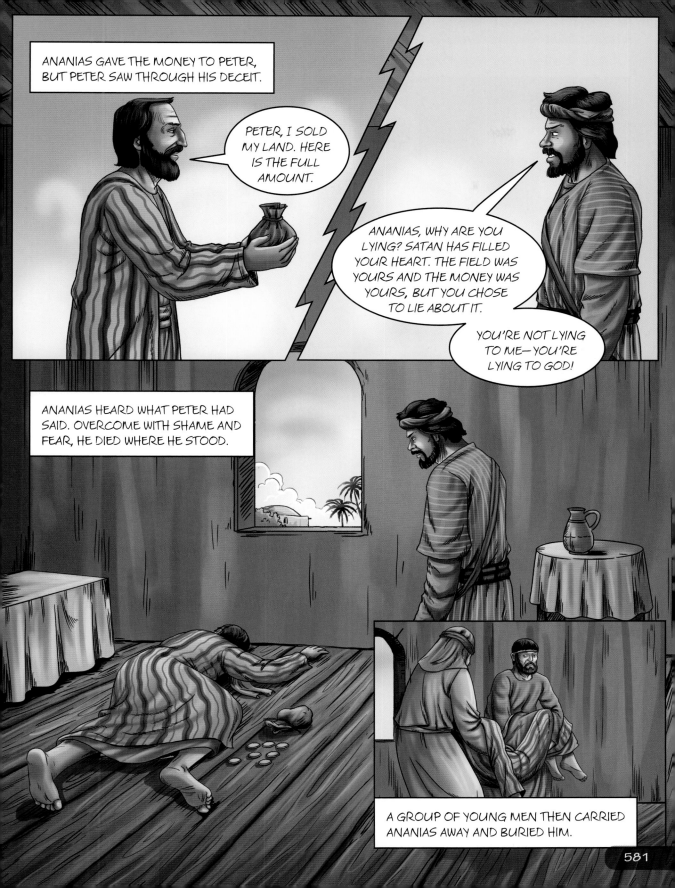

ANANIAS GAVE THE MONEY TO PETER, BUT PETER SAW THROUGH HIS DECEIT.

PETER, I SOLD MY LAND. HERE IS THE FULL AMOUNT.

ANANIAS, WHY ARE YOU LYING? SATAN HAS FILLED YOUR HEART. THE FIELD WAS YOURS AND THE MONEY WAS YOURS, BUT YOU CHOSE TO LIE ABOUT IT.

YOU'RE NOT LYING TO ME—YOU'RE LYING TO GOD!

ANANIAS HEARD WHAT PETER HAD SAID. OVERCOME WITH SHAME AND FEAR, HE DIED WHERE HE STOOD.

A GROUP OF YOUNG MEN THEN CARRIED ANANIAS AWAY AND BURIED HIM.

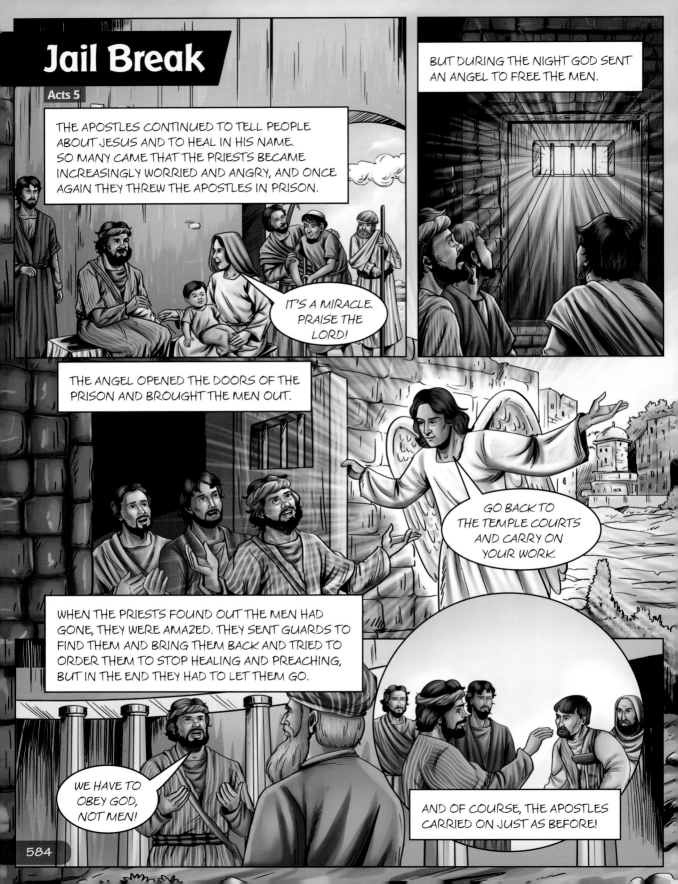

Stephen, the Martyr

THE BELIEVERS WERE GROWING IN NUMBER DAILY. TO MAKE SURE EVERYTHING WAS SHARED FAIRLY, THEY CHOSE SEVEN GOOD MEN TO BE IN CHARGE OF DIVIDING THE FOOD SO THAT THE APOSTLES COULD CONCENTRATE ON TEACHING THE WORD OF GOD AND ON PRAYER.

ONE OF THESE MEN WAS STEPHEN. HE WAS FULL OF THE HOLY SPIRIT AND HAD GREAT FAITH.

BUT STEPHEN'S ENEMIES MADE UP LIES ABOUT HIM, AND HE WAS BROUGHT BEFORE THE HIGH COUNCIL TO BE TRIED. HE FACED HIS ACCUSERS BRAVELY, HIS FACE SHINING LIKE THAT OF AN ANGEL.

YOU HAVE BETRAYED AND MURDERED GOD'S GREATEST MESSENGER. GOD GAVE YOU HIS LAW, BUT YOU DON'T OBEY IT.

LOOK! I SEE HEAVEN AND THE SON OF MAN STANDING AT THE RIGHT HAND OF GOD!

LORD, DO NOT HOLD THIS AGAINST THEM!

THIS WAS TOO MUCH FOR THE COUNCIL, WHO DRAGGED STEPHEN AWAY AND STONED HIM TO DEATH.

EVEN THEN, STEPHEN'S LAST THOUGHTS WERE NOT FOR HIMSELF.

Philip and the Ethiopian

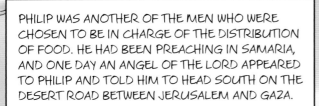

PHILIP WAS ANOTHER OF THE MEN WHO WERE CHOSEN TO BE IN CHARGE OF THE DISTRIBUTION OF FOOD. HE HAD BEEN PREACHING IN SAMARIA, AND ONE DAY AN ANGEL OF THE LORD APPEARED TO PHILIP AND TOLD HIM TO HEAD SOUTH ON THE DESERT ROAD BETWEEN JERUSALEM AND GAZA.

AS HE WALKED, PHILIP MET AN ETHIOPIAN OFFICIAL ON HIS WAY HOME FROM JERUSALEM, WHERE HE HAD GONE TO PRAY. HE WAS READING FROM THE BOOK OF ISAIAH.

SIR, YOU LOOK PUZZLED. CAN I HELP?

CAN YOU EXPLAIN THIS TO ME?

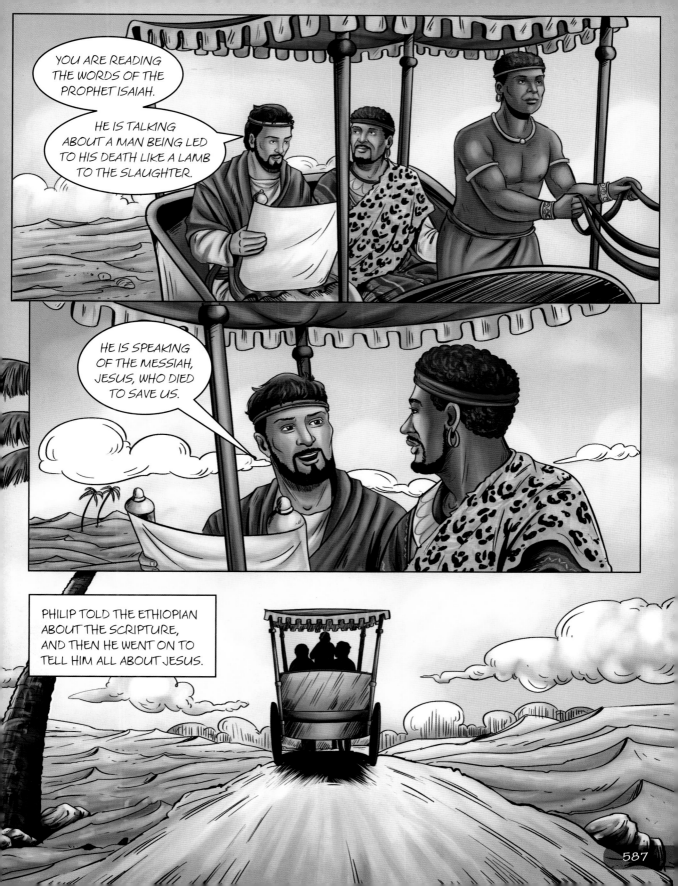

587

A Special Woman

Acts 9

IN JOPPA THERE LIVED A GOOD WOMAN NAMED TABITHA, WHO WAS A FOLLOWER OF JESUS. SHE LOVED TO HELP PEOPLE AND GIVE MONEY TO THOSE IN NEED, AND SHE MADE CLOTHES FOR THE POOR.

BUT SADLY TABITHA BECAME ILL AND DIED. WHEN HER FRIENDS LEARNED THAT PETER WAS PREACHING NEARBY, THEY BEGGED HIM TO COME AND HELP.

PLEASE HELP, PETER!

PETER WENT WITH THEM. THEY TOOK HIM TO HER ROOM. HE SENT EVERYONE AWAY AND PRAYED. THEN HE SPOKE TO TABITHA.

TABITHA, STAND UP!

TABITHA OPENED HER EYES AND STOOD UP. THEN PETER CALLED THE MOURNERS BACK INTO THE ROOM, AND THEY WERE FILLED WITH JOY AND PRAISE FOR GOD.

HERE IS YOUR FRIEND BACK WITH YOU!

PRAISE THE LORD!

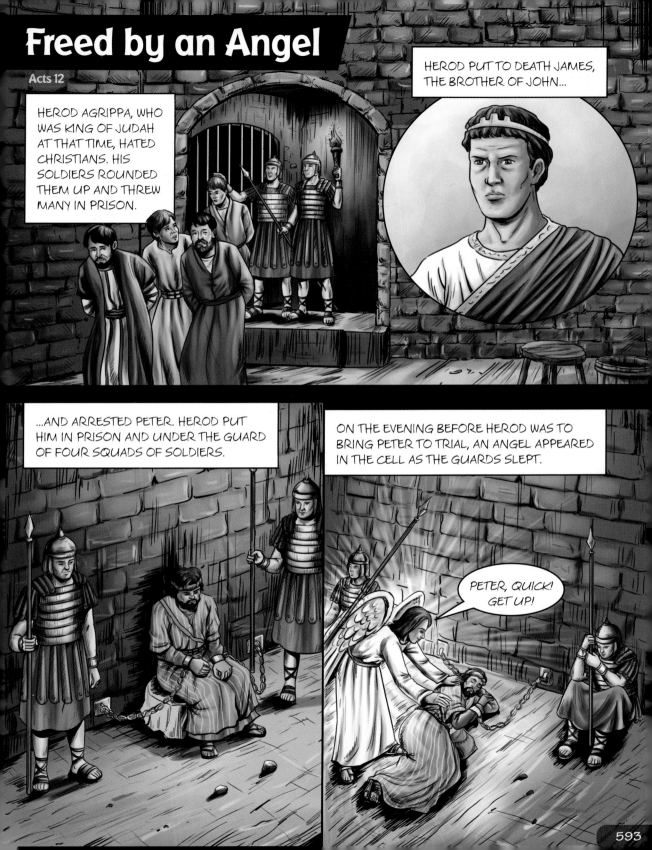

Freed by an Angel

Acts 12

HEROD AGRIPPA, WHO WAS KING OF JUDAH AT THAT TIME, HATED CHRISTIANS. HIS SOLDIERS ROUNDED THEM UP AND THREW MANY IN PRISON.

HEROD PUT TO DEATH JAMES, THE BROTHER OF JOHN...

...AND ARRESTED PETER. HEROD PUT HIM IN PRISON AND UNDER THE GUARD OF FOUR SQUADS OF SOLDIERS.

ON THE EVENING BEFORE HEROD WAS TO BRING PETER TO TRIAL, AN ANGEL APPEARED IN THE CELL AS THE GUARDS SLEPT.

PETER, QUICK! GET UP!

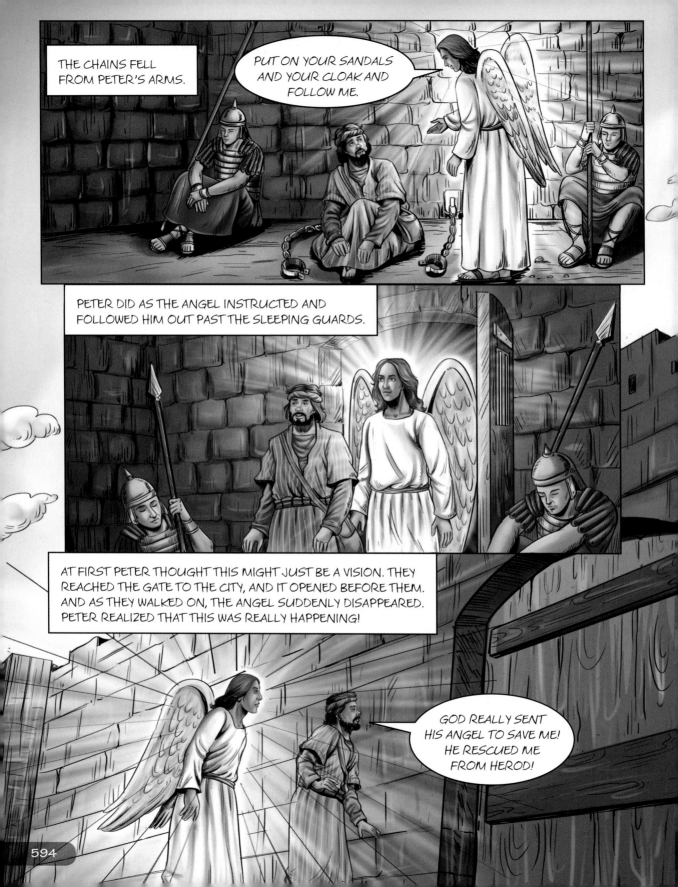

THE CHAINS FELL FROM PETER'S ARMS.

PUT ON YOUR SANDALS AND YOUR CLOAK AND FOLLOW ME.

PETER DID AS THE ANGEL INSTRUCTED AND FOLLOWED HIM OUT PAST THE SLEEPING GUARDS.

AT FIRST PETER THOUGHT THIS MIGHT JUST BE A VISION. THEY REACHED THE GATE TO THE CITY, AND IT OPENED BEFORE THEM. AND AS THEY WALKED ON, THE ANGEL SUDDENLY DISAPPEARED. PETER REALIZED THAT THIS WAS REALLY HAPPENING!

GOD REALLY SENT HIS ANGEL TO SAVE ME! HE RESCUED ME FROM HEROD!

594

Hero Profile
Paul—Spreading the Word

BORN: TARSUS (IN MODERN-DAY TURKEY) CIRCA AD 1–5

DIED: PROBABLY IN ROME CIRCA AD 67

LINEAGE: OF BENJAMITE DESCENT

SAUL OR PAUL?

IT WAS FAIRLY COMMON FOR THE JEWS AT THAT TIME TO HAVE TWO NAMES, ONE HEBREW AND THE OTHER LATIN OR GREEK. WHILE SAUL WAS HIS JEWISH NAME, SAUL WAS ALSO A ROMAN CITIZEN AND BECAME BETTER KNOWN BY HIS LATIN NAME, PAUL. HE POSSIBLY FELT THIS NAME WAS MORE APPROPRIATE FOR HIS MISSIONARY WORK LATER ON IN HIS LIFE.

THE SWORD OF THE SPIRIT

ARTISTS SUCH AS RUBENS AND REMBRANDT DEPICTED PAUL WITH A SWORD AND A BOOK. THE SWORD IS SAID TO SYMBOLIZE THE MANNER OF HIS DEATH. ALTHOUGH THE BIBLE DOES NOT SAY WHEN OR HOW PAUL DIED, MANY BELIEVE THE EMPEROR NERO ORDERED HIS EXECUTION IN ROME AROUND AD 67—AS A ROMAN CITIZEN, HE HAD THE RIGHT TO BE PUT TO DEATH BY HAVING HIS HEAD CUT OFF WITH A SWORD, RATHER THAN BY CRUCIFIXION. THE BOOK SYMBOLIZES HIS WRITINGS, WHICH HE REFERRED TO AS "THE SWORD OF THE SPIRIT."

Saul Sees the Light

Acts 7–9

THERE WAS A MAN NAMED SAUL FROM TARSUS. HE WAS A JEW WHO BELIEVED THAT THESE NEW CHRISTIANS WERE TROUBLE-MAKERS AND HERETICS. THEY CLAIMED THAT JESUS WAS THE MESSIAH! HE THOUGHT THIS WAS BLASPHEMY. AND HE BELIEVED HE WAS DOING GOD'S WORK WHEN HE ARRESTED THEM AND EVEN EXECUTED THEM.

...AND PUT THEM AND THEIR HUSBANDS, SONS, AND BROTHERS INTO PRISON.

HE DRAGGED WOMEN OUT OF THEIR HOMES...

HE EVEN WATCHED AS THE APOSTLE STEPHEN WAS STONED TO DEATH.

SAUL DISLIKED THE CHRISTIANS SO MUCH THAT HE ASKED THE HIGH PRIEST OF JERUSALEM TO SEND HIM TO DAMASCUS IN SYRIA SO HE COULD BRING BACK AND IMPRISON THE BELIEVERS.

IF I FIND ANYONE WHO BELIEVES IN THE WAY, I'LL BRING THEM BACK IN CHAINS.

THE HIGH PRIEST GAVE SAUL HIS BLESSING, AND HE BEGAN A JOURNEY TO DAMASCUS.

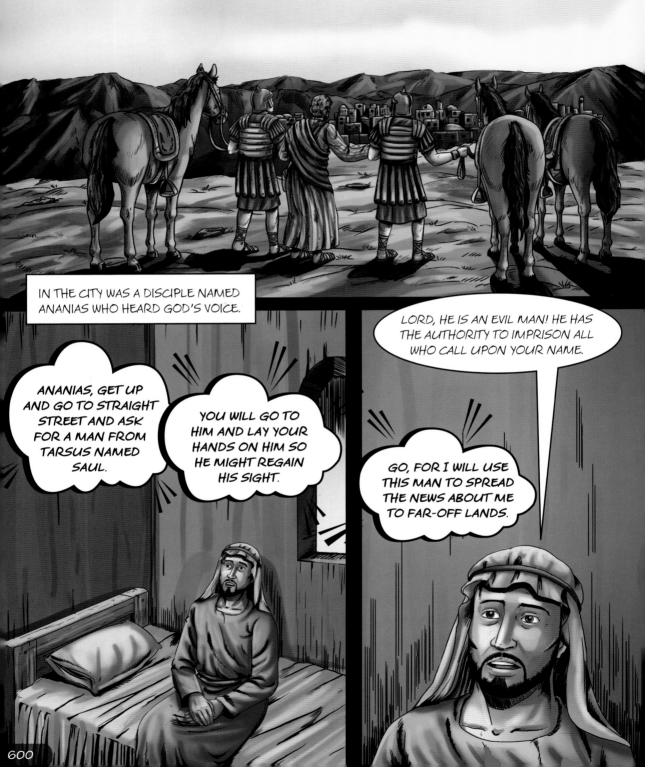

601

Escape in a Basket

Acts 9

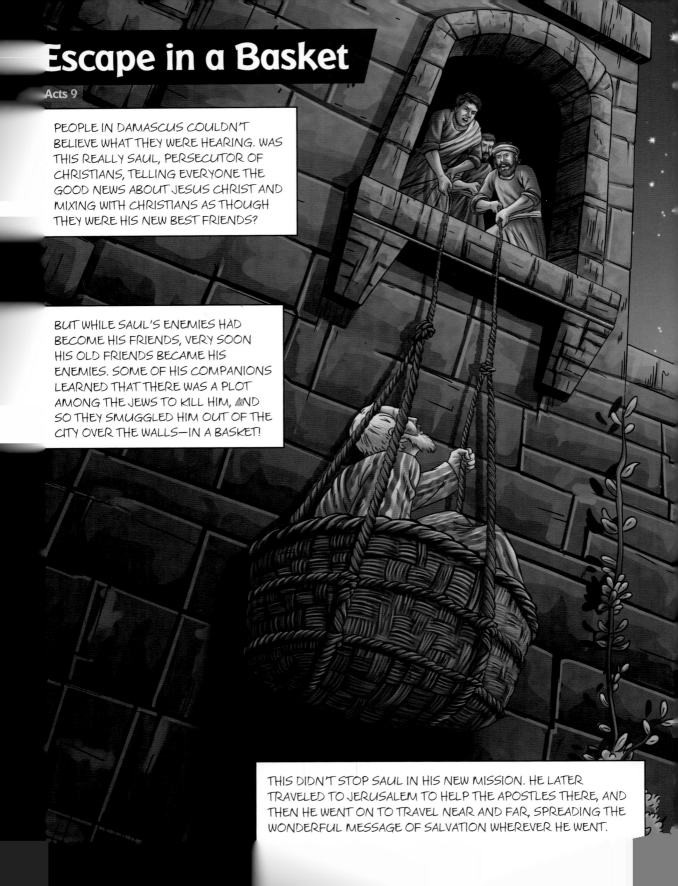

PEOPLE IN DAMASCUS COULDN'T BELIEVE WHAT THEY WERE HEARING. WAS THIS REALLY SAUL, PERSECUTOR OF CHRISTIANS, TELLING EVERYONE THE GOOD NEWS ABOUT JESUS CHRIST AND MIXING WITH CHRISTIANS AS THOUGH THEY WERE HIS NEW BEST FRIENDS?

BUT WHILE SAUL'S ENEMIES HAD BECOME HIS FRIENDS, VERY SOON HIS OLD FRIENDS BECAME HIS ENEMIES. SOME OF HIS COMPANIONS LEARNED THAT THERE WAS A PLOT AMONG THE JEWS TO KILL HIM, AND SO THEY SMUGGLED HIM OUT OF THE CITY OVER THE WALLS—IN A BASKET!

THIS DIDN'T STOP SAUL IN HIS NEW MISSION. HE LATER TRAVELED TO JERUSALEM TO HELP THE APOSTLES THERE, AND THEN HE WENT ON TO TRAVEL NEAR AND FAR, SPREADING THE WONDERFUL MESSAGE OF SALVATION WHEREVER HE WENT.

Struck Blind

Acts 13

GOD HAD A SPECIAL TASK FOR PAUL. HE TOLD PAUL AND A MAN NAMED BARNABAS TO GO ON A JOURNEY TO SPREAD THE GOOD NEWS TO PEOPLE WHO HAD NOT YET HEARD ABOUT JESUS. THIS WAS THE FIRST OF PAUL'S MISSIONARY JOURNEYS.

PAUL'S MISSIONARY JOURNEYS

→ PAUL'S FIRST MISSIONARY JOURNEY
→ PAUL'S SECOND MISSIONARY JOURNEY
→ PAUL'S THIRD MISSIONARY JOURNEY
→ PAUL'S VOYAGE TO ROME

FIRST THEY WENT TO CYPRUS WHERE THE ROMAN GOVERNOR SENT FOR THEM. ONE OF HIS ATTENDANTS WAS A SORCERER NAMED ELYMAS WHO TRIED TO STOP THE GOVERNOR FROM LISTENING TO PAUL.

THEY'RE TELLING YOU NOTHING BUT LIES!

YOU ARE THE SON OF THE DEVIL! YOU TRY TO TURN THE LORD'S TRUTH'S INTO LIES! BUT YOU WILL BE STRUCK BLIND!

INSTANTLY, THE SORCERER'S EYES CLOUDED OVER, AND HE COULD SEE NOTHING.

I CAN'T SEE! I CAN'T SEE!

THE GOVERNOR WAS SO AMAZED THAT HE BECAME A CHRISTIAN.

On the Road

Acts 13

PAUL AND BARNABAS NEXT SAILED TO THE LAND WE KNOW AS TURKEY, GOING FROM TOWN TO TOWN, PREACHING THE GOOD NEWS. IN ANTIOCH IN PISIDIA THEY SPOKE TO EVERYONE THEY COULD FIND, BOTH GENTILES AND JEWS.

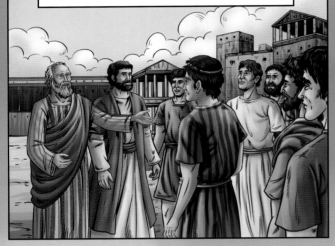

THE NEXT WEEK ALMOST THE WHOLE CITY TURNED UP AT THE SYNAGOGUE TO HEAR THEM SPEAK. SOME OF THE JEWS WERE ANGRY AT THIS. PAUL INSISTED THAT HIS MESSAGE WAS FOR THE GENTILES AS WELL AS THE JEWS.

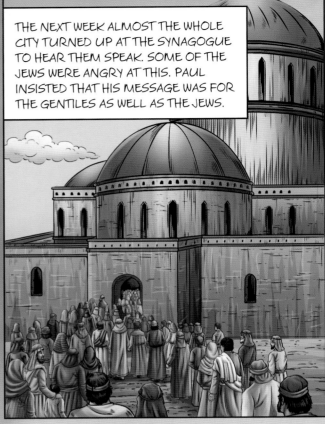

SOME OF THE JEWISH LEADERS THREW PAUL AND BARNABAS OUT OF TOWN.

WE NEED TO GET RID OF THEM!

BUT THE APOSTLES WERE DETERMINED TO SPREAD THE GOOD NEWS AND CONTINUED ON THIER WAY.

Off to Macedonia

Acts 15–16

SOME TIME LATER PAUL SET OFF ON ANOTHER MISSIONARY JOURNEY. THIS TIME HE TOOK A MAN NAMED SILAS WITH HIM. THEY WENT BACK TO SOME OF THE NEW CHURCHES THAT PAUL HAD SET UP TO HELP THE PEOPLE.

IT'S GOOD TO SEE YOU AGAIN!

TELL ME HOW YOU HAVE BEEN GETTING ON.

ONE NIGHT PAUL HAD A STRANGE DREAM. HE SAW A MAN FROM MACEDONIA ASKING FOR HELP.

COME TO MACEDONIA, PAUL! PLEASE HELP US!

PAUL AND SILAS TRAVELED TO MACEDONIA THE NEXT DAY AND CAME TO THE CITY OF PHILIPPI. THERE THEY MET A WOMAN NAMED LYDIA, WHO OPENED HER HEART TO THE WORD OF GOD AND WELCOMED THE MEN INTO HER HOME.

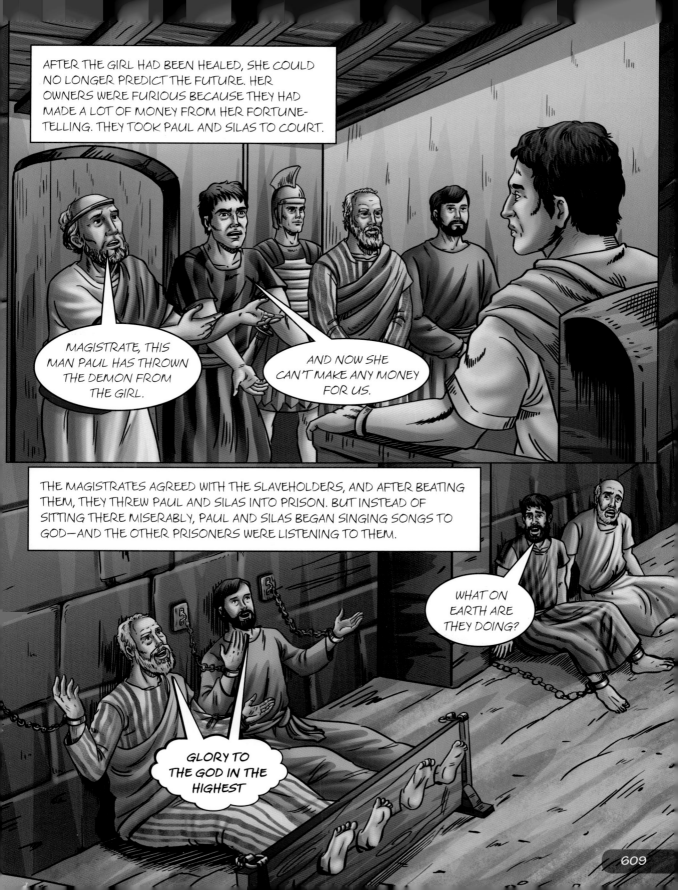

The Earthquake

Acts 16–17

THAT NIGHT AN EARTHQUAKE SHOOK THE PRISON, OPENING THE ENTRANCE.

CONVINCED THAT PAUL AND SILAS HAD ESCAPED, THE JAILER DREW HIS SWORD TO KILL HIMSELF. HE HEARD PAUL CALL OUT, AND WALKED INSIDE THE CELL TO SEE...

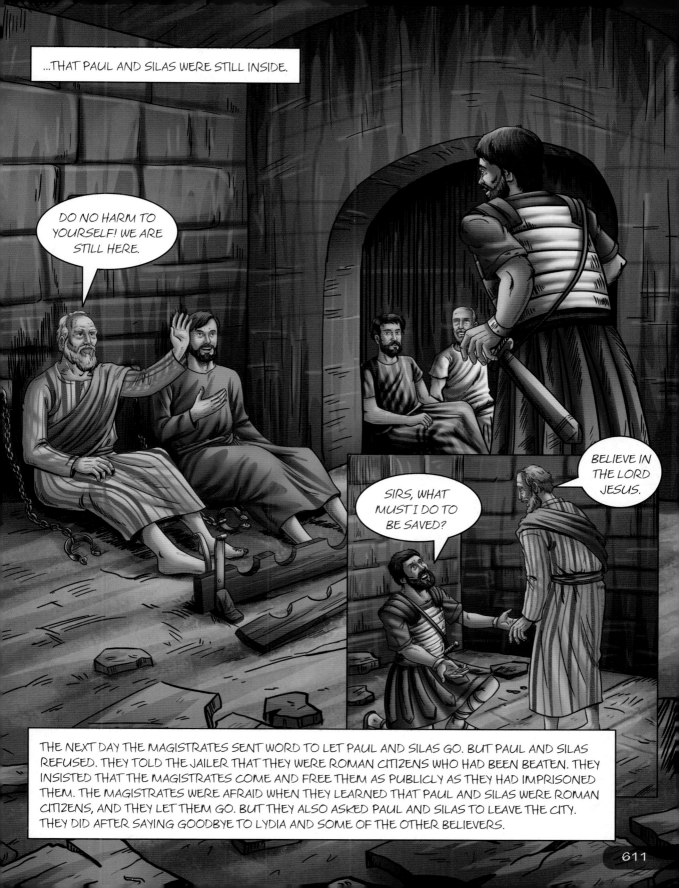

...THAT PAUL AND SILAS WERE STILL INSIDE.

DO NO HARM TO YOURSELF! WE ARE STILL HERE.

BELIEVE IN THE LORD JESUS.

SIRS, WHAT MUST I DO TO BE SAVED?

THE NEXT DAY THE MAGISTRATES SENT WORD TO LET PAUL AND SILAS GO. BUT PAUL AND SILAS REFUSED. THEY TOLD THE JAILER THAT THEY WERE ROMAN CITIZENS WHO HAD BEEN BEATEN. THEY INSISTED THAT THE MAGISTRATES COME AND FREE THEM AS PUBLICLY AS THEY HAD IMPRISONED THEM. THE MAGISTRATES WERE AFRAID WHEN THEY LEARNED THAT PAUL AND SILAS WERE ROMAN CITIZENS, AND THEY LET THEM GO. BUT THEY ALSO ASKED PAUL AND SILAS TO LEAVE THE CITY. THEY DID AFTER SAYING GOODBYE TO LYDIA AND SOME OF THE OTHER BELIEVERS.

Riot at Ephesus

Acts 19

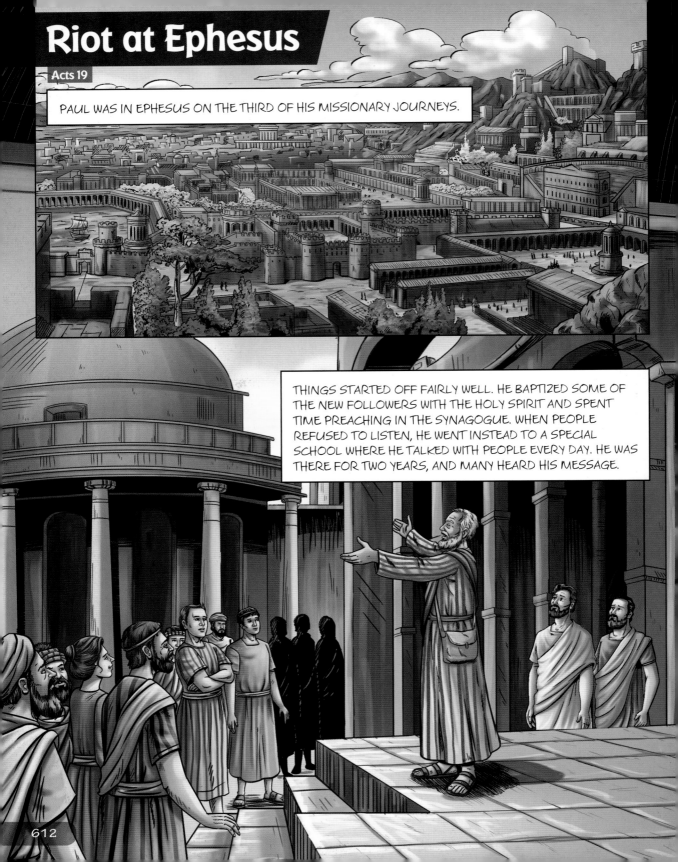

PAUL WAS IN EPHESUS ON THE THIRD OF HIS MISSIONARY JOURNEYS.

THINGS STARTED OFF FAIRLY WELL. HE BAPTIZED SOME OF THE NEW FOLLOWERS WITH THE HOLY SPIRIT AND SPENT TIME PREACHING IN THE SYNAGOGUE. WHEN PEOPLE REFUSED TO LISTEN, HE WENT INSTEAD TO A SPECIAL SCHOOL WHERE HE TALKED WITH PEOPLE EVERY DAY. HE WAS THERE FOR TWO YEARS, AND MANY HEARD HIS MESSAGE.

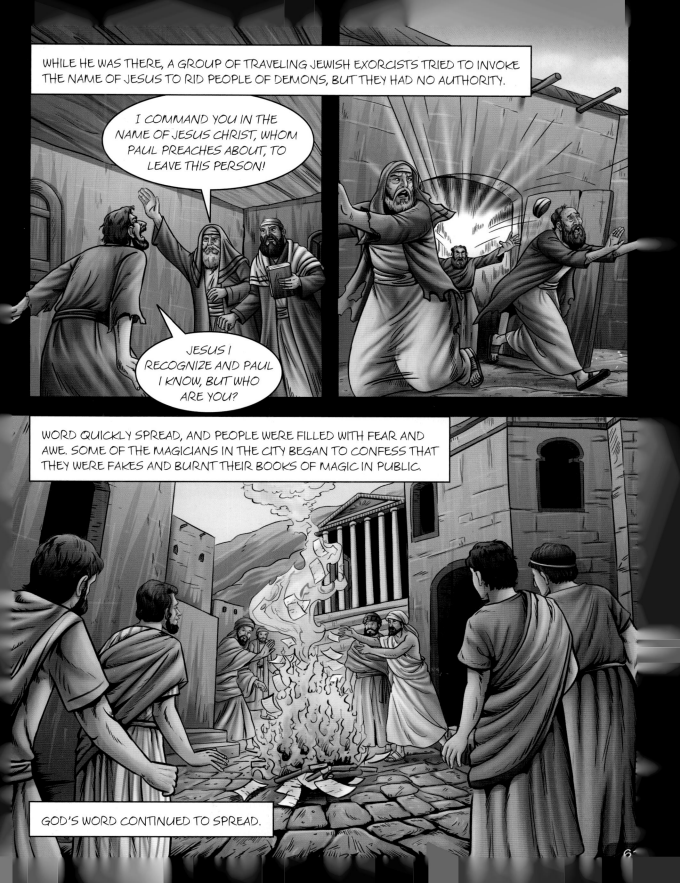

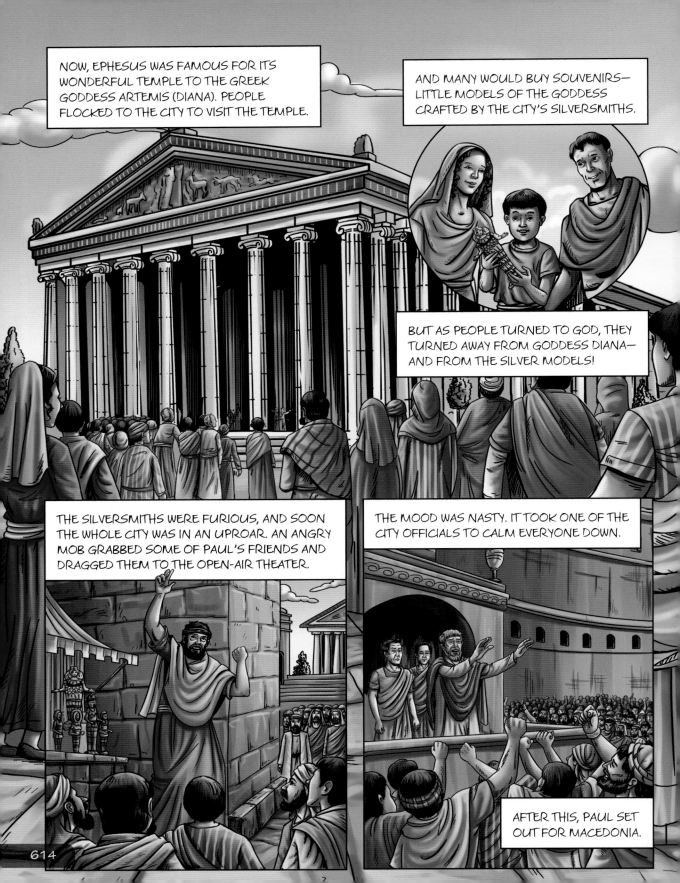

A Big Fall

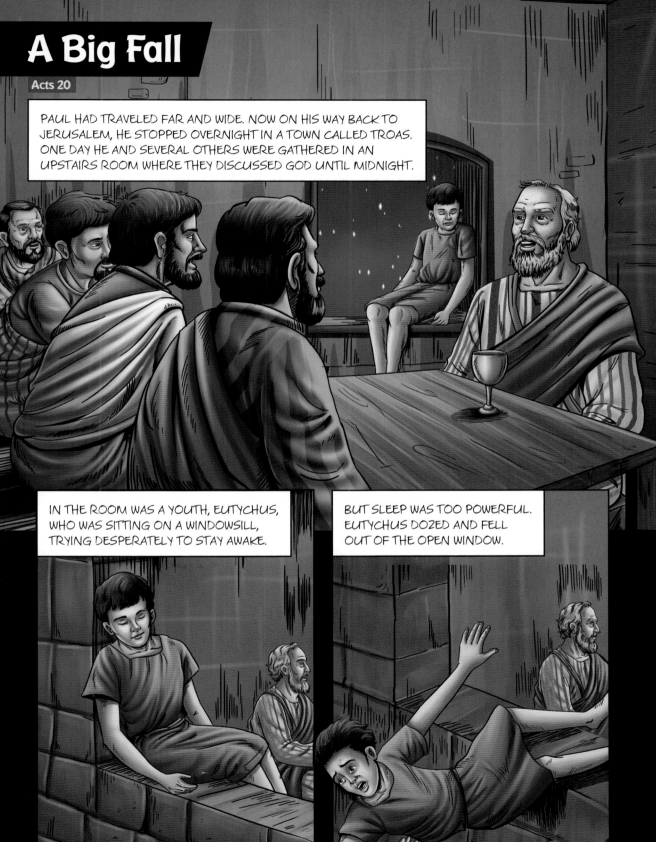

Acts 20

PAUL HAD TRAVELED FAR AND WIDE. NOW ON HIS WAY BACK TO JERUSALEM, HE STOPPED OVERNIGHT IN A TOWN CALLED TROAS. ONE DAY HE AND SEVERAL OTHERS WERE GATHERED IN AN UPSTAIRS ROOM WHERE THEY DISCUSSED GOD UNTIL MIDNIGHT.

IN THE ROOM WAS A YOUTH, EUTYCHUS, WHO WAS SITTING ON A WINDOWSILL, TRYING DESPERATELY TO STAY AWAKE.

BUT SLEEP WAS TOO POWERFUL. EUTYCHUS DOZED AND FELL OUT OF THE OPEN WINDOW.

PAUL CRADLED EUTYCHUS IN HIS ARMS.

THE BOY STOOD UP. HE WAS ALIVE, AND EVERYONE WAS AMAZED!

PAUL THEN WENT UPSTAIRS TO EAT.

THE PEOPLE ALL WENT BACK UPSTAIRS WITH PAUL AND LISTENED TO HIM UNTIL DAYBREAK!

DON'T BE ALARMED. HE'S ALIVE!

Please Don't Go

Acts 20

PAUL'S FRIENDS DIDN'T WANT HIM TO GO TO JERUSALEM. THEY KNEW IT WOULD BE DANGEROUS THERE FOR HIM AND BEGGED HIM TO STAY.

PLEASE DON'T TRY TO CHANGE MY MIND. THIS IS WHAT I HAVE TO DO. I AM READY NOT ONLY TO BE PUT IN CHAINS FOR JESUS BUT TO DIE FOR HIM.

BEFORE HE LEFT, PAUL PRAYED WITH HIS FRIENDS. THEY KNEW THAT THEY WOULD NEVER SEE HIM AGAIN.

Trouble in Jerusalem

Acts 21–22

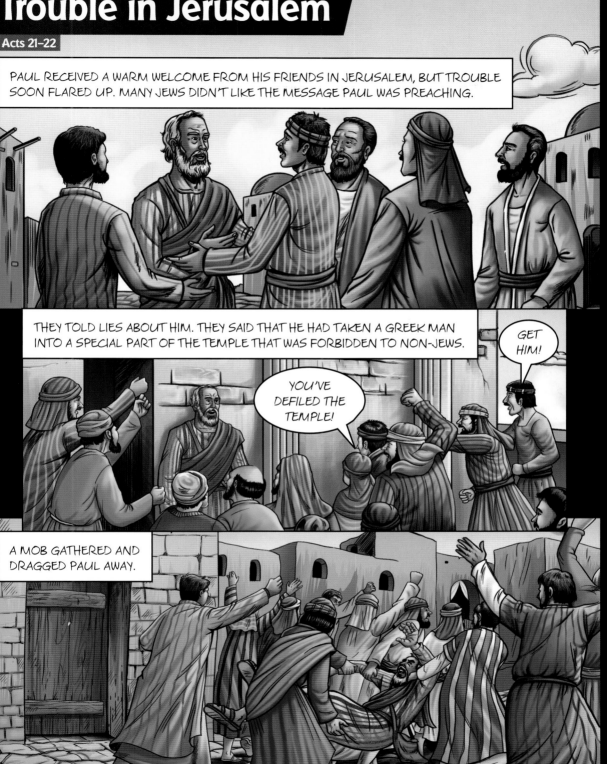

PAUL RECEIVED A WARM WELCOME FROM HIS FRIENDS IN JERUSALEM, BUT TROUBLE SOON FLARED UP. MANY JEWS DIDN'T LIKE THE MESSAGE PAUL WAS PREACHING.

THEY TOLD LIES ABOUT HIM. THEY SAID THAT HE HAD TAKEN A GREEK MAN INTO A SPECIAL PART OF THE TEMPLE THAT WAS FORBIDDEN TO NON-JEWS.

GET HIM!

YOU'VE DEFILED THE TEMPLE!

A MOB GATHERED AND DRAGGED PAUL AWAY.

THE CROWD WAS IN A FRENZY AND WANTED TO KILL PAUL.

BUT FORTUNATELY FOR PAUL, THE ROMAN COMMANDER LEARNED OF THE UPROAR AND RUSHED TO STOP THEM.

GRAB THAT MAN AND BRING HIM TO SAFETY!

GET RID OF HIM!

Conspiracy and Confusion

Acts 22–26

THE COMMANDER SENT PAUL BEFORE THE JEWISH COUNCIL TO SEE WHY HE HAD BEEN ACCUSED BY THE MOB, BUT THE COUNCIL ONLY ARGUED AND SENT HIM BACK. SOME OF HIS ENEMIES PLOTTED TO KILL HIM, AND SO THE COMMANDER SMUGGLED PAUL OUT OF THE CITY AT NIGHT AND SENT HIM TO ROMAN HEADQUARTERS AT CAESAREA.

IN CAESAREA NOBODY SEEMED TO KNOW WHAT TO DO WITH PAUL EITHER. HE SPOKE TO FIRST ONE ROMAN GOVERNOR AND THEN ANOTHER. ALTHOUGH HE HAD DONE NOTHING WRONG, THEY STILL KEPT HIM UNDER GUARD. IN THE END HE DEMANDED, AS WAS HIS RIGHT AS A ROMAN CITIZEN, TO BE HEARD BY THE EMPEROR IN ROME. BEFORE HE LEFT, HE WAS SEEN BY KING AGRIPPA, WHO FOUND NO FAULT IN HIM.

IF IT WERE UP TO ME, I WOULD SET YOU FREE. BUT YOU HAVE ASKED TO GO TO ROME, SO TO ROME YOU MUST GO.

The Storm and the Shipwreck

Acts 27–28

PAUL AND SOME OTHER PRISONERS BOARDED A SHIP, ESCORTED BY A ROMAN CENTURION NAMED JULIUS. THINGS BEGAN SMOOTHLY. THEY CHANGED SHIPS MID-JOURNEY, BUT THEN THE WEATHER CHANGED.

DO YOU THINK CAESAR WILL HEAR YOUR CASE?

I DO! I BELIEVE GOD IS WITH ME.

AS THE SHIP SAILED ACROSS THE MEDITERRANEAN, STORMS BEGAN TO RISE UP, AND STRONG WINDS BLEW THE SHIP OFF COURSE.

PAUL TRIED TO WARN THE CAPTAIN AND JULIUS THAT IT WOULD BE DANGEROUS TO CONTINUE, BUT HE WAS IGNORED.

MEN, I CAN SEE THIS VOYAGE MIGHT KILL US. IT'S TOO DANGEROUS TO GO ON.

PILOT! KEEP THE COURSE STEADY AND SET SAIL FOR CRETE.

DAYS PASSED, AND THE STORM CONTINUED TO RAGE. DESPERATE AND TERRIFIED, SOME OF THE SAILORS TRIED TO LEAVE IN ONE OF THE LIFEBOATS.

BUT PAUL WARNED JULIUS AND THE CAPTAIN THAT ALL MUST STAY WITH THE SHIP TO BE SAVED.

UNLESS THE MEN STAY WITH THE SHIP, THEY WILL DIE.

THE SOLDIERS LISTENED TO PAUL. THEY CUT THE ROPES OF THE LIFEBOAT AND SET IT ADRIFT.

FINALLY THEY SAW LAND, BUT SUDDENLY THE SHIP STRUCK A SANDBAR. THE BOW WAS WEDGED TIGHTLY AND COULD NOT BE MOVED. THE STERN BROKE APART UNDER THE POUNDING OF THE WAVES.

WORRIED THAT THE PRISONERS WOULD TRY TO ESCAPE, THE SOLDIERS WANTED TO KILL THEM. BUT JULIUS ORDERED EVERYONE TO SWIM TO LAND.

THOSE WHO COULD SWIM JUMPED OVERBOARD. OTHERS GRABBED WOODEN PLANKS AND OTHER DEBRIS FROM THE SHIP. EVERYONE REACHED THE SHORE SAFELY.

ALL ARRIVED ALIVE ON MALTA, WHERE THEY STAYED THE WINTER.

FINALLY PAUL REACHED ROME. ALTHOUGH HE WAS PLACED UNDER GUARD, HE WAS STILL ALLOWED TO RECEIVE VISITORS AND SO CONTINUED TO SPREAD THE MESSAGE TO NEW PEOPLE.

The Epistles

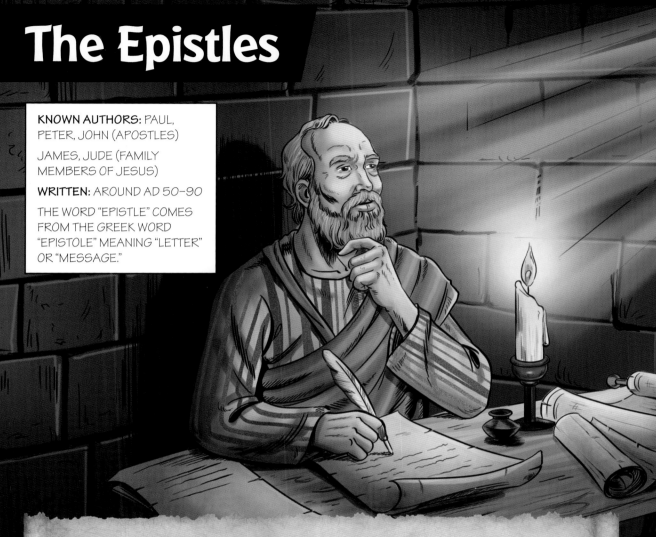

KNOWN AUTHORS: PAUL, PETER, JOHN (APOSTLES)

JAMES, JUDE (FAMILY MEMBERS OF JESUS)

WRITTEN: AROUND AD 50–90

THE WORD "EPISTLE" COMES FROM THE GREEK WORD "EPISTOLE" MEANING "LETTER" OR "MESSAGE."

THE POWER OF THE PEN

OF THE 27 BOOKS THAT MAKE UP THE NEW TESTAMENT, 21 ARE EPISTLES—LETTERS WRITTEN TO CHURCHES OR INDIVIDUALS. PAUL IS BELIEVED TO HAVE WRITTEN AT LEAST 7 OF THEM, AND UP TO 13 HAVE TRADITIONALLY BEEN ATTRIBUTED TO HIM. THESE ARE REFERRED TO AS THE PAULINE EPISTLES.

THE OTHER BOOKS ARE KNOWN AS THE GENERAL EPISTLES AS THEY WERE NOT ADDRESSED TO SPECIFIC PERSONS OR CHURCHES BUT WERE MEANT FOR GENERAL CIRCULATION AMONG ALL THE CHURCHES. THESE INCLUDE JAMES, 1 AND 2 PETER, 1, 2, AND 3 JOHN, AND JUDE.

PRISON AND PASTORAL

OF THE PAULINE EPISTLES SOME (EPHESIANS, PHILIPPIANS, COLOSSIANS, AND PHILEMON) ARE KNOWN AS THE PRISON EPISTLES BECAUSE THEY WERE WRITTEN WHEN PAUL WAS UNDER HOUSE ARREST IN ROME. OTHERS WERE WRITTEN TO INDIVIDUALS TO GIVE ADVICE ABOUT PROVIDING PASTORAL CARE AND ARE KNOWN AS THE PASTORAL EPISTLES.

The Greatest of These Is Love

Romans 5, 8; 1 Corinthians 12–13

PAUL WROTE MANY LETTERS. EVEN BEFORE HE WAS IMPRISONED IN ROME, HE WROTE LETTERS TO THOSE HE HAD MET ON HIS TRAVELS, OFFERING ADVICE, CRITICISM, ENCOURAGEMENT, AND LOVE. HIS HELP WAS INVALUABLE TO THOSE WHO WERE STARTING UP THE NEW CHURCHES, AND HIS ADVICE AND COMFORT ARE AS RELEVANT AS EVER.

BEFORE HE TRAVELED TO ROME, PAUL WROTE TO THE BELIEVERS THERE:

I believe that our present suffering is not worth comparing with the glory that will be revealed in us—and suffering itself produces perseverance, and so character and hope! If God is for us, who can be against us? He did not even spare His own Son, but gave Him up for us all. If He did this, won't He freely give us all things? There is nothing that will ever be able to separate us from the love of God which is ours through Christ Jesus our Lord—not hardship, or persecution, or hunger, or poverty, or danger, or death.

PAUL WROTE TO THE PEOPLE SETTLING IN CORINTH:

Many of you have been given wonderful gifts by the Holy Spirit, but don't get bigheaded. Everyone has his or her part to play. Each is part of the whole body. If I could speak every single language in the world, but didn't love others, I would be no more than a noisy gong. If I had the gift of prophecy or such great faith that I could move mountains, it would mean nothing if I didn't have love. I could give all I owned to the poor and suffer hardship, but it would be meaningless if I didn't feel love. Love is patient and kind. It isn't jealous, boastful, proud, or rude. It isn't selfish, cross, vengeful, or spiteful. Love protects and trusts and hopes. It is steady and true, and it never, ever gives up. Three things will last forever—faith, hope, and love—and the greatest of these is love.

628

Faith in Christ

Galatians 2–5; Colossians 3; Ephesians 6

PAUL KNEW THAT THE TRUE PATH TO GOD IS THROUGH BELIEF IN JESUS—NOT JUST FOLLOWING RULES AND RITUALS. HE WROTE TO THE CHURCH IN GALATIA:

You are made right with God by faith in Jesus, not by obeying the law. If following all the rules were enough, then Christ wouldn't have needed to die! You received the Holy Spirit because you believed the message about Jesus, not by obeying Moses' law. So don't become hung up on all the rules. Christ set us free—so stay free! Don't become slaves to the law!

HE SENT A SIMILAR MESSAGE TO THE COLOSSIANS:

Don't spend too much time thinking about the old rules. Think about the things of heaven— not the things of earth!

PAUL TOLD THE BELIEVERS IN EPHESUS:

Be strong in the Lord. Our enemies aren't made of flesh and blood, so put on every piece of God's armor. Then you can stand firm, with the belt of truth buckled around your waist, and with the breastplate of righteousness. Let your feet be shod with the readiness that comes from the gospel of peace, and take up the shield of faith. And take up the helmet of salvation and the sword of the Spirit, which is the Word of God.

629

Fight the Good Fight

1 & 2 Timothy

TIMOTHY WAS ONE OF PAUL'S FRIENDS. PAUL THOUGHT OF HIM LIKE A SON AND WROTE TO HIM TO ENCOURAGE HIM. HE TOLD HIM NOT TO LISTEN TO PEOPLE WHO SAID HE WAS TOO YOUNG BUT TO CONTINUE TO SET A GOOD EXAMPLE. HE ALSO SPOKE OF PEOPLE WHO WERE OBSESSED WITH MONEY AND POSSESSIONS:

Some people think they can become rich by being a Christian. Giving your life over to God can make you rich—but not in the way they think! We come into this world with nothing, and when we die we take nothing with us. So we shouldn't be longing for money and expensive clothes and possessions. The love of money is the root of all evil. It only leads to unhappiness. We should be content with what we have and feel rich in God. And if we do have lots of money, we should do good things with it and help those who are not so well off!

TOWARD THE END OF HIS LIFE, PAUL WROTE TO TIMOTHY FROM PRISON:

I am suffering and have been chained like a criminal, but the word of God cannot be chained. Remind everyone:

If we die with Him, we will also live with Him.
If we endure hardship, we will reign with Him.
If we deny Him, He will deny us.
If we are unfaithful, He remains faithful, for He cannot deny who He is.

As for me, my life has been an offering to God. The time of my death is near. I have fought a good fight, I have finished the race, and I have kept the faith. Now I look forward to my reward, which the Lord will give me on the day of His return—a reward not just for me but for all who eagerly await His coming!

NO ONE KNOWS FOR CERTAIN WHAT HAPPENED TO PAUL, BUT MANY BELIEVE THAT HE WAS EXECUTED WHILE IN ROME UNDER THE ORDERS OF EMPEROR NERO.

Run the Race

Hebrews; James; 1 & 2 Peter; 1 John

THE NEW TESTAMENT IS ALSO MADE UP OF LETTERS BY THE APOSTLES PETER AND JOHN AND BY JAMES AND JUDE, WHO WERE RELATED TO JESUS.

NO ONE CAN BE CERTAIN WHO WROTE THE LETTER TO THE HEBREWS, BUT IT ENCOURAGES THE READER TO BE FILLED WITH FAITH, LIKE NOAH, SARAH, AND MOSES:

Let yourself be filled with faith. Cast off the things that weigh you down so you have the strength and endurance to run the race set before us!

JAMES TOLD HIS READERS THAT IT WAS NOT ENOUGH TO SAY YOU HAVE FAITH:

What good is it to say you have faith but don't show it by your actions? Words are not enough—faith is not enough, unless it produces good deeds!

PETER WROTE:

You face hardship and suffering, but don't despair! Instead, be glad—these trials make you partners with Christ in His suffering. They will test your faith as fire tests and purifies gold. Remember there is wonderful joy ahead. Don't be disheartened if it seems a long time in coming—God wants everyone to repent. But the day of the Lord will come unexpectedly, so be prepared!

THE APOSTLE JOHN WROTE:

God is love. He showed how much He loved us by sending His one and only Son into the world so that we might have eternal life through Him. Since He loved us that much, let us make sure that we love one another so that God can live in us and we can live in God, and when the day of judgement comes, we will not have to fear anything. Perfect love drives out all fear! We love one another because He loved us first.

John's Revelation

KNOWN AS: THE REVELATION OF SAINT JOHN THE DIVINE

THE BOOK OF REVELATION

THE APOCALYPSE (FROM THE GREEK WORD "APOKALYPSIS" MEANING "UNVEILING" OR "REVELATION")

WHICH JOHN?

TRADITIONALLY, THE BOOK OF REVELATION HAS BEEN ASSOCIATED WITH JOHN, THE APOSTLE, BUT MANY MODERN SCHOLARS DOUBT THAT. SOME IDENTIFY HIM AS "JOHN THE ELDER," BUT HE IS OFTEN SIMPLY REFERRED TO AS "JOHN OF PATMOS," IN RECOGNITION OF THE ISLAND ON WHICH IT IS GENERALLY BELIEVED THE BOOK WAS WRITTEN.

BOOK OF PROPHECY

IT IS THE ONLY PROPHETIC BOOK IN THE NEW TESTAMENT. JOHN'S VISION DESCRIBES FUTURE EVENTS AT THE END OF THE WORLD, INVOLVING THE FINAL REBELLION BY SATAN AT ARMAGEDDON, GOD'S FINAL DEFEAT OF SATAN, AND THE RESTORATION OF PEACE TO THE WORLD.

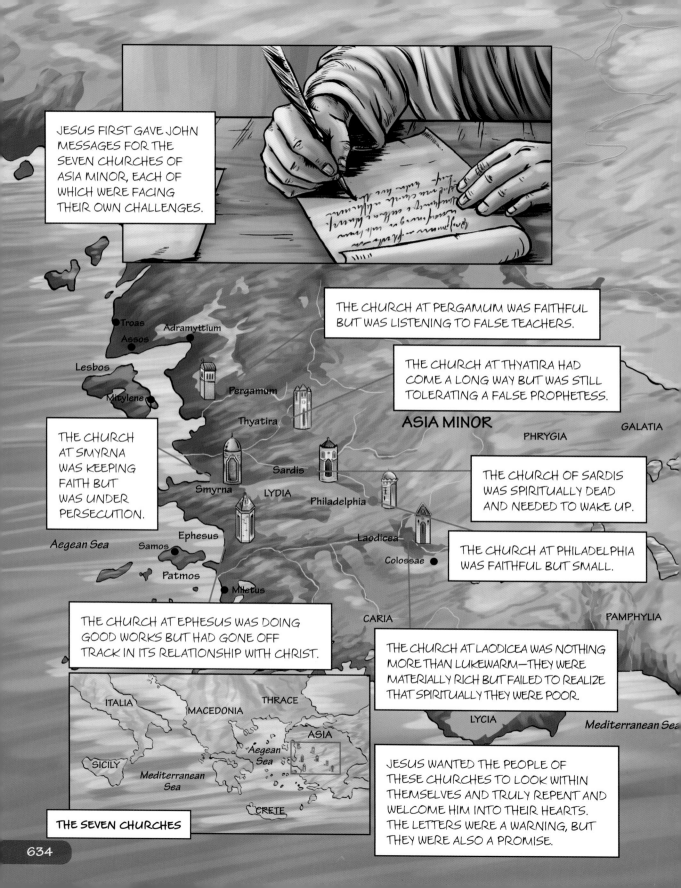

JESUS FIRST GAVE JOHN MESSAGES FOR THE SEVEN CHURCHES OF ASIA MINOR, EACH OF WHICH WERE FACING THEIR OWN CHALLENGES.

THE CHURCH AT PERGAMUM WAS FAITHFUL BUT WAS LISTENING TO FALSE TEACHERS.

THE CHURCH AT THYATIRA HAD COME A LONG WAY BUT WAS STILL TOLERATING A FALSE PROPHETESS.

THE CHURCH AT SMYRNA WAS KEEPING FAITH BUT WAS UNDER PERSECUTION.

THE CHURCH OF SARDIS WAS SPIRITUALLY DEAD AND NEEDED TO WAKE UP.

THE CHURCH AT PHILADELPHIA WAS FAITHFUL BUT SMALL.

THE CHURCH AT EPHESUS WAS DOING GOOD WORKS BUT HAD GONE OFF TRACK IN ITS RELATIONSHIP WITH CHRIST.

THE CHURCH AT LAODICEA WAS NOTHING MORE THAN LUKEWARM—THEY WERE MATERIALLY RICH BUT FAILED TO REALIZE THAT SPIRITUALLY THEY WERE POOR.

JESUS WANTED THE PEOPLE OF THESE CHURCHES TO LOOK WITHIN THEMSELVES AND TRULY REPENT AND WELCOME HIM INTO THEIR HEARTS. THE LETTERS WERE A WARNING, BUT THEY WERE ALSO A PROMISE.

ASIA MINOR

PHRYGIA

GALATIA

Troas
Assos
Adramyttium
Lesbos
Mitylene
Pergamum
Thyatira
Sardis
Smyrna
LYDIA
Philadelphia
Ephesus
Aegean Sea
Samos
Patmos
Miletus
Laodicea
Colossae
CARIA
PAMPHYLIA
LYCIA
Mediterranean Sea

ITALIA
MACEDONIA
THRACE
ASIA
Aegean Sea
SICILY
Mediterranean Sea
CRETE

THE SEVEN CHURCHES

IN HIS VISION, JOHN SAW A DOOR IN HEAVEN OPEN.

A VOICE TOLD JOHN TO LOOK BEYOND THE DOOR. THERE HE SAW A HUGE THRONE SURROUNDED BY TWENTY-FOUR OTHER THRONES, EACH WITH AN ELDER SITTING ON THEM.

JOHN SAW FOUR LIVING CREATURES, EACH WITH SIX WINGS.

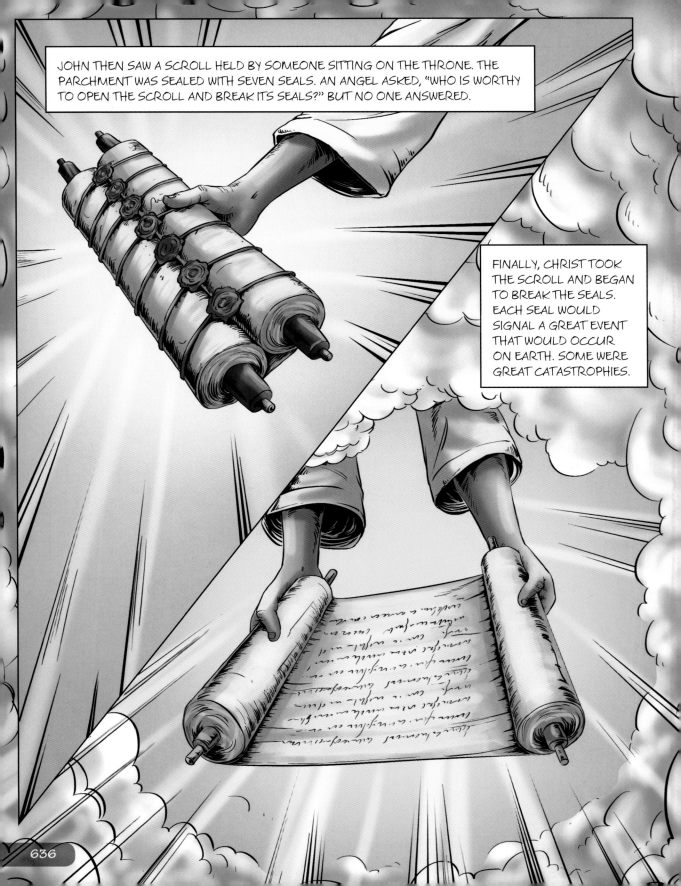

JOHN THEN SAW A SCROLL HELD BY SOMEONE SITTING ON THE THRONE. THE PARCHMENT WAS SEALED WITH SEVEN SEALS. AN ANGEL ASKED, "WHO IS WORTHY TO OPEN THE SCROLL AND BREAK ITS SEALS?" BUT NO ONE ANSWERED.

FINALLY, CHRIST TOOK THE SCROLL AND BEGAN TO BREAK THE SEALS. EACH SEAL WOULD SIGNAL A GREAT EVENT THAT WOULD OCCUR ON EARTH. SOME WERE GREAT CATASTROPHIES.

WHEN THE FIRST SEAL WAS BROKEN, A VOICE LIKE THUNDER CRIED OUT, "COME FORWARD!" A RIDER ON A WHITE HORSE APPEARED. HE CARRIED A BOW AND WAS GIVEN A CROWN. HE WENT OUT TO CONQUER AND SYMBOLIZED CONQUEST.

WHEN THE SECOND SEAL WAS BROKEN, A RED HORSE APPEARED, AND ITS RIDER WAS GIVEN A GREAT SWORD AND SYMBOLIZED WAR.

WHEN THE THIRD SEAL WAS BROKEN, A BLACK HORSE APPEARED. HIS RIDER CARRIED A PAIR OF SCALES IN HIS HAND AND SYMBOLIZED STARVATION OR FAMINE.

WHEN THE FOURTH SEAL WAS BROKEN, A FOURTH RIDER ON A PALE HORSE APPEARED. THE RIDER'S NAME WAS "DEATH," AND HADES FOLLOWED HIM.

THE OTHER SEALS WERE BROKEN AND AN EARTHQUAKE ROCKED THE PLANET. THE SUN DARKENED, AND STARS FELL FROM THE SKY. WHEN THE SEVENTH SEAL WAS BROKEN, SEVEN ANGELS WITH TRUMPETS STOOD BEFORE GOD, SIGNALING HIS WRATH.

WHEN THE FIRST ANGEL BLEW HIS TRUMPET, HAIL AND FIRE HURLED DOWN TO EARTH.

WHEN THE SECOND ANGEL BLEW HIS TRUMPET, A BURNING MOUNTAIN WAS HURLED INTO THE SEA.

AS EACH TRUMPET BLEW, A DIFFERENT CALAMITY STRUCK EARTH. THE ULTIMATE BATTLE BETWEEN GOOD AND EVIL HAD BEGUN.

639

JOHN'S VISION CONTINUED. AN ANGEL CAME DOWN FROM HEAVEN HOLDING IN HIS HAND THE KEY TO THE ABYSS. HE SEIZED THE DRAGON, WHO IS THE DEVIL, AND CAST HIM INTO THE BOTTOMLESS PIT. SATAN WOULD BE SHUT UP AND PEACE WOULD REIGN ON EARTH FOR A THOUSAND YEARS...

...BEFORE ONE FINAL, DREADFUL WAR BETWEEN SATAN AND THE PEOPLE OF GOD. BUT AT THE END SATAN WOULD BE CAST INTO A LAKE OF FIRE.

The Holy City

JOHN SAW THAT THEN WOULD COME THE TIME OF THE FINAL JUDGMENT. HE SAW A GREAT WHITE THRONE AND THE ONE SITTING IN IT, AND HE SAW THE BOOK OF LIFE WHICH WOULD BE OPENED, AND ALL WOULD BE JUDGED ACCORDING TO WHAT THEY HAD DONE. THEN THE WICKED WOULD ALSO BE CAST INTO THE LAKE OF FIRE, ALONG WITH DEATH AND HADES.

THEN JOHN GOT A GLIMPSE OF THE NEW HEAVEN AND EARTH. HE SAW THE HOLY CITY, COMING DOWN OUT OF HEAVEN LIKE A BEAUTIFUL BRIDE, AND HEARD A VOICE SPEAKING FROM THE THRONE.

NOW GOD'S HOME IS WITH HIS PEOPLE! HE WILL LIVE WITH THEM, AND THERE SHALL BE NO MORE DEATH, GRIEF, CRYING, OR PAIN!

FOR HE IS THE FIRST AND THE LAST, THE BEGINNING AND THE END!

THE HOLY CITY SHONE WITH THE GLORY OF GOD. IT'S TEMPLE WAS THE LORD GOD ALMIGHTY AND THE LAMB. THE RIVER OF LIFE RAN THROUGH ITS CENTER. THE CITY HAD NO NEED FOR THE SUN OR THE MOON, BECAUSE THE GLORY OF GOD SHONE ON IT, AND THE LAMB WAS ITS LAMP.

I AM COMING SOON!

AMEN. COME, LORD JESUS!